# SHOES

# Contents

# SHOES

## The Meaning of Style

Elizabeth Semmelhack

REAKTION BOOKS

Published by Reaktion Books Ltd
Unit 32, Waterside
44–48 Wharf Road
London N1 7UX, UK

www.reaktionbooks.co.uk

First published 2017

Designed by Sophie Kullmann

Printed and bound in Slovenia
by Gorenjski tisk storitve

A catalogue record for this book
is available from the British Library

ISBN 978 1 78023 834 0

# Introduction

## LE CHOIX DIFFICILE

SOULIERS, DE PÉRUGIA

*Modèles déposés. Reproduction interdite.*

What is a shoe? The answer seems obvious: a shoe is something worn on the foot to protect it and to aid mobility. Yet most shoes are tasked with functions far beyond the merely practical, and more often than not their design and use are driven by social rather than physical demands. Take, for example, wing-tip oxfords and 'sensible' heels. Both are considered appropriate, sometimes even compulsory, office footwear, yet nothing in their design is related to the physical demands unique to the business environment. Indeed, it could be argued that heels hinder both comfort and movement in the office. In addition, although both types of shoe are understood as part of proper business attire, they are hardly interchangeable. A typical male banker is not free to wear oxfords one day and high heels the next. His choice is not dictated by any biological imperative but rather by the social meanings that have been invested in footwear – meanings that are so deeply embedded that even if he altered nothing else about his outfit, choosing 'inappropriate' footwear would open him up to criticism. High heels might bring the greatest derision but if he chose to wear foot-baring sandals, sturdy boots or even, until recently, status sneakers, his footwear would likewise be regarded by many as out of place. How can a simple change of footwear carry so much significance? How has footwear come to play a central role in the construction of social identity? How have certain types of footwear or specific footwear brands come to encapsulate social ideas, including entire lifestyles and belief systems? And how have we arrived at this current 'shoeaholic' moment, where footwear has become so heavily invested in both social and economic value?

These are some of the questions that will be grappled with in this book as it explores the role of footwear far beyond its uses in protecting the foot. This book offers no typologies. It is not a study of construction techniques, or a catalogue of shifting styles. It is about the significance and signification of footwear in relation to culture, history, economics and the construction of social identity. In particular, it will consider how some footwear has been used to

This 1920s advertisement for André Perugia shoes captures the challenge of making just the right choice when selecting a pair of shoes. Jean Grangier, 'Le Choix Difficile', in *La Gazette du Bon Ton*. French, 1924–5.

protect power structures and perpetuate cultural values, while other footwear has been worn in protest against prevailing cultural norms, despite simultaneously being an unabashed product of consumer capitalism.

Footwear is, and historically has been, critical in performing gender, asserting allegiances, proclaiming status and expressing rebellion. Over time, widely varying styles have been assigned meanings that have become so normative and so easily read that they function as nonverbal statements used to convey meaning, from broad social alliances to more subtle statements of individuality. The current cultural importance of footwear is a direct product of industrialization, and the unprecedented variety of footwear available at a wide range of price points has allowed more consumers the opportunity to construct increasingly nuanced expressions of social identity through footwear choice.

Indeed, the current availability of diverse footwear is stunning. At the time of writing, a quick look at the Nordstrom website, just one of many North American retailers, reveals an expansive selection of over 15,000 distinct models for sale. Broadly organized into men's, women's and children's categories, the footwear on offer is further subdivided by footwear type, with the assumption that the average shopper will be able to understand these groupings easily, or, to put it another way, is fully literate in the meanings of these different styles. If a desired shoe cannot be found at Nordstrom, there are thousands of other businesses, both brick-and-mortar and online, vying for consumers' attention with ever-changing and enticing new models. For consumers interested in more unique offerings, second-hand retailers, vintage stores and auction websites provide access to a wide variety of footwear from the past.

Contemporary consumers also have access to a broad range of shoe-inspired items. Home decor novelties such as shoe-shaped Christmas ornaments and flip-flop-referencing hors d'oeuvre trays vie for consumer attention with sneaker-inspired key chains and tote bags embellished with depictions of high heels. In addition to purchasing actual shoes and shoe-related items, people are also increasingly consuming information on footwear. Shoe-themed websites and blogs abound on the Internet, as do Pinterest boards and Instagram and Facebook pages dedicated entirely to images of footwear. People post shoe 'selfies', read footwear-focused books, visit shoe-themed museum exhibitions and wait in long lines to have their shoes signed by famous designers.

The current cultural importance of footwear is not simply the result of the ever-increasing variety and availability of footwear but also coincides with the loss of many other accessories of dress that had traditionally served to establish gender and class identity. Hats, for example, were worn for centuries by both men and women until the mid-twentieth century. Losses such as this have put greater pressure on footwear to establish and relay differences between male and female, adult and child, rich and poor, while simultaneously promoting group identity within both wider society and subcultures. One of the more paradoxical uses of footwear has been the use of mass-produced shoes and multinational brands as a means of crafting individual self-expression. Today the rising importance of individualism feeds shoe consumption, and many people's wardrobes feature a range of footwear that allows the wearer to perform a multiplicity of social identities. The workplace self, leisure-time self, celebratory self, athletic self and rebellious self can now all be communicated through different types of shoes.

The ever-growing importance of footwear raises a surfeit of complex issues; nevertheless, with a volume of this size it is necessary to retain a somewhat limited scope. To that end, this book will focus on four essential footwear archetypes central to expressions of social identity in the twentieth and twenty-first centuries in Western societies: the sandal, the boot, the high heel and the sneaker. These four broad categories of footwear tread through the same moments in time but offer startlingly different and unique insights into these periods, each illuminating larger historical, social and cultural issues.

Chapter One begins with the reintroduction of the sandal into Western fashion at the end of the eighteenth century, centuries after it was abandoned at the end of the Roman Empire. Since the moment of that reintroduction, the sandal has often been worn by those attempting to push the boundaries of acceptability, with the most eccentric wearers often promoting the sandal's connections to a perceived exotic 'Other', such as with the mid-nineteenth-century Indian-inspired sandals worn by British 'simple lifers' or the Levant-referencing 'Jesus' sandals worn by mid-twentieth-century hippies. Periodically, sandals have also been embraced by high fashion, and when worn in such contexts have functioned in seemingly depoliticized ways. This tension between the proverbial 'raw' and the 'cooked' has made sandals the footwear of leisure and play and of elegance and refinement, but also the footwear of personal eccentricity and radical politics. The place of sandals in gendered public nudity also forms a central theme of the chapter.

Chapter Two explores the relationship between boots and ideas of power, domination, masculinity and uniformity. Prior to the second half of the nineteenth century, boots were the domain of men, and had long been the footwear of action, of hunting and warfare. In the later nineteenth century, industrialization and concomitant urbanization challenged the importance of the boot as an item of fashion in the daily wardrobes of many men. However, it remained paramount to nineteenth-century empire building, particularly in the American West, and associations of rugged individualism remain embodied in the cowboy boot. Although boots lost their place in many men's wardrobes they became important items of dress in women's fashion, and by the end of the nineteenth century women's boots were increasingly eroticized, as this chapter will explore. In the mid-twentieth century, boots were pressed into service by those who sought to express group cohesion through their footwear choice, including many subcultures such as motorcycle gangs and skinheads. Since the second half of the twentieth century, boots have functioned more as elements of costume, co-opted by fashion and brought into mainstream dress in myriad ways.

Chapter Three looks at the origin of the heeled shoe in Western Asia, where it was first worn by men for horseback riding. The chapter then considers the heel's adoption and adaptation in Western fashion in the seventeenth century and its transformation into an icon of frivolous yet manipulative, hypersexualized femininity. The heel's relationship to perceived feminine irrationality and its destabilizing role in gender politics, from women's suffrage to today, form a central theme, as does the heel's relationship to the erotic and its use in pornography. The chapter examines the increasing importance of high heels in women's dress and the development of a cult of genius around celebrity high-heel designers. The reasons for the typical Western discomfort regarding men wearing heels, and its relationship to Darwinian and eugenicist concepts of idealized masculinity, are also considered.

Chapter Four looks at the evolution of the sneaker from its debut in the middle of the nineteenth century as an item of status to the rise of sneaker culture in relation to new technologies, shifting ideas of masculinity, and expressions of class, status and privilege. The role of the Muscular Christianity movement and the importance of physical culture in the increased popularity of sneakers in the nineteenth century is explored, as is the influence of eugenics and fascism on the democratization of sneakers in the 1930s. The sneaker's loss of status in the post-Second World War baby boom, as well as its resurrection as a status symbol during the 'Me' generation and the advent of sneaker culture in the 1970s, form key sections of the chapter. It also addresses the inculcation of men into the fashion economy through the 'sneakerfication' of men's fashion and the attendant challenges of attempting to balance paradigmatic conceptions of masculinity with men's increasing participation in fashion con-sumption traditionally considered a female preoccupation.

Finally, the Conclusion explores the role of industrialization as a central driver in the growth of meanings associated with footwear. The ever-increasing number of shoes and items that reference footwear that are flooding the twenty-first-century marketplace has allowed the vocabulary of footwear styles to become a prominent part of the construction of social identity. The history of foot-wear production has moved from the long tradition of bespoke shoemaking to the de-professionalization of the craft and its mechanization; today, challenges as well as opportunities are posed by automated manufacture and 3D printing. The chapter also asks questions about the future of footwear production in a post-industrial age. The impact of hyperproduction in footwear and how the fires of desire are stoked in a post-scarcity market are also discussed, including how the product of multiple anonymous labourers supports the cult of celebrity around named designers.

In the chapters ahead, the often paradoxical roles played by these four types of footwear in both larger ideologies and more personal identities, as their meanings shift over the decades, will be elaborated. Yet, more than simply telling the fascinating history of each of these styles of footwear, the goal of this work is to shed light on why we choose the shoes we do, and what we think we are saying through our choices.

# I  Sandals: Eccentricity

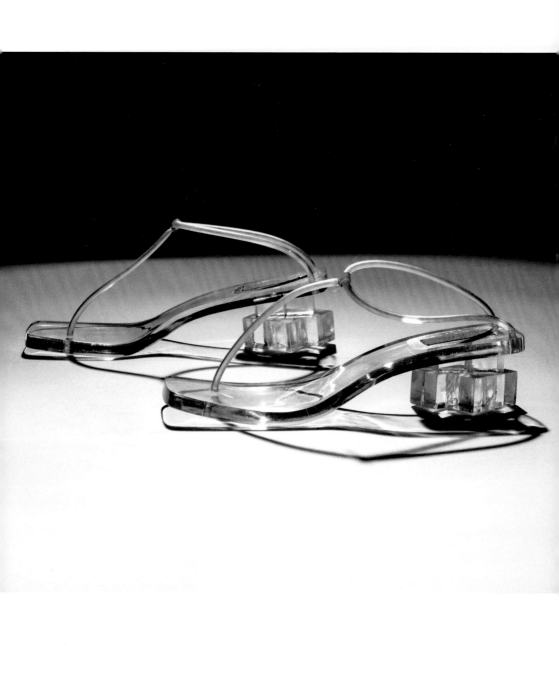

Ah, little barefoot sandals brown and still,
Do you long to be a-roaming on the hill,
Flashing down the garden way,
Fellows with the winds at play –
Are you weary waiting wingless, silent, chill?
Mary White Slater, 'Barefoot Sandals', 1917

Her sandals ravished his eyes,
Her beauty captivated his mind,
The sword cut through his neck!
Judith 16:9

Of all the different types of footwear, sandals are perhaps the hardest to pin down. Both their meaning and form are mutable. Sandals have been worn by mythological heroes, sainted figures and, from a Western perspective, exotic 'Others'. Sandals are also the footwear of summer, of relaxation and play. They can be red-carpet-worthy and yet are also the footwear of the politically discontent. The type of footwear deemed to be sandals has also changed dramatically over the years. In the nineteenth century, shoes with ribbons that laced around the leg were called sandals, while in the early twentieth century it was perforations in a shoe's upper, the part of the shoe that encloses the foot, that helped to identify it as a sandal. Currently, a sandal can be as simple as a flip-flop or as complex as a strappy stiletto, as long as most of the foot is bare.

The basic sandal, consisting of a flat sole with straps, is one of the earliest types of footwear.[1] Tutankhamun's tomb contained examples made of finely plaited vegetable fibre, as well as leather, ornamented with precious metals and beads made of rare stones.[2] The lacing or unlacing of sandals formed part of the erotic iconography of ancient Greece; goddess Aphrodite famously used a sandal to defend herself from the advances of Pan. The sandals worn by

This pair of I. Miller sandals are both classicizing and futuristic at the same time. Their simple thongs harken back to antiquity while the use of clear materials is fashion forward. American, 1965–9.

the Israelite heroine Judith ravished the eyes of the Assyrian general Holofernes, and her beauty distracted him for long enough to allow her to behead him.

Greek and Roman sandals ranged in complexity from the relatively simple thong sandal to the sandal boot, which often featured both elaborate decoration and intricate strapping. In Roman culture, sandals were just one of many types of footwear, and wearing them was dictated by complex codes of dress. When a grain ship dating from around 201 CE was recovered from the Rhine river, archaeologists discovered that every member of the crew had at least one pair of shoes and one pair of sandals with them, suggesting there were different functions for each type of footwear.[3]

Despite their widespread use across the far-flung Roman Empire, sandals fell out of favour throughout Europe after the empire's collapse and were only reintroduced as an item of fashion well over a

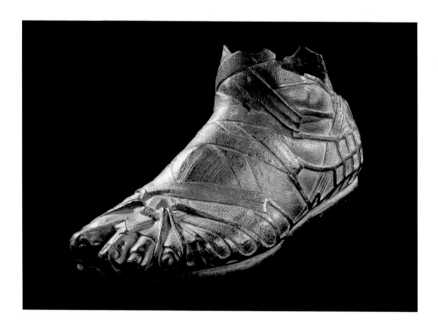

(*above*) This bronze sculpture of a sandal-clad foot from ancient Rome captures the complexity of many Roman sandals. Roman, 1st century CE.

(*left*) The simple design of these elegant ancient Egyptian sandals is still in use today. Ancient Egyptian, 332 BCE–395 CE.

thousand years later, at the turn of the nineteenth century. Yet during these years of desuetude, sandals were not forgotten. Churches were filled with portrayals of biblical characters wearing sandals; sandals adorned the feet of classical sculptures; and when Europeans began to engage in wide-ranging seafaring trade, they became aware of the array of sandals worn by 'Others' in foreign lands. Indeed, although sandals may not have been worn as daily dress in the West, images of them were everywhere, occupying a space in the European imagination that was by turns sacred, classicizing, humble and exotic. Few dared to wear sandals, but those who did, such as members of certain Catholic orders, wore them to signal their rejection of worldliness. Even today, some sandals retain a soupçon of this meaning and remain the footwear associated with the radicalized.

Sandals were reintroduced into women's fashion around the turn of the nineteenth century, as part of a larger interest in all things classical. The discovery and archaeological excavations of the ancient Roman towns of Herculaneum and Pompeii in the eighteenth century, and

In the 18th century, women's footwear described as 'sandals' were full shoes with decorations that suggested sandal straps. English, 1790–95.

the growing political and philosophical interest in Greek rationalism, gave birth to neoclassicism. By the end of the century, the enthusiasm for Greek democracy and the fashions of antiquity signalled a new world order. The revolutionary personifications of Liberty, the French Marianne and the American Columbia were clad as the classical goddess Libertas, wearing classicizing gowns and, when shod, sandals. Despite these models, sandal-inspired footwear in women's fashion of the end of the eighteenth century bore little relation to the sandals of antiquity. Instead, the fashionable 'sandals' of the 1790s were actually low-heeled shoes that completely concealed the foot. The only aspect of this footwear connoting 'sandal' was the decorative appliqué on the uppers, which suggested sandal straps. However, by the time of the French Directory at the close of the eighteenth century, a few adventurous French women dared to expose their toes by wearing true sandals. These *Merveilleuses*, or 'Marvellous Ones', wore shockingly diaphanous gowns as well as sandals that

This daring turn-of-the-century sandal was worn by the Italian actress Clara Novello. Although her toes would have been exposed, the sandal also features a pink satin lining that would have concealed the majority of her foot. Italian, 1795–1805.

EVENING DRESS.

Engraved for N.º 41. New Series of La Belle Assemblee. Feb.ry 1.st 1813.

revealed the feet *à la grecque*. It was a fashion, along with the eccentric dress of their male counterparts, the *Incroyables* (Incredibles), designed to fly in the face of the French Revolutionary politics that had so recently attempted to regulate all manner of behaviours, including dress, during the merciless Reign of Terror.

One *Merveilleuse* was the influential social figure Thérésa Tallien, who reportedly wore sandals that laced up her legs and revealed her naked feet, ornamented with jewel-studded toe rings. Despite the supposed political intent of this style, most adopters were criticized for being more devoted to fashion than politics. As the *Literary Magazine, and American Register* noted in 1804,

> To judge of the political tenets of these belles from their exterior, a stranger would be often led into error. He might naturally conclude them to be republicans, since they have, in general, adopted the Athenian attire, though they have not, in the smallest degree, the simple manners of that people. Their arms are bare almost to the shoulder; their bosom is, in great measure, uncovered; their ancles [sic] are encircled by narrow ribands, in imitation of the fastenings of sandals ...[4]

By the turn of the nineteenth century such extremes had become passé, and while an antique flavour continued to inform fashion, women adopted less shocking styles and did not dare show their toes.[5] Instead, most women opted for more demure shoes that concealed the foot and only suggested a 'sandal' through decoration such as ribbons that could be tied around the ankle or calf. A report from 1810 in *Hibernia Magazine* describes footwear typical for the period:

> The Grecian sandal, in the form of a half boot, cut out to display the lace stocking, made in white, blue, or pale-pink kid, bound and laced with silver, is in high estimation at Bath; it is admirably calculated to display a fine foot to advantage.[6]

Everything in this fashion plate, the hairstyle, gown and lace-up sandals, reflects the influence of neoclassicism on early 19th-century women's fashion. English, 1813.

Although ideas about sandals informed women's footwear fashions, sandals in men's dress were completely absent. Napoleon may have worn sandal-inspired shoes to his coronation, but he was clearly an exception rather than trendsetter, at least in regard to sandals.

As the nineteenth century progressed, women's fashion continued to embrace footwear that made reference to sandals, with the flimsy, satin slipper-sandal with ribbons that tied around the ankle or up the leg being the most popular. A humorous article from 1807 titled 'The London Shoemaker' illuminates the increasing importance of the shoemaker in the early years of the nineteenth century as well as the ludicrous delicacy of some women's footwear. The celebrated shoemaker in question was 'a man of fashion and elegance, a paragon of taste'. A pair of his shoes 'arrived at six o'clock, were admired till eight, put on at nine, worn until bed time, and laid aside in the morning by the maid'. In the morning, the owner was shocked to see that the shoes were worn out, and the shoemaker was sent for:

> 'Impossible – let me see – Ah, bless me! . . . How long did you wear them?'
> 'I walked in them but two hours.'
> 'Walked in them, Madam, walked. Oh then, it is not to be wondered at; why, Madam, those shoes were made only to wear, and not to walk in.'[7]

Indeed, the insubstantial footwear worn by many women in the early nineteenth century was clearly not designed to sustain strenuous wear. Instead, it was intended to reflect the new feminine ideals that were beginning to emerge. Women were positioned as the centre of the emotional and spiritual life of their homes, rather than as members of the larger political world. Eighteenth-century Rousseauian ideas of female sentimentality and the importance of childhood merged with the newly recoded Protestant ideals that privileged the role of motherhood within the family, and motherhood came to be seen

The delicate flats fashionable in the first half of the 19th century reflected the new cultural emphasis on femininity in relation to domesticity. This pair by Melnotte are reminiscent of ballet shoes. French, first half of the 19th century.

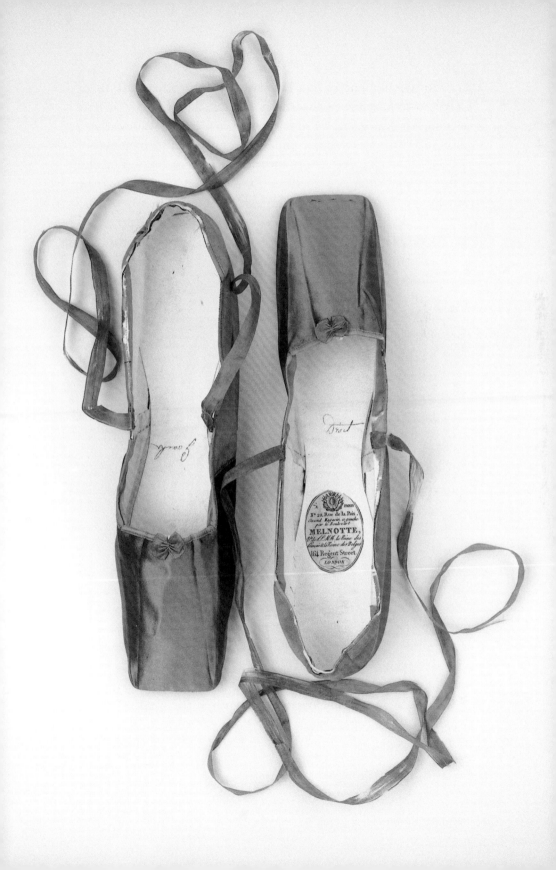

as a fundamental female trait that united all women, transcending socioeconomic and even racial barriers. This 'cult of domesticity', as it came to be called, argued that the proper place for women was in the home. Attempts to step beyond these confines were commonly met with condemnation or derision, and the delicate footwear fashionable at the time was often used by critics as a means of ridiculing those who dared to step into the public realm:

> Considering the damp, muddy, state of the streets at this time of year, I am equally amazed and delighted to see the ladies, almost universally, going about in thin shoes. This elegant fashion beautifully displays the conformation of the ankle-joint; but to the surgeon it has another recommendation. I behold the delicate foot, separated scarcely by the thickness of thin paper from the mire. I see the exquisite instep, undefended but by a mere web. I meditate on the influence of cold and wet upon the frame; I think of the catarrhs, coughs, pleurisies, pneumonies, consumptions, and other interesting affections, that necessarily must result from their application to the feet; and then I reckon up the numbers of pills, boluses, powders, draughts, mixtures, leeches, and blisters which will consequently be sent into the fair sufferers, calculate what they must come to, and wish I had the amount already in my pocket.[8]

If women of privilege who only navigated the muddy byways from time to time were the focus of ridicule, the working-class women who populated the public realm were often objects of both scorn and suspicion. They were assessed as having been pushed there by economic need, and the silk sandal-slipper had no place on their feet. Instead, working-class footwear was often hardwearing ankle boots made of more durable leathers or textiles.

One of the only professions that required the wearing of the fashionable sandal-shoe was ballet. In the nineteenth century, ballet shifted from being an entertainment associated with the French

Marie Taglioni was one of the first female dancers to rise *en pointe*. She darned the edges of her fashionable 'sandals' to give herself greater stability. A. E. Chalon and R. J. Lane, *Mademoiselle Taglioni*, 1831, lithograph.

court to becoming a bourgeois obsession, in which young ballet dancers were the focus of male desire. The dainty, feminine foot shod in a pair of silk sandals was already an eroticized object:

> a lady's shoe, worn with crossing sandals [ribbons], gently curving over the instep and around the ankle, is immeasurably superior to the plain, quaker-like, old maid affair . . . Did women but know how much these slender lines of ribban add to their appearance . . . they would never put on a shoe without such an appendage.[9]

Ballerinas heeded this advice. The sandal-slipper was perfect for dance: the ribbons kept the slipper on the foot and the soft silk uppers allowed for movement of the foot. The fashion in women's footwear for straights – that is, shoes with neither lefts nor rights – was also perfect for ballet as it created a pleasingly symmetrical presentation of the feet. The trend for straights in the early nineteenth century was part style and part industrialization. Shoemakers had made footwear with lefts and rights for centuries but straights were more economical; they required only one shoe last per pair rather than a left last and a right last and were one of the earliest ideas for speeding up production. Eventually refinements in manufacturing allowed for lefts and rights to be more easily made and straights were abandoned in fashion, yet they have persisted to this day in footwear for ballet.

The ethereal mood demanded by the Romantic ballets of the 1830s and '40s called for the ballerinas to seem otherworldly. To that end, pointe work was invented. Although some male dancers had ventured to dance on their toes in the late eighteenth century, Marie Taglioni is often credited with being the first ballerina to dance *en pointe*, in 1832 in the ballet *La Sylphide*, choreographed by her father. In order to perform the challenging steps, Taglioni began to darn the sides of the toes of her shoes, allowing her to stay *en pointe* for brief yet breathtaking moments, transforming her slippers into nascent pointe shoes.[10]

While appearing on stage was not an activity many 'respectable' women pursued, the industrial age was opening up more socially sanctioned opportunities for women to be more active, and the seaside sojourn became fashionable. Leisure activities such as visiting the beach had long been the domain of the privileged, and in the nineteenth century the newly wealthy pursued similar amusements for reasons related to both relaxation and status. By the 1830s the invention of railways permitted increasing numbers of people to reach resort towns with ease, and with these holidays came new wardrobes for women and girls, including bathing attire and bathing sandals. 'No one presumes to bathe without shoes, and these are strapped on by means of bright-coloured sandals,' wrote an author in 1876 whose sentiments reflected the longstanding cultural requirement that women's bodies be concealed.[11] Women were encouraged to enjoy the beach but the maintenance of modesty was paramount,

Eugen Sandow was considered a specimen of masculine perfection in the late 19th century and he often flaunted his physique wearing little more than a pair of classicizing sandals. Napoleon Sarony, *Sandow, No. 9*, 1893.

and the 'sandals' women wore remained similar to the sandal-shoes that they had worn earlier in the century: closed-toed shoes of which the laces alone suggested classical sandals. Women's bathing suits hid practically every inch of the body, and woollen bathing stockings and cotton bathing 'sandals' completely covered the legs and feet. Even with these precautions, some beaches segregated women from men. Bathing machines, which allowed women to change in private and to enter the water directly, were also popular. In a cultural environment like this, women's toes never had a chance.

In contrast, men were permitted to flaunt their naked feet at the beach, but only if they were wearing swimwear. When dressed, their feet had to be concealed within shoes. Toe-exposing sandals were unthinkable. The only men allowed to wear sandal-inspired footwear were professional strongmen or those who pursued physical culture, a physical fitness and strength training movement that began in the nineteenth century. In postcards and posters, men displayed their physiques costumed in ways that suggested the classical past, including strappy footwear. Children, regardless of gender, were encouraged to wear 'sandals' similar to those worn by women, to

(*above*) Typical lace-up bathing shoes. The uppers are made of red cotton and the soles of cotton-covered cork. American or Canadian, 1895–1915.

(*left*) This stereograph shows the typical bathing costume, including lace-up 'sandals', of the day. Strohmeyer and Wyman, *Vacation Sports at the Seaside* (1890s).

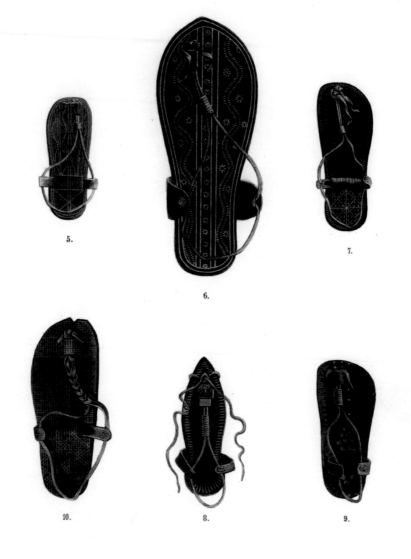

This illustration is of 'exotic' sandal types from Akhmim, Egypt. Colour plate from *Antike und Frühmittelalterliche Fussbekleidungen aus Achim-Panolois* (1895).

help prevent injury caused by stepping on glass or other sharp objects that could be found in the sand, yet period images provide ample proof of children being able to enjoy the sand between their toes, without wearing any footwear. Despite these sartorial inconveniences, going to the beach became a favourite pastime in the nineteenth century, and the popularity of bathing sandals helped to establish the cultural connection between sandals and play.

The privileged in the nineteenth century did not simply rely on the seaside for escape from daily life. Many sought adventure through international travel, and even those who stayed at home eagerly read about faraway lands where sandals were a feature of local dress. Newspaper reports and magazine articles described the clothing worn in distant places and frequently remarked on footwear. In this context, sandals from foreign lands became synonymous with both the exotic and the 'primitive'. The fashion sandal, with its ribbons or straps that went up the leg, was associated with elegance and sophistication, while sandals from other cultures were, as one journalist put it, not the footwear of 'civilized white races of women who wear French-heel shoes' but instead were in fashion among 'the ebony beauties that Ryder Haggard declares exist in the central regions of Africa, [or] the chocolate-tinted Venuses beloved by the many rajahs of India's empire'.[12] At the height of nineteenth-century colonial expansionism, the sandalled 'Others' of distant lands impressed themselves onto the Western imagination. The popularity of Orientalist paintings and Japanese prints conjured up places in which the naked foot was protected by only the most minimal of footwear. The establishment of the British Raj in India in the middle of the century made all things Indian of particular interest within the metropole, and indeed the reintroduction of sandals into British dress was inspired by Indian examples.

As the world opened up, some people in Europe and the United States began to view the traditions and teachings from other cultures with interest and curiosity. Foreign 'Others' seemed to hold the secrets to health and tranquillity. These Western devotees believed that the modern age, with all its industrialization, urbanization and, above all, 'over-civilization', had removed mankind from its natural element to the detriment of both body and mind. In the United States, transcendentalism, which combined Eastern spiritualism with Yankee Puritanism, advocated the love of nature and simplicity in all things, including dress and footwear. 'Better moccasins, or sandals, or even bare feet, than a tight shoe,' wrote Henry David Thoreau, one of the main exponents of transcendentalism, in his journal in April 1850.[13] Indeed, the sandal was becoming a symbol of the rejection of mainstream society in favour of moving towards the goal of living a more pure and independent life.

For many, the pursuit of a more 'authentic' life became political. In the middle of the century, both abolitionists and the women's rights activists who emerged out of the anti-slavery movement turned to the sandalled image of Libertas. In her flowing gown and sandalled feet, images of the Roman goddess beseeched onlookers to consider the inequity of denying people the right to vote. When the Statue of Liberty, in her cloak, gown and sandals, was unveiled in 1886, suffragettes chartered a boat and circled Liberty Island, yelling through a megaphone that if Lady Liberty were to step off her pedestal she would not have the right to vote in either America or France.[14] The reference continued into the twentieth century: the Woman Suffrage Procession in Washington, DC, in 1913 featured a number of women dressed as Columbia or in classicizing dress, including sandals, in emulation of Libertas. Such associations between women's suffrage and Lady Liberty would eventually lead to the booted male Uncle Sam replacing the statue as the principal icon of the United States.[15]

Women's suffrage was not the only movement that politicized the sandal. It became the footwear of choice in the latter half of the nineteenth century for many who sought a new vision of the world, including advocates for dress reform. The Irish activist Charlotte Despard, who dedicated her life to the plight of the poor and suffrage for all, embraced the tenants of the Rational Dress Reform Movement and dispensed with tight-laced corsets and adopted sandals, becoming an icon of female radicalization. Despard's sartorial choices were

shared by other women and the look quickly became an established stereotype. Decades later George Orwell would decry it, describing women who dressed in this manner as members of 'that dreary tribe of high-minded women and sandal-wearers and bearded fruit-juice drinkers who come flocking towards the smell of "progress" like bluebottles to a dead cat'.[16] Men too embraced sandals. The British socialist Edward Carpenter, an advocate of the 'simple life', is credited with introducing sandal-wearing into England. Inspired by the writings of Thoreau, Carpenter sought an enlightened existence that included the embracing of homosexuality, vegetarianism, pacifism, socialism and dress reform. In his quest for liberation, he abandoned many aspects of fashionable attire, including shoes, which he claimed were 'coffins for the feet'.[17]

Carpenter saw no practical reason for the habitual donning of shoes except tradition, and asked that, just as democracy 'redeems

Edward Carpenter wearing his handmade sandals with socks. Alfred Mattison, *Self in Porch*, 1905.

that lowest and most despised of the people', it 'must redeem also the most menial and despised members and organs of the body', thereby linking the freedom of the individual and his body to liberation for all, and in turn further politicizing sandals.[18] Carpenter's interest in sandals led him to ask his friend Harold Cox, who went to India in 1885 to take a professorship in Aligarh, to acquire sandals for him there. Cox obliged and sent him two pairs of Kashmiri sandals.[19] Carpenter loved them and began to make replicas for himself and for friends at his home in Millthorpe, Derbyshire. He started offering sandals for sale, and before long sandals, often worn with socks, became a signifier of 'simple life' radicalism in England. One of the principal places to observe people in sandals was at Letchworth, the first 'garden city', in the early twentieth century. This thoughtful urban

Raymond Duncan's commitment to classical dress, including sandals, can be seen in this photograph. Like his parents, young Menalkas also wears handmade sandals. Bain News Service, *Raymond Duncan*, 1912.

plan was peopled with sandalled citizens who held a wide variety of political and lifestyle views from ideals of pacifism to vegetarianism. Sightseers flocked to Letchworth to gawk at the curious inhabitants. One newspaper reporter described the clothing of a woman as she walked past him, writing that she was 'not only hatless and obviously corsetless, she is also stockingless. And instead of shoes she wears primitive sandals.'[20] The use of the pejorative word primitive was telling, but there was also an appreciation of the ruddy good health and freedoms the proponents of simple living enjoyed. The article continues: 'Her walk is sinuous and graceful. All the children, boys and girls, are stockingless also, their legs brown and hard as walnut.' Further on, the writer also comments on the elegance of other sandal-clad 'beauties', many of whom would have been wearing sandals made by Carpenter or by those whom he had trained.

Although America had no Edward Carpenter, it did have Isadora Duncan, and, more importantly for the history of sandals, it also had her older brother Raymond. Like Carpenter, the Duncans espoused the quest for a simpler, more spiritually and artistically integrated life. Isadora expressed herself through dance and dress. Barefoot and clad in flowing gowns that imitated the attire of Greek goddesses, she shocked and thrilled audiences with her performances, while her personal and professional exploits filled the scandal pages in the United States and Europe, bringing her classicizing nakedness into mainstream consciousness. Raymond Duncan also lived an unconventional life and like his sister admired the 'simplicity' of Greek attire. He married a Greek woman and the couple dressed only in classical garb, including sandals, to the amazement of all who saw them. His Grecian dress may have had political and social reform aspirations, but it was frequently the focus of ridicule. Shortly after returning to the U.S. in the middle of January 1910 to do a lecture tour, Raymond Duncan's young son Menalkas and his maternal aunt were accosted by a police officer because of the scant garments they were wearing in the dead of winter. The aunt was put in jail and, in his tunic and sandals, Menalkas was taken to the Children's Society. Raymond showed up in similar attire to retrieve his son; the press declared that his appearance 'was utterly unlike anything recorded in the annals of society'.[21]

The scandalizing sandals worn by the Duncans were crafted by Raymond himself. He agreed with a well-known physician that

> we have never improved on the Greek and Roman footgear, though I am not such a dreamer of dreams as to suppose for a moment that our fashionable ladies will ever become sensible enough to take to sandals, even for the seaside. Besides, even if they are so inclined, boot makers and the hosiers would hardly encourage them in their ideas, as it would bode ill to their prosperity.[22]

Despite this discouraging forecast, the sandal was beginning to make inroads into fashion, and later in the century shoe manufacturers and retailers would promote this new style not as a substitute form of footwear but as an additional necessity in stylish wardrobes.

It was not, however, the sandal's relationship to eccentricity or radical thought that would cause it to be accepted by the fashionable; rather, it was its relationship to health. In Britain, the *Reading Eagle* reported in 1901 that the wearing of sandals without stockings had become a fad in London parks. The association with freedom and play made sandals especially appropriate for children's attire and the healthy benefits of 'barefoot' sandals were often touted. The following year a reporter in France wrote,

> English sandals are a novelty . . . English children go stockingless but sandaled and even their elders are now acquiring a belief in the system. Women who have pretty feet are, of course, not averse to following the fad but it is one that is not likely to be generally adopted here, for most French women cramp their pedal extremities too much for them to be symmetrical.[23]

This pair of children's 'barefoot sandals' featured cut-outs to encourage 'healthy' air circulation. Canadian, early 20th century.

Tango boots featured sandal-like laces and were worn for evening wear, although this illustration from the cover of *Puck* depicts a woman in swimwear in a pair at the beach. Tango boots, French, 1910–20. Jack Held, 'Just between Friends', *Puck*, 29 August 1914.

For all its notoriety, the barefoot sandal still did not actually reveal much of the foot. Instead, it simply featured perforations on the vamp, the part of the shoe that covers the forepart of the foot, or it featured wide strips of leather that completely encased the foot. Both these approaches increased ventilation but did not fully reveal the feet. For some, the increased popularity of wearing 'barefoot' sandals without hose continued to smack of the 'lower orders'. Sandals and savagery were never far removed from each other in the popular mind, and people were warned

> You must bear in mind that the foot of the well-bred child is a very tender thing, and no amount of running wild will ever make the cuticle as hard as that of a savage child . . . therefore, that the risks run of getting dirt which may be poisonous into scratches on the feet, owing to their being partially exposed . . . are greater than the thing is worth, for poisoned blood is a thing which can never be properly cured.[24]

In the days before antibiotics, this concern, it must be said, had some basis in reality.

Despite comments like this, many physicians began to advocate the wearing of sandals without socks. The *New York Times* reported in 1912:

> This innovation is highly approved by medical men here, who think that by exposing the foot and part of the leg to the air the physical system is much strengthened. Two physicians who have made a special study of the subject, Prof. Raymond and Dr. Charlier, declare that 40 per cent of delicate girls can have their health restored by discarding stockings in Summer.[25]

In the 1910s, sandal-inspired footwear appeared again in women's fashion. Some examples, as in the past, simply featured ribbons to be laced up the leg, but the more daring wore actual toe-revealing and flat-soled sandals. In 1914, the popular French actress Jeanne

Provost appeared one evening with her bare feet shod in pretty sandals. The press reported her as saying, 'it is delightful to have one's feet quite free.'[26] The article ended by stating that Provost had started the trend for the 'trouser skirt', intimating that a fashion for sandals was sure to follow.[27] Slowly but surely, the idea of women wearing toe-revealing sandals was starting to enter into the cultural consciousness; however, sandals themselves languished as a fashion accessory.

The sandal in menswear remained next to impossible. In 1917 an article in the *San Jose Evening News* attempting to promote the wearing of sandals as a means of conserving resources during the First World War wrote:

> perhaps it is useless to expect that all men and women will ever adopt the comfortable and sensible custom of wearing sandals but it is to be hoped that the time will come when a portly business man can walk down the street wearing sandals without having the police stop him on the theory that he has just escaped from Agnews.[28]

Given that Agnews was a local insane asylum, it is clear that men would have to wait before they could comfortably don sandals.

At the close of the First World War, men in sandals continued to be viewed with suspicion – an opinion only reinforced by the return of Raymond Duncan's son to the news headlines around Christmas in 1920. This time, Menalkas had run away from his father's home in Paris and, much to the merriment of the press, abandoned his traditional garb for trousers and shoes. An article in the *New York Times* bore the headline, 'Trouserless Home Greets Menalkas . . . Boy Sighs for Modernity . . . Wanted to Enjoy His New Clothes and Know at Least One Non-vegetarian Christmas'. In the article, Menalkas is described as not wishing to be returned to his father's house, 'preferring his nice gray suit to the chlamys and sandals' and hungering 'for the turkey and mincemeat which he had promised himself in celebration of his first modern Christmas'.[29]

Sandals were central to the sartorial expression of a number of other notable people in the 1920s, in addition to the Duncans. The celebrated African American entertainer Josephine Baker kept the sandal's connection to exoticism and the 'primitive' alive in people's imaginations. The Indian political activist Mahatma Gandhi advocated for Indian independence and self-sufficiency, and kept sandals political by wearing *chappals* that he had made himself.[30] The spectacular discovery of Tutankhamun's tomb in 1922 revealed numerous pairs of the young pharaoh's sandals, including an elegant pair in gold. Sandals could also be found in popular media. They were worn by the thousands in Cecil B. DeMille's silent film epic *The Ten Commandments* (1923), and in 1926 gilded sandals adorned the feet of the actress Vilma Bánky in the incredibly popular

The sandals worn by Mahatma Gandhi (right) contrast with the footwear worn by the poet Rabindranath Tagore (left) and were probably made by the civil rights leader himself. Unknown photographer, possibly late 1920s.

Shoes with woven uppers were considered airy summer wear in the 1920s.
The style was inspired by the traditional footwear of the Balkan region and was
known as the 'Lido sandal' after the pool area on a cruise ship. Swiss, made by
Bally, 1926.

movie *The Son of the Sheik*, also starring Rudolph Valentino. However, these multitudinous examples of sandals did little to spark fashion's interest in toe-exposing footwear.

The lack of interest in wearing foot-baring sandals is especially curious considering the radical transformations in women's fashion in the 1920s. Clothing had become quite revealing – hemlines rose to the knee, necklines plunged and arms were bared – and it seemed like a perfect moment for the archetypal sandal to finally be embraced. Instead, sandals in the 1920s most commonly referred to a high-heeled shoe that featured an upper made of woven leather and some form of strapping, typically a T-strap. Like children's 'barefoot' sandals of the previous decades, the majority of women's sandals in the 1920s were in reality more solid than strappy, and as with children's sandals could also be used to signify play. The most popular of these were the so-called Lido sandals, named after the famed beach in Venice, Italy, and subsequently, pool decks on cruise ships.[31] Lido sandals, deemed appropriate from boardwalk to garden party, featured intricately woven uppers and were touted as being made in Czechoslovakia, inspired by the uppers found on traditional Czech footwear called *opanke*.[32] Evening sandals were also popular, but despite descriptions such as 'the less of the evening sandal there is, the smarter it is for the season', dressy shoes remained just that: shoes.

At last, in 1926 *Vogue* reported that 'At the Lido, woven shoes were very smart [but] the really smart beach sandals show beautifully pedicured toes.'[33] Toes were on the verge of becoming fashionable. Resort wear and sun tanning had become popular among the wealthy who wintered in Palm Beach and on the French Riviera, and dress codes for the beach were starting to shift. Another *Vogue* article about appropriate beach attire at the Lido in Venice included drawings of two types of toe-revealing sandals.[34] One was a shoe that revealed the toes, called in later advertisements a 'Moroccan pyjama sandal', and the other was a wooden-soled sandal with two instep straps, identified as a 'Chinese clog'. The article also noted that when about to swim one put on rubber swim shoes, but that 'the longer one stayed at the Lido, the more often one forgets the shoes',[35] suggesting that women were finally able to bare their feet at the beach. Although these exoticizing Moroccan pyjama sandals and Chinese clogs continued to show up from time to time throughout the rest of the 1920s in relation to seaside attire, foot-baring sandals were rarely seen beyond the beach.

Pedicures, like sandals, were suggestive of exoticism, but they were also evocative of luxury. Chinese chiropodists beautified Parisians' feet, and foot care products and toenail polish were quickly becoming good business, especially as the criticism of hedonism was balanced by a focus on overall foot health. By the end of the decade, the female foot was polished and poised enough to be seen. The always prescient French shoe designer André Perugia offered cork-soled sandals strapped to the foot with linen bands for beachwear, and a strappy sandal with a slight wooden platform sole and gilded straps studded with rhinestones for evening wear in 1929, pointing to the direction fashion would soon take.

At the end of the decade sandals for men became part of the platform for men's dress reform. The Men's Dress Reform Party in Britain captured the attention of the press by promoting sandals and clothing that they deemed, 'healthier and better for men . . . with as much profit to their health and appearance as women have recently achieved'.[36] Yet revealing the male body remained problematic: 'in a given bunch of ten men you can find more strange looking bumps, curves and angles, also jints, than they is in a jigsaw puzzle. No, sir, I say, keep 'em covered up long as possible until we can breed a race of men that are pleasing to the eye in the raw.'[37] This letter to the editor in response to men's dress reform was itself very revealing. Creating a race of 'perfected men' was to be a political aim in countries around the world as a second world war began to brew, and ideas related to racial superiority and physical perfection would stoke fascist fires.

Finally, in the 1930s after the stock market crash, the naked foot was permitted to be a part of fashionable women's dress. 'Dancing feet are out of bondage – sandals are bare-toed, bare-heeled', *Vogue* proclaimed in 1931.[38] High-heeled sandals became the epitome of

This sandal with grosgrain straps is typical of the new toe-exposing footwear becoming popular for women in the 1930s. Swiss, made by Bally, 1934.

evening elegance, while peep-toe shoes that revealed just a bit of the toes were considered fashionable for daywear. Simple strappy sandals for leisure were especially popular – they were cheap. 'If you're a smart little poor girl, or a thrifty little rich girl, you may reduce your summer wardrobe to the nth power of efficiency by living in beach clothes this season', an article advised in 1930.[39] An advert for toe-revealing Shadow Sandals directed to United States shoe retailers for the summer of 1931 described the sandals on offer as 'evolved to meet the peculiar conditions of this unusual year . . . ridiculously low-priced – and few women will be able to deny themselves a pair or two. This is merchandise . . . timed to the public-purse – and timed to the merchant's need of profit.'[40] Indeed, the fact that sandals could be made with less material than regular shoes and were easily mass-produced did make them a less expensive alternative. The full-colour advertisement featured brightly hued sandals with names that evoked the classical past. In 1931 the marketing and fashion retail consultant Amos Parrish commented on the new vogue for sandals and described it as coming into women's fashion 'via the children's department'.[41] For the fashion-minded, it was precisely the sandal's connections to youthful exuberance and play that assimilated it into the everyday wardrobe.

Despite the new associations between sandals and play, politics and economics remained central to their use. The popularity of sandals in fashion was in fact closely linked to politics and economics. The 1930s saw unprecedented numbers of people with time on their hands. The New Leisure, as it was called in the United States, was the result of the overall reduction in the hours of the working week, due in part to legislation and in part to the Great Depression. Those faced with chronic unemployment were encouraged to engage in inexpensive activities such as going to local beaches or municipal pools. Carl Carmer wrote in 1936 for *Vogue*:

> The rich seek their country homes, their clubs, their yachts. Those not so fortunate rush to near-by waters, where cottages and hotels are as close to each other as their city homes.

Sparsely clad, they sun themselves on body-strewn beaches, swim in droves, dance on crowded piers, parade the 'board-walks' in milling throngs.[42]

Soon the inexpensive fashions used for these pursuits, including breezy beach pyjamas and open-toed sandals, also began to transition into loungewear worn at home, appropriate even for hostess attire. The strappy evening sandal that was 'so much in favor with the smartest women seen at Paris parties'[43] continued to feature elaborate cut-outs and strapping edged with light-catching gilt leather that did not seem to speak to frugality and yet proved to offer an economic advantage. Sandals in gold and silver metallic kid went with everything, meaning women no longer had to match their foot-wear to the colour of their gowns.[44] Likewise, the pedicures required to bare one's feet were encouraged as much for health as for style: 'If the fad takes, and becomes a fashion, women will have less foot ills in the future,' declared an article in 1932 reporting on the trend.[45]

Exoticism remained linked to the sandal. In 1935 the designers Elsa Schiaparelli and Alix (Germaine Émilie Krebs, who later adopted the name Madame Grès) presented collections of Indian-inspired evening dresses paired with low-heeled sandals that *Vogue* described as appropriate for dancing girls.[46] In 1936 Schiaparelli herself was featured in *Vogue*, photographed vacationing in Tunisia wearing a pair of wooden platform sandals reminiscent of traditional *qabâqib* (tall stilted sandals worn in Turkish baths), and the caption for the image described her as having 'gone native'.[47] Although the French couturier Madeleine Vionnet's classicizing gowns cried out for sandals à la Raymond Duncan, it was the platform footwear from the Renaissance that inspired the next step in sandal design.

Platform shoes had not been in fashion since the seventeenth century, when women in Italy and Spain were mounted on high platform footwear called chopines, but in the 1920s platforms suddenly came back into fashion as beachwear. The French shoe designer André Perugia designed several models. Schiaparelli also paired cork platforms with her beach pyjamas in 1929, and *Vogue* advocated high-platform cork beach shoes the following year. But platforms as fashionable streetwear was a new idea, introduced by the Italian shoe designer Salvatore Ferragamo in the 1930s.

Ferragamo had moved from his native Bonito in southern Italy, first to Boston in 1914 to assist his brothers working at a cowboy-boot making factory and then to Santa Barbara, finally setting up shop in Los Angeles in 1923, where he rose to fame making shoes for both film studios and celebrities. Among his Hollywood commissions at that time was the order to create seemingly innumerable sandals for DeMille's *The Ten Commandments*. In his autobiography Ferragamo writes that the fashion that he 'ached to alter was the closed-toe shoe . . . I began to dream about putting women's feet in sandals.'[48] As he was fulfilling his order for costume sandals, he began to offer other sandals of his own design to a number of movie 'extras' he had come to know.[49] The style did not catch on, however, until after a princess from India ordered five pairs in different colours, and Ferragamo 'Roman sandals' became a hit in Los Angeles. He received a commission to make footwear for Douglas Fairbanks and it is believed that he created the platform shoes worn by the 'Mongol' prince in the 1923 silent film *The Thief of Bagdad*. These theatrical boots were inspired by a design created by the film's assistant art director, in which he had sketched a wedged heel. In the coming years, sandals, platforms and wedges would be transformed by Ferragamo into items of fashion.

Despite his success in the United States, Ferragamo returned to Italy in 1927 eager to expand his business using Italian shoemakers – but his timing could not have been worse. The worldwide economic depression, coupled with Italy's own economic and political upheaval, led to a shortage of conventional shoemaking materials. Ferragamo's inventive mind set to work. One of the materials that he turned to was cork, and his inspiration was the Renaissance chopine. There were two principal forms of chopine: the Italian chopine, which was made of wood, and the Spanish chopine, made of cork. Italian chopines, specifically Venetian ones, reached remarkable heights but were typically worn concealed beneath the skirt of women's dresses

Thus go the Ladies in Spain upon their Pattens.

at the end of the sixteenth century.[50] In contrast, Spanish chopines were worn fully visible, and as a result were often excessively bejewelled or gilded. As accessories of ostentatious display, Spanish chopines were important luxury goods and their use in upper-class women's dress led the Spanish archpriest Alfonso Martínez de Toledo, Queen Isabella of Spain's confessor, to lament at the end of the fifteenth century that there was not enough cork in Spain to satisfy women's demands for these platform shoes.[51] Of the two forms of chopine, it seems to have been the Spanish model that most inspired Ferragamo. In contrast, the French shoe designer Roger Vivier referenced the Venetian style when he sketched a high platform sandal in 1937. Vivier first offered his design to Herman Delman, head of Delman Shoes, but after it was rejected as being too radical, he offered it to Schiaparelli, who paired it with a long neoclassical gown that covered the footwear in the Venetian style. The credit, however, goes to Ferragamo for transforming the platform over the next decade into an icon of luxury and one of the most fashionable forms of footwear.

Spanish chopines were highly ornate platform overshoes worn by women as markers of status for centuries. They fell out of fashion in the 17th century but inspired the fashion for platforms in the 1930s. Spanish, c. 1540.

(*above*) The wedge platform of this sandal is accentuated by the interplay between matt black suede and reflective silver kid. Salvatore Ferragamo's platforms inspired myriad designers in both Europe and America. European, late 1930s.

(*right*) Salvatore Ferragamo invented the wedge as an orthopaedic shoe but it quickly became a fashion staple. This pair of black satin evening wedges was worn by the actress Ruth Gordon. Italian, made by Ferragamo, 1938–40.

The multicoloured and gilt platform sandals that Ferragamo designed took the fashion world by storm in the late 1930s, inspiring a new form of footwear. His other innovation, the wedge, was also commonly used to make sandals. The design was originally orthopaedic in purpose, but fashion embraced it immediately. Both these types of sole, the platform and the wedge, helped to redefine the fashionable silhouette. As a visually unusual type of footwear, platform-soled sandals provided an instant update to women's dress and proclaimed the wearer as fashion-forward.

'Men unanimously, don't like them. They are deprived, they say of one of their favourite sights, a delicately high instep teetering along on a French heel. Women, however, are buying the wedge-heeled shoes in droves, partly because these types are comfortable, partly because they are considered smart and mostly because they are new,' reported the *New York Times* in 1940.[52] Criticisms lobbied against platforms and wedges echoed criticisms of chopines centuries earlier, such as Cosmo Agnelli's screed written in 1592:

> Women think that strutting around from this magnificent perspective makes them alluring, but true beauty consists in proper proportions. Elongating your legs with heels that are a quarter or even half an arm's length leaves you looking like a monster.[53]

The heightened nakedness of the foot offered by platform and wedge sandals could have been alluring, yet somewhat counter-intuitively there was mounting evidence that men apparently seemed to find the exposure of the female foot singularly unattractive. The *Pittsburgh Press* wrote:

> Golden and silver sandals may have graced the feet of Grecian goddesses on Olympian evenings. But ever since modern women and girls were induced to adopt them for daytime street wear we have suffered frequent fits of shudders at the spectacle of dusty heels and bulging bunions unconcealed by the gleaming straps.[54]

The foot-concealing high-heeled shoe seemed to have been favoured by men and certainly remained the predominant form of footwear in men's erotica.

This division between fashionable and sexually alluring footwear would become increasingly important during the years of the Second World War. The professed male disdain for platforms and wedges made them useful footwear choices when husbands and boyfriends were away at war. Throughout the war years, most women wore 'sensible' shoes, often with low wedges, as they helped with the war effort, but when women needed dressier footwear many donned the platform sandals deemed unattractive by men, thus allowing women to continue to participate in fashion while simultaneously discouraging unwanted male attention. The industry journal *Boot and Shoe Recorder* of 17 January 1942 discussed these shoes, writing: 'They may look like a lot of foolishness to you, but you'd be surprised how many, even so-called very sensible women, like a thoroughly frivolous shoe now and then.'[55] The platform sandal, with its connections to leisure and play, was perhaps the most uplifting footwear choice women could make.

In North American men's fashion, sandals remained peripheral, despite reports such as the one in the *Palm Beach Post* in 1939 that noted:

> Phenomenon sandals. For decades, it has gone without saying that one of the more important clauses of the bill of rights safeguarded bedraggled sneakers as the standard summer footwear. Come this summer . . . men are grabbing every kind of exotic hoofery from Norwegian moccasins to wood-soled shoes and South Sea rope sandals – stuff that previously would have drawn a snort if seen on anybody except a museum statue.[56]

European men had begun to sport a male version of the 'barefoot' sandal, but in North America they remained questionable and most men avoided them.

During the war, many traditional shoemaking materials were rationed, pushing shoemakers to use a range of materials to make footwear. This pair of platform sandals was made using vegetable fibre. Probably French, 1938–45.

One of the challenges facing the integration of sandals into the male wardrobe was that men in sandals continued to convey the idea of radicalism. George Orwell's book *The Road to Wigan Pier*, published in 1937, was a call to socialism and featured a critique of why the movement was not more universally accepted. He wrote that the ideals of socialism, justice and liberty were buried because 'the very word "Socialism" calls up . . . a picture of vegetarians with wilting beards, of Bolshevik commissars (half gangster, half gramophone), of earnest ladies in sandals, shock-headed Marxists.'[57] Orwell continues, writing that the cause would be helped if 'the sandals and pistachio-coloured shirts could be put in a pile and burnt . . . [and] the more intelligent kind of Socialist stop alienating possible supporters in silly and quite irrelevant ways'.[58] He warns that if these sartorial issues which cause many people to flinch with revulsion are not addressed, 'fascism may win'. His predictions were timely, for as Orwell was writing, fascism threatened the world, and by the end of the decade the Second World War was being waged.

Throughout war-torn countries, women began to wear simple sandals out of necessity. Limited resources were available but many makers showed remarkable inventiveness and a lively engagement with their charge. In Italy, shoemakers were lauded for returning to their classical roots and offering up thin-strapped sandals reminiscent of ancient models.[59] In France, exaggeratedly high platform sandals became a symbol of wartime resistance, as they were showy and appeared to fly in the face of wartime privation. *Vogue*, reporting on French fashion during the war, commented that French women realized that,

> saving only benefited the Germans. The more material the French used, the less the Germans got. The more workers employed to produce French clothes, the fewer would be conscripted for Germany . . . about 1942 came rebellious signs of fashion bravado . . . high wooden clogs pedaled bicycles . . . frivolity was one way a Frenchwoman said to the Germans that although they took her country, took away her liberty of speech and action, they could not break her spirit.[60]

In 1947, Salvatore Ferragamo won the prestigious Neiman Marcus Fashion Award for his Invisible Sandal, which featured clear nylon straps inspired by fishing line. Italian, made by Ferragamo, 1947.

Platform sandals could be easily made out of non-rationed materials such as cork and some textiles or fibres such as straw and raffia. Their popularity increased during the war years, but as the war neared its end the platform's days became numbered.

Reports from post-war Paris complaining about the ill effects of platform footwear on gait announced the end of the style. Christian Dior's ultra-feminine New Look of 1947 revolutionized fashion and called for a new form of footwear. Ferragamo's Invisible Sandal from that same year was both forward-looking and *retardataire*. The straps of the sandal were inspired by clear fishing line and pointed to the increasing nakedness of the female foot in fashion, but the cantilevered wedge sole covered in reflective silver kid was, like the platform, destined to be discarded. Fashion was putting greater emphasis on the high heel as it moved women's attire into greater alignment with men's erotic ideals. Elegant high-heeled sandals once again became popular for evening wear but, unlike their 1930s predecessors, they featured the new, more attenuated stiletto heel and thinner straps. Indeed, the earliest narrow all-steel heel, the precursor to the invention of the stiletto, was designed by André Perugia in 1951 and was held to the foot using just two thin straps. The fashion for high-heeled sandals quickly caught on and was even deemed formal and dignified enough for Queen Elizabeth II to wear to her coronation: in 1953 she ascended the throne in a pair of toe-revealing gilt sandals created by Roger Vivier, who designed them for Rayne, the British shoe manufacturer with a Royal Warrant to the Queen.[61]

The strappiness of the evening sandal was mirrored in the minimal construction of flat-soled summer sandals. As early as 1944, thong sandals were being promoted in fashion. One *Vogue* article from 1945 claimed that the new thong sandals were directly related to the war: 'They can't possibly be worn with stockings. They couldn't have happened before the war, because we hadn't learned to go barefoot.'[62] Another *Vogue* spread claimed that the new 'barely there' sandals were not reminiscent of Julius Caesar or of Raymond Duncan,[63] yet there was no doubt that these sandals were classicizing in form. A love affair with Italy, so recently an enemy nation to the Allies, was

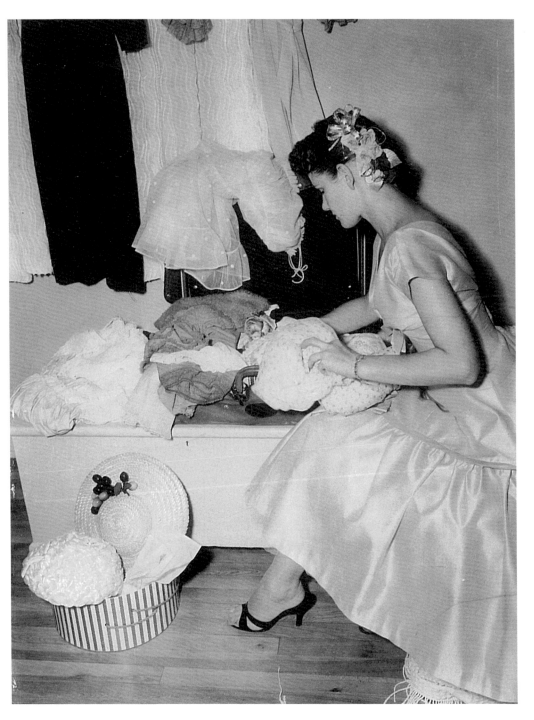

By the 1950s, barely-there high-heeled sandals were popular for dressy occasions. Canadian, 1957.

in the air, and Italian sandals reminiscent of days gone by were everywhere, as attested to by the pair worn by Audrey Hepburn in *Roman Holiday* (1953). This new fashion revived the connection between leisure and sandals – a point made clear at the end of the film, when Hepburn's royal character marks her return to duty by abandoning her sandals and stepping into a pair of 'serious' high heels.

It was during the war that the ballet flat, a descendant of the early nineteenth-century satin sandal-slipper, also came into fashion. In 1944 the American fashion designer Claire McCardell reportedly put her models in textile ballet slippers because of wartime restrictions on footwear materials, creating a fashion that remains popular to this day. As with the Italian sandal, Audrey Hepburn helped to popularize the style. By the 1950s, the ballet flat became the footwear choice of the ingénue.

Despite the popularity of sandals in women's fashion, sandals in men's dress still possessed counter-cultural associations. The post-war romance of 'bumming' around Europe, and their prominence in the garb of many European intellectuals, gave sandals cachet, but it was the emergence of the West Coast beatnik that further cemented the 'alternative' associations of the sandal in the 1950s. Herb Caen of the *San Francisco Chronicle* coined the label 'beatnik' in 1958, the year after Jack Kerouac's *On the Road* was published. The name stuck and lent the subculture a decidedly negative association that played on old-school Bolshevist tropes and current Cold War fears. The stereotyped uniform of the late 1950s beatnik was khakis, turtlenecks and sandals, with or without socks. Beatniks quickly became the poster children of nonconformism and their dress was both highly imitable and frequently spoofed. Henri Lenoir, owner of the Vesuvio Café, a favourite with beatniks in San Francisco, lampooned the whole concept and put a sign in his window advertising a 'beatnik kit', complete with turtleneck, sunglasses and sandals.[64] On the East Coast, beatniks could escape to Provincetown on Cape Cod and purchase sandals from Menalkas Duncan, who despite his youthful rejection of his father's lifestyle had grown up to become a renowned sandal-maker.

These well-worn sandals belonged to the former prime minister of Canada, Pierre Trudeau. He wore them to 'bum around the world' as a young man. European, 1948–9.

For the more conventional man, however, wearing sandals remained unthinkable. In 1948 an article predicted that sandals would soon be available for men in gold and silver. This was seen as calamitous: 'the day when men start wearing 'em is likely to be recorded, in the story of American civilization's decline and fall, as one of the sadder footnotes.'[65] Meanwhile, another piece quipped,

> These new sandals for men are too fast for me. Saw what I thought was a barefoot boy of 40-odd on Fifth Ave. last night, only to discover he wore sandals. Just a sole and a strap between his toes. He wore shorts too. Dressed like that, I'd feel as in one of those nightmares when you suddenly find yourself in a crowd of people – *sans* clothing.[66]

It may have been the nakedness revealed by the wearing of the sandal that most men rejected, but it was precisely this exposure that kept the sandal in women's dress, a feature taken to a humorous level in the following decade with Beth Levine's completely upper-less sandals of 1965.

As the 1950s progressed, foot-revealing sandals were becoming a part of everyday women's dress. For daywear in the summer many women continued to wear the simple barely-there sandals inspired by Italian models, and for the evening, stiletto-heeled sandals had become de rigueur. Ferragamo designed numerous sandals in the 1950s, including his famous Kimo cage sandal, which came with a 'sock' in gold kid or satin that could be worn with the sandal to change its look. He even took out a patent on this high-fashion version of socks-and-sandals.

Around the house, women began also to wear the Japanese rubber thong sandals that flooded the market in the 1950. The earliest flip-flops, as they would come to be called because of the sound they made when worn, were marketed to women as shower shoes and were at first called by their Japanese name, *zori*. Japan was already mass-producing rubber footwear in the 1930s, and after the war manufacturers such as the Hiroshima Rubber Company

In the mid-1960s, shoe designers played with the idea of designing upper-less footwear. This pair, embellished with Garden-of-Eden-like foliage, were worn glued to the foot. They were never mass-produced. American, designed by Beth Levine, made by Herbert Levine, 1965.

began exporting rubber *zori* to the United States and beyond. Easy to wear and remarkably cheap, flip-flops soon eclipsed other forms of beach sandals as the emblem of summer relaxation. The flip-flop became part of the southern California surfer culture, and in Australia and New Zealand these rubber sandals were integrated into daily dress.[67]

The 1950s also saw the widespread use of the type of sandal that would come to be known as the jelly. Based on the design of French fisherman sandals, the first jelly was patented in France by Jean Dauphant in 1954.[68] By 1955, the jelly had become the first injection-moulded sandal. They became particularly popular in many African countries; in Eritrea, the jelly became a national symbol of resistance and a statue of a pair of jellies stands in the heart of the city of Asmara, commemorating the fight for independence. *Shida*, as the sandals are called, were worn by guerrilla fighters starting in the 1960s and, given the lack of a uniform, were the one item of dress all fighters wore.[69] The style was also popular in South America, from where it was later reintroduced into American fashion in the 1980s, creating a short-lived craze for these sandals in vivid, jewel-like colours.

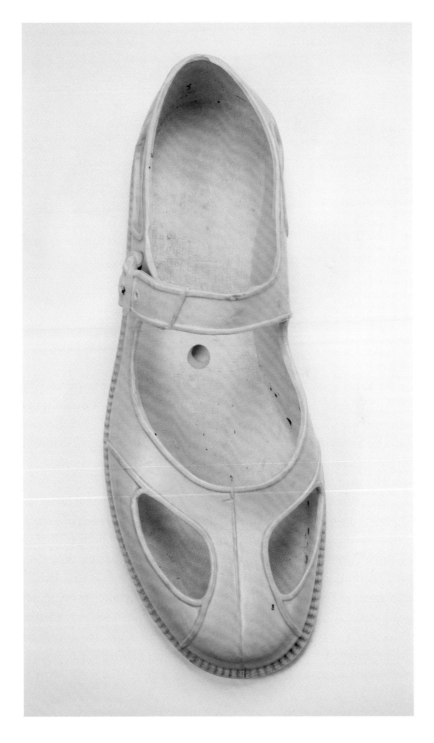

(*above*) The Sandak sandal was one of the earliest injection-moulded forms of footwear. It was made in France for the West African market. French, 1955.

(*left*) This pair of humble Bata flip-flops was worn by the Dalai Lama. Indian, 21st century.

By the 1960s, social unrest had given rise to a wide variety of movements that challenged the status quo. The Civil Rights Movement, women's liberation and environmentalism reflected a desire for cultural change. Much of this wide-ranging discontent found expression through unconventional dress, and, specifically, in sandal-wearing. Counter-culture 'hippies' pressed sandals, often from foreign countries, into their politically motivated sartorial style. As Hunter S. Thompson wrote in 1967 for the *New York Times Magazine*, 'Hippies despise phoniness; they want to be open, honest, loving and free. They reject the plastic pretense of 20th-century America, preferring to go back to the "natural life," like Adam and Eve.'[70] À la Edward Carpenter, they preferred the handmade to the mass-produced and the flip-flop, although cheap and readily available, remained a signifier of surfer, and not hippie, culture. Imported Indian *chappals* and Mexican *huaraches* were the choice for many

(*above*) Intricately woven *huaraches* from Mexico became popular in the 1960s. Mexican, made by José Martinéz, 2014.

(*right*) Birkenstocks were first embraced for their orthopaedic properties but became icons of liberal politics. German, 1990s.

hippies and, as with radicals from earlier periods, their association with exotic 'Otherness' lent them an air of alluring authenticity. In addition, sandals were seen as reviving connections to spirituality, and they went on to become the chosen footwear for many 'Jesus people' or 'Jesus freaks', who evolved out of the hippie movement in the early 1970s. For most people, handmade leather sandals were viewed as the regalia of those who chose to 'drop out' of mainstream society.

It was in this milieu that the famous Birkenstock sandal was popularized in America. In 1966 the dress designer Margot Fraser began importing Birkenstocks after finding that wearing a pair alleviated her severe foot pain. 'All the exercises the doctor told me to do, like standing on a phone book and grabbing it with my toes (which made me feel like a hero if I did it for three minutes), I did automatically with these sandals.'[71] As with Dr Martens, another form

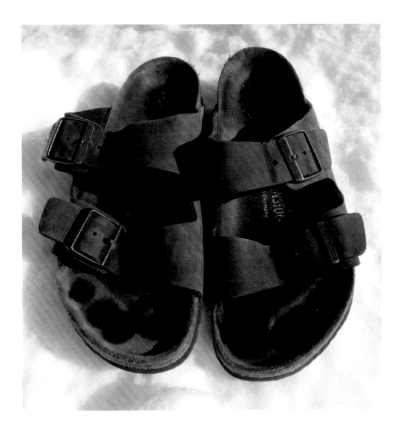

Dr Scholl sandals were designed to tone the legs and feet when worn.
Their specially sculpted footbed required the foot to continually grip and flex.
American, made by Dr Scholl, 1980.

of counter-culture footwear, Birkenstocks were originally created by a German. In 1902, Konrad Birkenstock, one in a long line of shoemakers going back to the eighteenth century, was asked to create supportive footwear for recuperating German soldiers. He developed an ergonomically-shaped insole using cork. The expertise of the company was primarily in crafting insoles, but in 1964 they released a suede-covered, cork-soled sandal called the Madrid, designed by Konrad's grandson Karl Birkenstock, and a classic was born. The ability of the sole to mould to the wearer's foot and its broad instep straps created a sandal that was easy to wear with socks and earned it a die-hard following. The sandal's association with comfort and health made it a natural choice for sale by health food stores, which were among its earliest distributors. Its anti-fashion aesthetic and the fact that many wore Birkenstocks with socks connected the style to the sandals worn by earlier simple life advocates and other 'malcontents'. In the 1970s, Birkenstocks became associated with hippies and others who sought a more 'authentic' lifestyle, especially those in the women's rights movement.

Dr Scholl's Exercise Sandal also came out in the 1960s. It too was promoted as footwear for good health, but, rather than being embraced by counter-culture adherents, this all-American sandal became a fashionable staple worn by young women as a means of exercising their feet and legs. 'The first great surge of popularity came when the London "birds" discovered the exercise sandal looked great with their minis.'[72] Indeed, long lengths of leg were revealed by miniskirts, and to complement the look fashion offered a range of options, from minimalist sandals to futuristic gladiator sandals that laced up the leg. Exoticism also informed the fashion, but it was exoticism with a tendency towards luxury rather than asceticism, and it smacked of Orientalism and decadence.

In men's fashion, the 'peacock revolution', which encouraged men to express greater individuality through dress, looked to other cultures and other times for inspiration, and the sandal seemed poised as a possibility for men; indeed, some African American men

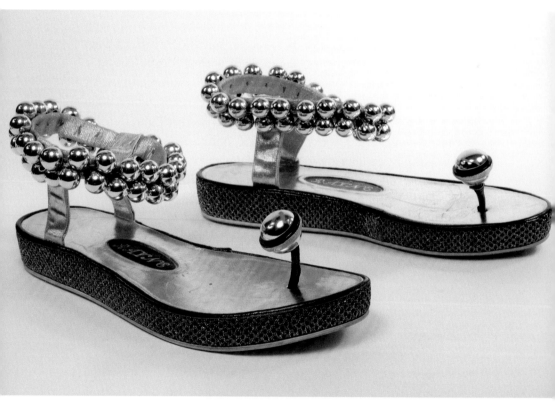

This pair of sandals by Rayne was inspired by Indian footwear and ankle jewellery. The toe-knob structure is modelled on the traditional *paduka*. British, 1967.

donned African sandals along with *dashikis* as part of the Black Pride movement in the mid-1960s. But for most 'straight-laced' white men, sandals continued to be taboo.

As political protest gave way to self-indulgent hedonism, and as disco eclipsed folk music, sandals as signifiers of play became a central theme in women's fashion. The high platform sandal, a reimagining of the 1940s style, was initially popular among teens and young women and was seen as an extreme fashion, especially when worn with socks. The trend was reported on in *Time* magazine: '[socks] . . . are most frequently worn with cork-soled, open-toed sandals or wedges . . . the most ardent socks supporters seem to be teens and the under-30 set who love the pizazz of a fashion leg.'[73] Women had worn sandals with stockings, but colourful socks were something new and the preference for thick, rainbow-hued socks marked the trend as juvenile. This connection to youth complicated the erotic value ascribed to platform sandals. Distaste for the style was not revived, however; the vintage vibe suggested an aura of childish dress-up, and from news reports to Hollywood films, platform sandals were depicted as part of the costume of sexually exploited children; Jodie Foster's character in *Taxi Driver* (1976) epitomized the look. As the *New York Times* put it,

> Today's composite of runaways in New York is not the Norman Rockwell *Saturday Evening Post* cover of the lovably defiant and appealing freckled 14-year-old boy with his clothes in a bandana tied to the end of a stick; it is a 14-year-old girl in platform soles and hot pants on the street corner on Eighth Avenue, asking passers-by whether they want a good time.[74]

Fashion also promoted the hypersexualization of the sandal: 'Think naked – more bareness is the rule. Sandals have been pared-down, stripped-away. And nothing lengthens the leg faster than a high, bare sandal!'[75] As the libidinous decade progressed, the quirky platform sandal was eventually replaced by the even more erotic

(*above*) British shoe designer Terry de Havilland designed many of the most fashionable platforms in the 1970s. British, 1972.

(*right*) High-heeled sandals replaced platforms as the most fashionable footwear in the second half of the 1970s, as disco fashions came to dominate. Italian, made by Benito Scardavi, 1975–9.

stiletto sandal. For most men, however, sandals continued to be taboo, too risky even in a period when some men were venturing out in high platform shoes and boots. But times were about to change.

The 1980s saw the revival of the peep-toe in women's fashion, but the decade was more about the 'power' pump than the playful sandal. Men's dress, however, saw the introduction of the first sports sandal, the Teva, in 1984. The Grand Canyon river guide Mark Thatcher invented the Teva after he noticed that many of his clients did not have appropriate footwear: sneakers became waterlogged and flip-flops were dangerously slippery when rafting. Thatcher contrived a solution, repurposing a Velcro watchband to make straps for a flip-flop, and the idea for a rugged, all-terrain sandal was born. The Teva

Tevas were designed for rugged wear and their associations with outdoor sports helped integrate sandals back into the male wardrobe. American, 1990s.

was a sandal for adventuring, not lounging, and its capacity to signify active rather than passive leisure, as well as its exorbitant price, finally made sandals acceptable to many men. One writer compared the Teva to a supersonic jet, saying, 'banish all thoughts of leather thongs or simple flip-flops: the latest adventure sandals have as little in common with these as the Concorde has to a paper dart.'[76]

As the idea of men in sandals became more acceptable, the once unisex flip-flop was also given a redesign to be gender-specific. In the 1990s, flip-flops for men featured heavier soles and thick leather or heavy nylon web thongs. They were available in hues from jungle green to dirt brown: colours that suggested off-road adventure. In contrast, flip-flops marketed to women began to be offered in candy colours, and many were extravagantly embellished with everything from rhinestones to plastic flowers. The Brazilian brand Havaiana, whose flip-flops had been a staple of the Brazilian wardrobe since the early 1960s, entered the world of high fashion in 1999 when Jean-Paul Gaultier featured their flip-flops on the runway. By 2001, the company was offering artisan-crafted flip-flops for the fashion market, and they were retailed in the U.S. and Europe in high-end stores.[77]

The popularization of 'Casual Fridays' in North America put new stresses on the male wardrobe, and suddenly the off-duty sandal made an appearance in the workplace. Rather than hiding behind the uniform of male authority, the suit and business brogue, Casual Fridays required that aspects of workers' leisure time be revealed at the office – and confusion ensued. Sneakers and jeans were the most common sartorial choice, but some men chose to reveal more and came to work in flip-flops or Tevas. Although these sandal choices conveyed a laid-back nature or an adventurous spirit, the flaunting of the naked male foot continued to be unsettling. Advice columns and op-ed pieces decrying the wearing of foot-revealing sandals exploded.

The anxiety over what type of footwear was appropriate for men and how much of their body should be made visible foreshadowed much larger shifts that would take place in men's fashion, as one astute reader of the *New York Times* pointed out in 1994. He wrote:

As men gain experience in dressing outside the rules, they'll develop the taste for fashion that fuels the women's clothing business. If menswear plays it smart, what it fears from Casual Fridays can help turn the industry around. Not angst, but opportunity.[78]

The increased body awareness introduced, in part, by sandal-wearing, encouraged male pedicures, fitness regimes that focused on muscle definition and the removal of body hair coined 'manscaping' at the turn of the twenty-first century.

If the integration of the sandal into men's dress was partially responsible for encouraging men to put greater thought into how they presented themselves, the strappy high-heeled designer sandal that came into women's fashion in the late 1990s simply signalled a perpetuation of ideas about what made a woman attractive. While the popular 'stripper shoe'-inspired sandal of the early 2000s linked sandals once again to play, although in this manifestation it was role-play and the wearer toyed with looking like a 'working girl'.

The resurgence in the popularity of the Birkenstock in the 1980s and '90s among university students and New Agers kept the Edward Carpenteresque association between politics and footwear alive as the 2000s began. The term 'Birkenstock liberal' was coined by conservatives in 2003 in relation to the Vermont Democrat Howard Dean's presidential aspirations. With a simple reference to a type of footwear, images of granola-crunching feminists, LGBTQ rights activists, bearded, tree-hugging environmentalists and other 'un-American undesirables' were immediately conjured up. The term Birkenstock liberal and the importance of footwear in the construction of social identity in the early 2000s was contemplated by Ginia Bellafante, who wrote:

The Birkenstock is a handy referent in a world increasingly prone to thinking about shoes as an infallible system of social and ideological classification. To say, for instance, that someone is a Manolo Blahnik woman – 'Manolo' now an expression in such wide use it appears on op-ed pages without exposition – is to suggest very efficiently that she is between 28 and 45, with a post-feminist orientation and an Austenesque appetite for marrying well. Shoes can telegraph a lot about someone – where a person has come from, landed or would like to go. And as codes to allegiances of class and style, shoes may be able to tell us how someone might vote.[79]

Although Bellafante's purpose was to poke holes in the association between Birkenstocks and Dean's ideology, her assessments were insightful – in the early 2000s a wide variety of types of footwear carried with them what appeared to be rigid social identities. This was particularly problematic for younger feminists, who sought to distance themselves from their sandal-footed forebears. As with all footwear, however, the meaning of Birkenstocks was fluid and mutable. The same year that 'Birkenstock liberal' was coined, Birkenstocks were also chosen to be included in the lavish Academy Awards gift bags. The actress Gwyneth Paltrow was seen wearing them, and the supermodel Heidi Klum was brought on board by the company to design new styles for both Europe and North America.[80] Dealers were unable to keep stock on the shelves; in 2014, nearly 20 million pairs of Birkenstocks were sold, and according to the *New Yorker*, Manolo Blahnik himself had admitted to wearing them.[81] The unfashionable was suddenly fashionable and, to some degree, the Birkenstock was depoliticized.

The 2010s saw sandals included in most people's wardrobes and yet they continued to cause anxiety; in particular, the exposure of men's bare feet in public remained a cause for consternation. While on holiday in Hawaii in 2011, Barack Obama, then president of the United States, was photographed wearing flip-flops while getting a snow cone with his youngest daughter. The press went mad. Many people found his flip-flops a better choice of beach footwear than that of former U.S. president Nixon, who 'famously came off like an uptight weirdo because of his bizarre habit of walking along the beach in his formal wingtip shoes'.[82] Experts were interviewed; most expressed surprise but also gave him a pass: 'I don't think this a big deal. Your footwear belongs to the occasion. If you're on the beach buying your daughter snow cones, I don't think you can beat him up for this. Now if he's wearing flip-flops to the State of the Union, that'd be different,' presidential historian Jane Hampton Cook was quoted as saying in the paper that broke the story.[83] Brian Moylan of Gawker wrote, 'Look, I am far more outraged that George W. Bush wore Crocs ... [Flip-flops] are disgusting, uncouth, and unattractive [but] he was on vacation. When you are not at work you don't have to answer to anyone.'[84]

The unsettling thing about men in sandals was not so much related to people's dislike of the aesthetics of the humble flip-flop, but rather was related to a cultural discomfort with seeing men's feet in sandals. 'My husband's feet are gnarled, horny, hairy and callused, and he insists on wearing flip-flops in the summer. Is there any way I can get him to get them groomed before he goes out in public?' asked a concerned wife to style advice columnist Russell Smith. 'The male foot, particularly as it ages, is not the most seductive body part,' he responded. He advised that her husband should wear running shoes or open-weave shoes, and also warned her to have her husband avoid 'the worst of all footwear, those ghastly Velcro rubber "sport" sandals, the pride of barbecuing mall dads in SUVs everywhere'.[85]

Men's footwear choices were becoming increasingly complex in the early part of the twenty-first century. Not only were men's feet deemed unseemly, but a number of popular leisurewear choices, including Tevas and the newly invented moulded, closed-cell resin Croc, were likewise frowned upon. The concern over the nakedness of the male foot highlighted the numerous contradictions surrounding the exposure of men's bodies. In North America, shirtlessness has been perfectly fine in the context of relaxation and sport, but bathing suits such as Speedos that allow for the appraisal of male genitals have been socially unacceptable. Men's legs can be revealed but only from the knee down. Feet are allowed to be fully nude in the backyard or at the beach, but slipped into a pair of sandals they become naked; framed by the sandals, they become objects of scrutiny. The naked foot can also suggest vulnerability. Indeed, sandals have long been the footwear choice of pacifists. Perhaps there is some truth in the nineteenth-century adage that 'even in his highest moments of ornament, a man should always bear about him a trace of the useful.'[86] The most common sentiment, though, remains discomfort at the sight of men's feet: 'Everyone seems to be able to agree on one thing: MEN HAVE DISGUSTING FEET THAT NAUSEATE EVERYONE AROUND THEM.'[87]

If making the male foot an object of the public gaze is uncomfortably feminizing, requiring men to pamper and pedicure their feet pushes the envelope too far for many men. The salon experience is described by many as one of sheer intimidation, from not wanting to giggle when having their feet touched to the discomfort brought on by running into other men in the hyperfeminine space that is the nail salon. Many articles, however, conclude with the author professing to being converted to pedicures:

> Surprisingly, upon entering the nail salon, there was no banner reading, 'Welcome To Sissytown, You Foppish Ponce!' Instead, there were just some chairs and magazines (even guy's ones) . . . In a way, I do see why most men refuse to get a pedicure . . . a nail salon is seriously uncharted territory for most of us.[88]

In response to the emerging need for male pedicures, 'men-only' spas have opened to cater to this new clientele.

Arguably, the sense of discomfort with seeing men's bare feet in sandals could have been alleviated by men reviving the old tradition of wearing socks with sandals. David Hayes's *Financial Times* article in 2013, 'Socks and the City: The Rise of the Man-sandal', reported on the 'brave' men daring enough to wear sandals beyond the beach, pointing to what little progress men's fashion had made in integrating the sandal into the male wardrobe and the long-standing disapproval of men who wear socks with sandals. Socks worn with sandals have generally been even more frowned upon than have men who bare their nude feet in sandals. Sandra Choi, creative director of Jimmy Choo RTW, has declared socks with sandals a definite 'no-no', while the high-end shoe designer Pierre Hardy is more open-minded, insinuating liberal politics into the discussion by equating the right to wear socks with sandals to the right to marry whomever one chooses.[89] Clearly, the ghost of Edward Carpenter continues to haunt the combination of socks with sandals.

Perhaps the most reviled footwear in recent times, however, has been Vibram's FiveFingers, which seems to fuse sandal and sock. Designed as a 'glove for the foot', FiveFingers conceal the foot yet simultaneously highlight each toe, in a way that many onlookers find disturbing. Another unsettling thing about the design was that the motivation for creating these shoes came from a desire to allow people's feet to engage, in a protected way, with the natural environment. It was a goal that smacked of health reform from Father Kneipps's much maligned nineteenth century 'grass cure', which encouraged walking barefoot through the morning dew, to the more recent devotees of barefoot running. Despite the fact that barefoot running had scientific support in Harvard studies on the biomechanics of running without footwear,[90] those wearing FiveFingers soon became pigeonholed as self-obsessed 'wellness enthusiasts':

> They became part of a whole look: the 'Aw, dude, I just finished this *killer* 10K' look. The look that suggests you've run straight from the trail to the Greek yogurt section of Whole Foods with this really smug, really *active* smile on your face. If you are one of these people, you know who you are and you are the worst.[91]

The trend for wearing shower-pool slides – or slip-on plastic sandals with a single instep strap – with socks also came to be associated with smug superiority. A variety of young men, from frat boys to athletes, have used this pairing to convey a kind of sartorial nonchalance. Sean Sweeny in his article 'How to Look Fly in Your New Slides', wrote:

Honestly, if you're currently a college student and don't have this look in your rotation, you're slipping. It's a perfect mix of 'I'm in shape because, look at me, I might be on the way to workout' and 'I'm taking everything as it comes', as well as 'I'm not that dude who takes an hour to get ready.'[92]

Despite the seemingly just-rolled-out-of-bed look of this style, rules do apply. The most popular slides feature clear branding and incorporate a hint of athletic masculinity into the sandal, connecting it to sneaker culture. The type of sock worn is also critical: tube socks,

Despite being casual, branding is central to the fashion for slides. Japanese, made by F. C. Real Briton, 2016.

themselves often branded, add to the look of athleticism by suggesting that the wearer will soon be or has recently been wearing sneakers for sport. Yet socks are also suggestive of undress and can insinuate the erotic into the ensemble. The style has become so popular that higher-end versions of these inexpensive sandals started being promoted in fashion, as Stu Woo and Ray A. Smith reported in 2015 in the *Washington Post*:

> Wearing socks with sandals – a source of endless ridicule for dads, German tourists and hippies – is allegedly in vogue. Calvin Klein Collection, Bottega Veneta, Marni and other luxury labels showcased the pairing at men's runway shows in June . . . Part of the credit, or blame, for the trend goes to the sports locker room. One recent afternoon before practice, about a dozen New York Giants players trotted out of the locker room to speak to the media. Half of them wore socks with sandals . . . athletes say they wear socks with sandals because they can. The locker room has no dress code.[93]

It is precisely this suggestion, that the wearer could not be bothered, that makes the style so interesting. Wearing socks and slides maintains long-standing tropes of desultory male interest in fashion while simultaneously encouraging consumption and brand alliances.

Despite the arrival of designer slides, even the most daring men currently do not wear sandals to formal functions. In recent years, some men have paired sneakers with tuxedos, but conservative lace-up oxfords or formal pumps, which men began wearing in the nineteenth century, remain the standard form of footwear for most when attending formal functions. Yet in women's fashion, strappy sandals have almost become a requirement of women's formal attire. These high-heeled sandals impart no suggestion of poverty or any disengagement from the world; rather, the high-heeled sandal with barely-there straps speaks to the long-established associations between sandals and Orientalizing or classicizing excess. The most expensive footwear to date is a pair of high-heeled sandals created

This pair of evening sandals was part of Prada's 2012 Spring/Summer collection and was inspired by luxury car design of the 1950s. Italian, made by Prada, 2012.

by Stuart Weitzman which were embellished with precious gems, including diamonds said to cost over $1 million. The dramatic contrast between men's formal dress, which conceals nearly every inch of flesh aside from the head and hands, and women's, which exposes broad expanses of the neck, chest, back, arms and legs, and is usually worn with foot-revealing evening sandals, reflects the perpetuation of many traditional conventions of gender, and makes sandals such as these perhaps the most highly gendered items of footwear in today's Western fashion.

## II Boots: Inclusivity

Boots! There is something, to my thinking, particularly imposing in that simple monosyllable. It conveys, to my mind, an idea of solidity, strength, swiftness, power of endurance, personal capacity: it images all the energetic and active properties of our nature.

*Household Words: A Weekly Journal*, 1855

We don't need boots for the most part, do we? It's just this kind of romantic image. Unless you're going to war or plowing the fields, they're not particularly practical. Boots are just so good-looking. It's all about vanity.

'Getting the Boot', *Vogue*, 1 August 1993

Boots have enabled humans to survive in challenging environments and to conquer enemies. They have long been worn to convey authority and they remain suggestive both of heroism and menace. Boots have been the footwear of advancing armies, lone cowboys, self-involved dandies, xenophobic skinheads and comic book superheroes. They have also been features of women's fashion, used to accentuate the leg, in turn becoming objects of desire themselves. In Western fashion, boots were traditionally the domain of men. Riding boots, linked to the status of horse ownership, were for many years signifiers of military might and upper-class privilege. Work boots, by contrast, have been emblems of physical labour and the rugged masculinity connected to 'traditional values' and manliness. Boots have also been used to establish group cohesion through the reinforcement of uniformity, be it military or counter-cultural. Since the twentieth century, boots as daily dress have largely lost their practical function and instead have become accessories of identity and fashion.

This pair of boots is said to have belonged to the Grand Écuyer of Napoleon III, who was in charge of the royal stables. Although they were ostensibly worn in relation to his responsibilities, their almost impossibly narrow design suggests that his real concern was fashion. French, late 19th century.

Although boots, which can be defined as coverings for the foot and part of the leg, have been worn since ancient times, they only became important accessories in men's fashion in the sixteenth century. As the Western world was expanding, boots became part of the uniform of military adventure and global exploration. Portraits of men in close-fitting boots and fine clothing reflected the impact of the widening world. 'For an Englishman's suite is like a traitor's bodie that hath beene hanged, drawn and quartered, and set up in severall places,' complained Thomas Dekker in 1606; 'His Codpeece is in Denmarke: the collor of his Dublet and the belly in France:... Polonia gives him the Boates [boots].'[1] He was right: contact with the greater world was changing how the English dressed, including the boots they wore. The Polish boot to which Dekker refers was connected to England's increased trade with Poland and other countries to the east. Indeed, it was via Western Asia that the heel was introduced into Western fashion, added to men's riding boots around the time that Dekker was grumbling.

In the early seventeenth century the most fashionable boots were made of fine suede that slouched around the ankles, with shafts that could be pulled up over the knee but were instead typically worn folded down to create large cuffs, which in turn were often festooned with lace-edged boot hose (linen socks worn over lace stockings to prevent the expensive hosiery from being damaged). A story by the English writer Thomas Middleton from 1604 included the assessment of the boots of a swaggering gallant: 'casting mine eyes lower, I beheld a curious pair of boots... in such artificial wrinkles... as if they had been starched lately and came new from the laundress's.'[2] The young man's overly studied and perfected state of rumpled elegance made him a laughing stock – he was clearly not attired for either work or war. By the middle of the seventeenth century, cavalier fashion gripped men's dress, including a taste for extravagant boots.[3] Centuries later, this sort of boot came to be associated with pirates, whose flouting of all the rules both moral and sartorial was thrilling.[4] This image of the swashbuckler in bucket boots was inaccurate; the style had passed from fashion by the end of the seventeenth century. Period

images invariably depict pirates in shoes, not boots, and texts from the time concerning pirates make no mention of boots at all. Instead, by the end of the century, boots had lost much of their currency in fashion and had returned to being primarily equestrian. Buttery suede was switched for heavy, often jacked leather (leather that has been thickened, typically through boiling), and all pretences towards booted elegance were abandoned.[5]

In the eighteenth century, boots were returned to fashion when country squires began to wear lighter, sleeker boots as part of daily fashion. The style first started in England but quickly spread across the Continent and North America; it was a look that would define the age. At first some disapproved of the trend: the fashionable Beau Nash, for example, supposedly attempted to 'civilize' the luxury watering place of Bath, which in the middle of the century rivalled

The slouchy boots worn by Charles I for this portrait were the height of elegant men's fashion in the early decades of the 17th century. Daniël Mijtens, *Charles I, King of England*, 1629, oil on canvas.

(*above*) Top boots – riding boots with a contrasting band of leather at the top – were popular among well-to-do men in the first half of the 19th century and remain an equestrian fashion today. French, 19th century.

(*left*) This boot was made of hard 'jacked' leather and features high stacked heels. It was clearly designed to be worn in harsh riding conditions. English, 1690–1710.

London as the most fashionable locale in all of Britain, by demanding that men abandon their boots for shoes and stockings. He employed all the weapons of ridicule

> to push his victories, he got up a puppet-show in which Punch came in booted and spurred, in the character of a country squire … [whose mistress] desires him to pull off his boots, 'My boots!' replies Punch, 'why madam, you may as well bid me pull off my legs! I never go without boots.'[6]

Despite Nash's attempt to curb boot-wearing, the tide had turned. The country squire look signalled profound changes in ideas about hereditary male privilege in relation to work. Revolutionary thoughts, such as 'all men are created equal', called for new constructions of masculinity that moved away from favouring privileged birth

Boots were given to little boys to mark their passage into boyhood, a moment of great pride for many. *See My New Boots*, published by Nathaniel Currier. American, *c*. 1856.

towards ideals that sought to unite men across socioeconomic levels and ideas linking masculinity to work began to be established. The wearing of riding boots represented these new ideas, even if the work being referenced was the business of managing one's estates. By the end of the century, a marked simplicity had begun to define French fashion as well, and the sleek equestrian boot became standard in many men's wardrobes.

By the turn of the nineteenth century, boots had become the pride of the gentleman's wardrobe: 'There may be other integuments, equally indicative of manhood, but there are none of which a male wearer is so proud of as his boots.'[7] A man's first pair of boots were often given to him as a child and marked his transition from infancy to youth, and the centrality of boots within men's fashion made them the principal form of footwear for all but the most formal occasions. In 1808 the British wit Edward Dubois mocked the ubiquity of boots:

> The universal adoption of boots, introduced only within the present generation, hath given an entirely new appearance to our national character. Our forefathers, misled by the maxims of antiquity, never thought of putting on their boots till they had ordered their horses.[8]

It was a militaristic age; revolution and imperialism required boots. The ostentatious Hessian boot which had become popular in part because the French Revolution made breeches worn with stockings and shoes held to the foot with glittering buckles a political issue linked to aristocratic excess and effete masculinity. In response, pantaloons worn with boots came into fashion after the Revolution. Designed to create a long, elegant line for the leg, they required that a strap attached to the hem of the trouser be slipped under the foot. Frequently, they were tucked into form-fitting Hessians featuring curvilinear top lines, invariably polished to a glass-like sheen and often ornamented with embroidery and silk tassels. The fashion for wearing them tight to the leg, so small and neat, made them the

(*above*) This Hessian boot with its slight heel and extravagant embellishment would have been perfect for pantaloons. Military fashion borrowed heavily from Eastern European dress in the early 19th century, including ornate embroidery and tassels on boots. Possibly Hungarian, early 19th century.

(*right*) Fashionable men in the early 19th century sought to cut an elegant figure in boots that were remarkably tight and often too small, as depicted in this caricature by M. Egerton, *New Boots*, 1827.

NEW BOOTS.

focus of both desire and mockery. A humorous piece in George Cruikshank's *Omnibus* from 1842 recounts a pair of Hessians so beloved that the author liked simply to 'draw them on, and sit with one knee crossing the other, to contemplate my favourite leg', wishing he were a centipede so that he could wear fifty pairs of Hessians at a time. The essay also includes an amusing nod to the fashion for making Hessians too small by telling of a French bootmaker described as 'some incredible genius [who] constructed a pair of boots, which Tom Thumb when a little boy could no more have got on than Cinderella's sister could the magic slipper'.[9] Hessians were the boots of military men but they were also the boots of dandies. In an age of increasing uniformity in men's dress, Hessians were doomed and were soon replaced by the Wellington.

The Wellington, named after the famous British military hero Arthur Wellesley, 1st Duke of Wellington, who defeated Napoleon at Waterloo in 1815, was a less fussy boot. In a letter to his bootmaker George Hoby, Wellington writes: 'The last boots you sent me were still too small in the Clf of the leg & about an inch & half too short on the leg. Send me two pair more altered as I have above directed.' Although some historians have extrapolated a great deal from this brief missive, it is unclear what the boot really looked like. Wellingtons *were* a bit looser and did not hug the leg as closely as Hessians, but to what extent Wellesley himself guided the design of his namesake boot remains unknown. Wellingtons lacked ornamentation, making them easier to wear under the trousers which were replacing pantaloons, yet they could also be worn with the trouser legs tucked in if the wearer desired.

Wellingtons may have been embraced for their functionality but they, like other boots, represented a considerable expense. Ankle boots were less costly and eventually replaced the taller Wellington in men's dress. The Congress boot, which featured elasticized gores on the side, was invented in the late 1830s by the British shoemaker Joseph Sparkes Hall and proved to be exceptionally popular with men and women alike. The Highlow, defined as 'a covering for the foot and ankle too high to be called a shoe and too low to be a boot',

The use of elastic gussets for footwear was invented by the British shoemaker Joseph Sparkes Hall in 1837. They were easy to take on and off yet also kept the line of the boot neat. Probably British, *c*. 1860.

laced closed and was also quite popular.[10] Like the Wellington, it was named after a military hero, the Prussian marshal Gebhard Leberecht von Blücher, who fought with Wellington at Waterloo. Blücher is said to have requested a boot for his infantry that could be quickly put on and could accommodate feet in a range of widths. The style was extremely successful and millions of infantry soldiers went into battle in versions of the Blücher during the nineteenth and twentieth centuries. The brogan, similar in structure to the Blücher yet typically of lower quality, was a tough working shoe-boot traditional in parts of Ireland and Scotland, the word *brog* being Gaelic for shoe. In the U.S., this inexpensive work boot was central to the development of the shoemaking industry as it was made in large quantities for slaves in both the American South and the West Indies.[11] Factories churned them out, but many were also produced by Northern farmers as a cottage industry during the winter months.

The Wellington became fashionable in the early 19th century and has remained a classic. The toplines of Wellingtons are often straight, but sometimes the front or back can feature a peak, as can be seen here. This pair was made by British bootmakers Faulkner & Sons. British, 1918–30.

These exceptionally cheap 'Negro brogans' were crudely made using stiff leather that often dug into the skin of the wearer. Narratives of slaves' lives often include memories of needing to stuff new footwear with rags in order to prevent injury, and of the greasing of the uppers in an attempt to make them more pliable.[12] Despite the fact that the majority of slaves were ill-shod and outfitted with only one pair a year, the brogan market was significant and it was a boon to the shoe manufacturers of the North. A British report in 1854 noted that,

> No inconsiderable quantity of the coarser kind of shoes called 'brogans' is disposed of for the use of slaves in the south . . . the northern manufacturers . . . have little reason to wish for a speedy termination of slavery.[13]

Some Southerners were desperate to make shoemaking a more local industry, and this was reflected in the high sale price paid for slaves

These brogans were said to have been worn by a prison guard at the notorious Confederate prison in Andersonville and reflect the state of footwear during the American Civil War, 1863–5.

with shoemaking skills. The former slave Cicely Cawthon recounted that the first slave her 'master' had was a shoemaker: 'They paid big money for him . . . He was 'bout as valuable as the blacksmith. I don't remember how much they paid for him, but it was big money.'[14] Despite these attempts to localize footwear production it remained a Northern monopoly, and once the Civil War commenced the want of footwear was keenly felt throughout the South.

Throughout the nineteenth century, well-to-do men were expected to wear their boots polished to a high gloss, regardless of type. The British dandy Beau Brummell supposedly had his servants polish his boots with champagne in order to achieve the correct lustre. While this account is likely apocryphal, the importance of polished footwear should not be underestimated. Cities and towns were filthy places and boots were constantly being soiled. The wealthy could rely on

This image of Union soldiers shows a range of footwear styles. The two men on the right wear boots, probably Wellingtons. The first man seated to the left has on Berlin work slippers and the man at the far right is wearing brogans. *7th New York State Militia, Camp Cameron, DC*, 1861.

servants to keep their boots shiny at home, and out on the street the services of shoeshine boys were available for a pittance. The demand for having spotless boots irked some: 'Is the circumstance that a man's boots are stained any smirch on his character? Why is a conventional black lustre better than aesthetic mud-tints? Why does society insist upon so much glitter on a man's feet, when it makes no objection to his having an unpolished brain?' complained 'A Sufferer' in a piece titled 'Boot-Blackmail' in *Life* magazine in 1886.[15] Yet men who disregarded the fashion of high polish opened themselves up to criticism that suggested they were shabby in character as well as dress, and bootblacks remained essential fashion workers throughout the nineteenth century:

> If you keep your head up, and look straight on as you push through our crowded streets, you will see what is an upper stratum of humanity . . . about two feet under the level of the man-life, there is a full current of boy-life also flowing in the crowd . . . Look down, then, and see this unnoticed boy-life. Nay, you must look down at it when a shoeblack points suggestively to your spattered boots.[16]

Penniless, homeless and often barefoot, bootblacks were seen as littering the urban landscape plying a trade that made them vulnerable to abuse and exploitation. They were often the focus of social anxiety, as reflected in numerous articles and books such as Horatio Alger's *Ragged Dick; or, Street Life in New York with the Boot Blacks* (1867), and in the creation of Ragged Schools, first in the UK and then in the U.S., which sought to educate such children and improve their living conditions and opportunities. 'Bootblack brigades' were charitable organizations that pooled the money earned by their member boot-blacks and used these funds to send the young boys to far-flung parts of the British Empire, including Australia and Canada:

> Sailor-life is just the thing for daring boys . . . so when these precocious youngsters are captured before they are really spoilt,

The title of this photograph, *Michael Mero, 2 West 4th St. Bootblack, 12 Years of Age, Working One Year of Own Volition. Don't Smoke. Out After 11 p.m. on May 21. Ordinarily Works 6 Hours per Day. Location: Wilmington, Delaware*, speaks to the efforts made to show bootblacks as entrepreneurial, disciplined and ambitious rather than as social pariahs.

These dark green satin 'Adelaide' boots would have offered minimal protection from the elements but they did cover the ankles. European, *c.* 1840s.

they make fine bold sailors, and, being sent far away from their old haunts and coteries, they have a new start in a fair field; for boys are now far better treated on board ship than they were some years ago.[17]

In women's dress, the boot was a relative newcomer. Short, front-lacing boots had been worn by some women at the end of the eighteenth century, when it became fashionable to walk along public promenades or up and down shopping streets, but it was not until the nineteenth century that boots were fully integrated into the fashionable woman's wardrobe. Like the ubiquitous flat-soled sandal-shoes popular in the opening decades of the nineteenth century, side-lacing boots made of delicate fabric that covered the ankles offered little protection from the elements, but unlike those slippers they were seen by some as offering a nod to modesty. In England, these boots were called Adelaides, in honour of the tight-laced queen consort of William IV who was said to be somewhat prudish. With the invention of the steel-cage crinoline, the boot became even more important. While the crinoline offered the advantage of creating a wide, full-skirted silhouette without the burden of wearing numerous petticoats, its steel structure was also remarkably sensitive to movement, causing it to rise up, revealing a woman's legs. One admirer quipped, 'its advantages are that the slightest movement shows the ankles, and a brisker one the knees, while a quick turn of the body, to say nothing of windy days, exhibits a greater more.' But another commenter shuddered, writing, 'who ever before knew what a world of bow-legs, turkey-legs and pigeon toes were concealed beneath the symmetrical folds of lace and muslin.'[18]

In an age when the phrase 'pretty ankle' was often all that was needed to convey a woman's attractiveness, boots were useful either to conceal ankle inadequacies or to enhance comely appendages. By the second half of the century, front-lacing and side-buttoning boots became prominent in fashion and boot shafts crept up the leg. As corsets constrained and accentuated the torso, these exceptionally form-fitting boots accentuated the shape of the foot and the calf.

Lola Montez, writing in 1858 in her book *The Arts of Beauty*, relayed the story of the

> celebrated Madam Vestris [who] used to have her white satin boots sewed on her feet every morning, in order that they should perfectly fit the exquisite shape of her foot . . . and it was said that she made more conquests with her *feet* than with her *face*, beautiful as it was.[19]

Those who did not wish to go to such extremes could turn to the French footwear manufacturer Jean-Louis François Pinet, who made the most desirable boots of the day. The short romantic story 'The Footprints on the Sand' from 1888 pivots on a pair of Pinet boots. A suitor is smitten after seeing an impression left by a tiny pair on the beach:

> it was no fat, comely Welsh girl who had imprinted that footstep upon the sand. The female inhabitants of Llandavid most certainly did not affect Paris boots, and Pinet was to them a name unknown. I fell to wondering what manner of woman owned that little foot . . . My walking dreams were haunted by a figure, small but beautifully moulded, with fairy hands and feet.[20]

The delicate embroidery that adorned many a pair of Pinet boots suggested the work of fairy hands but was in fact the daily toil of the seven hundred embroiderers employed by the manufacturer. These embroiderers did piecework, meaning that they were paid by the upper, not by the hour, and most likely laboured long, arduous days for nominal pay. Their work is breathtaking in its botanical accuracy and detail, yet, for all their efforts, these women would not have been able to afford a pair of Pinets. Instead, they would have worn mass-produced boots in leather, possibly embellished with a bit of machine embroidery, or perhaps they might have acquired boots from used

The flowers and scrollwork in neutral 'wheat' coloured silk added restrained but still sumptuous embellishment to these elegant and expensive ruby-red boots by the Parisian footwear manufacturer François Pinet. French, *c.* 1875–85.

clothing dealers, taking any footwear in need of repair to the myriad out-of-work shoemakers who, because of industrialization, were now forced to become cobblers – repairers rather than makers of shoes.

As the century progressed, women's feet and footwear, including boots, were becoming increasingly eroticized without regard to class. The craze among upper-class women in England and France to have casts made of their legs and feet reflected this. An article in the Philadelphia paper the *Evening Telegraph* from 1870 reported on this fad:

> One lady the wife of a mayor in the provinces, came to London and had two casts taken of her leg – one nude, and one with the neat little shoe, stocking and garter. Strange to say . . . the leg with the stocking and garter produced an effect much further removed from modesty than the leg quite unclad.[21]

In alignment with the writer's sentiments, there was a trend in contemporary pornography to depict women naked with the exception of footwear. This trope served to eroticize women's footwear further, in both fantasy and real life.

The materiality of boots also became a focus of eroticism. It should come as no surprise that fetish boots emerged at this time. The English writer Frederick Locker-Lampson wrote in his poem 'My Mistress's Boots':

> O, where did hunter win
> So delectable a skin
> For her feet?
> You lucky little kid,
> You perished, so you did,
> For my sweet!

The psychiatrist Richard von Krafft-Ebing's reference book on sexual practices from 1886, *Psychopathia Sexualis*, included a number of shoe fetish – or, more commonly, boot fetish – case studies.

These boots were designed to look like a stockinged leg in a shoe. A glimpse of the boot's shaft would have tantalized the onlooker. Swiss or German, 1890s.

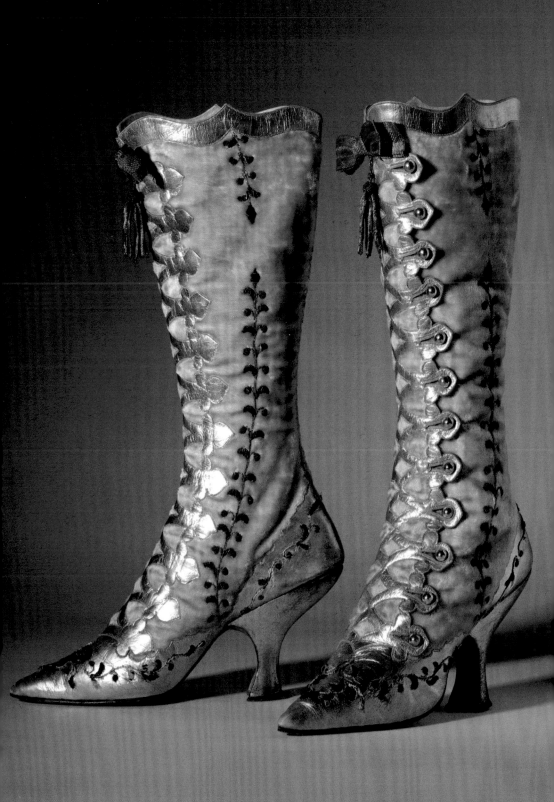

According to one 'patient', 'these perversions of men are well known in many houses of prostitution – a proof that these are not so very infrequent.'[22] Some patients simply described the desired boots as elegant, but others specified they be leather; one even fantasized about the brutal death of the animals required to make the boots.[23] The sheen of patent or highly polished leather was also commonly commented on by enthusiasts and has remained a central feature in fetish footwear to this day.

While fetish boots met the desires of a very specific market fashionable boots at the end of the century also incorporated many eroticizing features. The heels rose higher, as did boot shafts, which now tightly hugged the ankle and the calf. Some boots were designed to look like stockinged legs in shoes, to give those who saw them the sensation of glimpsing the forbidden leg. Others, such as barrette boots, featured strapping or cut-outs that allowed the actual stockinged leg to be seen. These styles not only upped the sexual ante of these boots but also foreshadowed the profound change in women's dress that would happen in only a few decades, when the boot would be abandoned and the stockinged leg fully revealed.

The changing times were also evidenced in women's increased participation in sports. From tennis to golf, many late nineteenth-century women embraced the opportunity to exercise and get fresh air. The invention of the bicycle was of particular interest to women and many enthusiastically embraced the freedoms cycling allowed. The shock of seeing women astride velocipedes, as they were called, was only matched by the shock of seeing what women wore while riding. The highly politicized bloomer that had created such a stir when donned by women's rights activists earlier in the century now became the fashion of choice for athletic activities. However, rather than tapering to the ankle like the original models, bicycle bloomers stopped at the knee, revealing a shocking expanse of leg – albeit it an expanse concealed by stockings and often boots. Yet many felt, as one reporter put it, that 'no woman yet born can contrive to look well in the loose, ugly Dutch trousers.'[24] Many women simply wore shoes on their excursions, but others wore specially designed

The "NEW WOMAN" AND HER BICYCLE.——THERE WILL BE SEVERAL VARIETIES OF HER.

bicycle boots that featured textile shafts laced up to the knee, which provided greater protection from both the elements and prying eyes. Regardless of costume, however, bicycles were seen as offering women new freedoms, even new romantic opportunities: 'Now the couple who desires to escape parental vigilance may wheel themselves into matrimony on the *tête à tête* bicycle.'[25]

The idea that women could ride astride was soon extended to horse riding. *Physical Education* noted the phenomenon in 1892, stating that: 'The popularity of bicycle riding among women has made it more possible for women to accept the idea of riding *en cavalier*.'[26] Although some women had ridden astride prior to the turn of the twentieth century, the more traditional way for women to ride was side-saddle, with their legs demurely draped to one side of the horse and concealed under their long-skirted riding habits. Although women had worn trousers under their habits since at least the 1870s, riding astride required shorter skirts. This new habit revealed trousered legs that were invariably covered by masculine knee-high top boots or butcher boots. The increasing popularity of polo,

This cartoon lampoons the range of women embracing bicycle-borne freedom and their bicycling attire. Frederick Burr Opper, 'The "New Woman" and Her Bicycle – There Will Be Several Varieties of Her', *Puck*, 19 June 1895.

(*above*) These riding boots were made by the British bootmaker Tom Hill and were worn by Diana Champ for riding astride. British, 1930s.

(*left*) While some women protected their legs when cycling by wearing spats, others wore speciality bicycle boots. British, 1895–1905.

first introduced into England by British soldiers returning from duty in India and Afghanistan in the late 1860s, also introduced the jodhpur, and by the early twentieth century the boldest women had abandoned the skirted habit altogether for jodhpurs and high, sleek riding boots.

For men, the knee-high boot had faded from fashion by the end of the nineteenth century. Horse riding was being replaced by mechanized modes of transportation and in Europe and the eastern United States, equestrianism was quickly becoming mainly recreational, although it should be noted that automobile drivers, particularly liveried ones, as well as motorcycle riders, continued to wear equestrian-inspired fashion, including jodhpurs and riding boots. Ankle boots remained in fashion; many featured textile uppers – like pseudo-spats – but it was the shoe that was now to signify masculine authority and industry. The sleek closed-tab oxford, the open-tab derby and the brogue, which could confusingly be either an oxford or a derby, suddenly became popular. A brogue (not to be confused with a coarse brogan, yet related by means of being a work shoe, albeit white-collar rather than physical labour) was simply a shoe that featured broguing: decorative punchwork and pinking.

In the American West, however, the horse and the boot remained paramount in both reality and imagination. One of the most enduring American icons, the cowboy, dates to the second half of the nineteenth century. Despite the indelible impression the cowboy made on the American psyche, the period of cattle herding was relatively short in American history. The cattle drives of the late 1860s to 1880s were made possible by the incursion of the railroad into the western plains. The 'iron horse' transported cattle to the stockyards in cities such as Chicago for slaughter. Driving thousands of cattle hundreds of miles to a railhead was hard, dirty work that required sturdy boots. The first cowboy boots were simply military boots pressed into civilian service. From images, it appears that most tended to be similar to those worn during the American Civil War: plain, broad-toed Wellingtons with maybe a Hessian or two in the mix. Early daguerreotypes and photographs of cowboys show them wearing a wide range of

In the opening decades of the 20th century, boots fell from favour and classic oxfords or derbys became the footwear of choice for the elegant man, as this Stetson advertisement attests. American, 1924.

boots, the majority quite plain. Some contend that cowboys would spend their hard-earned cash on luxuries such as customized boots after reaching the railheads in Kansas, and that it was these boots that first began to shape the modern cowboy boot. This theory is compelling. The first Kansas cow town, Abilene, had a bootmaker named Thomas C. McInerney, who set up shop in 1868 to provide custom-made boots, and by 1870 over 120 bootmakers were working in Kansas making bespoke footwear, from pull-on cowboy boots to lace-up packer boots.[27] The most famous cowboy bootmakers today trace their history back to this period of the open range. The Hyer Boot Company (recently renamed the Olathe Boot Company) opened shop in Olathe, Kansas, in 1875, while Justin Boots was established in Spanish Fort, Texas, shortly after, in 1879.[28] Some early cowboys do display a bit of swagger by purposely leaving out their boot pulls, and heels had substantially increased in height by the 1880s, but the stylized and highly ornamented cowboy boot would have to wait for rodeo bravado to invent and for Hollywood to popularize.

If the railroad gave birth to the cowboy, it also caused his demise when it brought an end to the long-range cattle drives as more and more rail transfers opened up across the country, making these long, difficult treks unnecessary. The invention of barbed wire and the closing of the frontier in 1890 reduced the open-range cowboy to a wage-earning hired ranch hand. The romance of the rugged individualism of these folk heroes of the open range, however, continued to live on in the media. A humorous account in *Puck* of an Easterner's misguided preparations for visiting Wyoming painted the picture many held concerning cowboys:

> Out in the Territories there are two classes – the 'cowboys' and the 'tenderfoots.' Such of the 'cowboys' as are not professional thieves, murderers and miscellaneous blacklegs . . . are men who, totally disregarding all the amenities of Eastern civilization, brook no restraint and . . . yield allegiance to no law save their own untamed passion . . . The 'tenderfoot' who

goes among them should first double his life insurance, and then be sure that he is 'well heeled.'[29]

Just as the wind-swept plains were being depleted of each and every bison and the threatening 'savage' warriors were being forced onto reservations, the myth of cowboy heroes gripped the popular American imagination. Dime novels told of the exploits of characters such as Buffalo Bill Cody, and by 1872, wearing theatrical interpretations of frontier clothing and full stage make-up, Buffalo Bill re-enacted his exploits on stage. By 1883 he had created his famous touring Wild West Show, featuring elements of what would become the rodeo, replete with elaborate costuming. For three decades this 'half-circus, half-history lesson' thrilled audiences across America and Europe.[30] Close scrutiny of photos of the costuming reveals that the iconic elaborately tooled cowboy boot had yet to be invented; even Buffalo Bill himself famously wore plain thigh-high riding boots made of unadorned leather.

With the exception of a few high heels, the majority of the boots worn by the cowboys in this photograph are plain, hardworking boots. C. A. Kendrick, *A Group of Cowboys*, c. 1904.

While many people flocked to Wild West shows at the dawn of the twentieth century, even more went to the cinema, where the western theme flourished. Films such as *The Great Train Robbery* of 1903, considered to be the first narrative movie, literally depicted cowboys in black and white – as either heroes who lived by the 'cowboy code' or disenfranchised 'free agents' who had become horse-mounted bandits. Costume as well as action was central to distinguishing the hero from the villain and cowboy boots became central to the iconography of this silver screen morality play.

If the cowboy boots of the Wild West spoke to unfettered freedoms in the early twentieth century, the button boots worn by suffragettes, with their menswear styling, reflected the growing demand for increased freedoms for women. In the opening decades of the century, women

This photograph of Sitting Bull with Buffalo Bill Cody, publicizing his Wild West Show, shows his thigh-high boots. William Notman Studio, *Sitting Bull and Buffalo Bill*, 1885.

marched through the streets protesting against their exclusion from the political process. The boots they wore as they demonstrated, like the women themselves, walked a very fine cultural line between acceptable aspiration and egregious transgression. Indeed, the clothing choices of the suffragettes were as closely scrutinized and criticized as the political changes that they advocated. The most common condemnations were that suffragettes were either too manly or too feminine, both assessments deeming them incapable of participating in politics. Many advocates of women's suffrage attempted to tread the middle line by wearing moderately heeled boots that proclaimed femininity, decorated with menswear detailing that suggested competence. This did little to assuage the naysayers, however, and suffragettes were frequently lampooned as being overly masculine in both ambition and attire. As the suffragettes were agitating for the right to vote in menswear-referencing boots, the advent of the First World War sparked a trend towards military-inspired outfits in women's fashion which featured shorter skirts paired with higher boots to cover the leg. Wartime restrictions on materials soon reduced the shaft height of women's boots, however, and after the war the boot was almost completely abandoned.

The outbreak of war put many men back into boots. Officers across the divides went into battle wearing riding boots that retained the traditional symbolism of military power and elite horseman-ship. Most soldiers wore laced ankle boots such as Blüchers with puttees, long strips of cloth that were wrapped closely around the calf. The Germans wore knee-high jack boots, similar to Wellingtons but made of heavy, thick and hard jacked leather, outfitted with metal hobnails, setting their distinctive uniforms apart from the Allies' and adding a terrifying dimension of sound to their approaching forces which transformed them into symbols of menace. The renowned American journalist Richard Harding Davis witnessed the invasion of Brussels on 20 April 1914:

> At the sight of the first few regiments of the enemy we were thrilled with interest. After they had passed for three hours in

one unbroken steel-gray column we were bored. But when hour after hour passed and there was no halt, no breathing time, no open spaces in the ranks, the thing became uncanny, inhuman. You returned to watch it, fascinated. It held the mystery and menace of fog rolling toward you across the sea . . . For seven hours the army passed in such solid column that not once might a taxicab or trolley car pass through the city. Like a river of steel it flowed, gray and ghostlike. Then, as dusk came and thousands of horses' hoofs and thousands of iron boots continued to tramp forward, they struck tiny sparks from the stones, but the horses and men who beat out the sparks were invisible.[31]

Davis's eloquent account would be echoed by many other witnesses who shared the experience.

Although the war years provided a boon to the shoemaking industries, particularly in the United States and England, most of the footwear issued to soldiers on all sides was substandard.[32] It was poorly made and unsuited to the intense rigours of marching, the muddy battlefields or the flooded trenches. Soldiers in shoddy, unlined boots suffered as water easily infiltrated their footwear and hobnails conducted the cold directly from the ground, sometimes causing their feet to literally freeze. Lack of proper footwear and inhospitable conditions were age-old problems of war, but in the opening years of the First World War they became almost insurmountable. Story after story from the Front high-lighted the importance of boots, with narratives ranging from the longing for them to their outright theft.[33] A report in the *New York Times* titled 'Saw War in the Trenches: Dutchman Horrified When Belgians Took the Boots of Dead Germans' remarked on the desperate need for boots which led young soldiers to risk their lives by leaving the trenches to take the boots from dead German soldiers, replacing them with their own worn-out shoes as a poignant gesture of respect.[34] Trench foot, which was at first thought to be a matter of low morale and malingering, was in fact caused by feet being continuously wet. If never

This propaganda poster of blood-soaked German boots captured the menace of the enemy during the First World War. The spur not only adds an aggressive edge to the image but also reflects the continued importance of the horse in warfare at the time. John Norton, *Keep These Off the U.S.A – Buy More Liberty Bonds*, *c*. 1918.

allowed to dry, the skin on the foot erupts with debilitating sores that often lead to infection. Trench foot felled tens of thousands of combatants in all the armies. In theory the problem was preventable, but in reality soldiers were hard pressed to stay dry. Clean, dry socks were a defence in combating trench foot and in all the warring countries calls went out for knitters to make socks as quickly as possible. British military orders issued in 1916 concerning trench foot convey the typical advice given to soldiers:

> It is absolutely necessary that all men, especially when in the trenches, be made to remove their puttees, boots and socks at least once a day, and to dry their feet and to treat them with whale oil or anti-frost-bite-grease, and then to put on dry socks . . . Spare socks must be taken into the trenches by all ranks . . . The Boots should be kept well greased in wet weather.[35]

Dry socks and attempts to waterproof boots with whale oil were one means of keeping feet dry; the introduction of the rubber Wellington was another.

In both Britain and the United States, rubber boots were issued to soldiers by the thousands in the effort to address the problems of trench foot. But despite being waterproof, the rubber boots introduced their own problems. They got stuck in the muck of the trenches and battlefields, and soldiers were frequently forced to abandon their trapped boots *in situ*. Another major problem was that the rubber did not breathe, which caused perspiration to collect in the boot. In addition, fully drying the insides of rubber footwear took at least 24 hours. Yet rubber Wellingtons were undeniably waterproof, and orders for them were immense. In 1915 the *New York Times* reported that the value of U.S. exports of rubber footwear had increased tenfold from the previous year, and once the U.S. entered the war demands further increased; the government ordered 5,500,000 pairs in 1918 alone. The rise of the famous British Wellington-maker Hunter Boot Ltd dates to these years, when the War Office commissioned 1,185,036 pairs of knee-high waterproof

boots.[36] Despite their problems, Wellingtons were superior to what the Germans had, and these trench boots were credited with contributing to the winning of the war.

By the end of the war, there was no romance to military boots; neither men's nor women's fashion reclaimed them. The term bootlegger may have been bandied about in the United States during prohibition, but it was wingtips and T-straps, not boots, that ruled the decade. For a brief moment in the early 1920s a fad emerged among young flappers to wear galoshes with the buckles unfastened and the long tops flapping against their shins. Inspired by the actor Douglas Fairbanks in *The Three Musketeers* (1921), the goal of the fashion was to lend a swashbuckling air to their attire.[37] An article in *Life* concerning the fashion reported that young women wore four-buckle galoshes:

With her unbuckled galoshes, tasselled hat and frank open expression, this image of a young 'flapper' captured both the new fashion and new mores emerging in the 1920s. *A Flapper Girl, c.* 1922.

from November to May regardless of weather [which] when worn turned down à la *Three Musketeers*, denotes youth or the desire to appear youthful. Lower buckle fastened denotes modest maidenhood. Two buckles fastened denotes caution. Three buckles fashion denotes approaching age.[38]

The trend was short-lived, and many erroneously credited the fad for the term flapper; the word had in fact long been used in fashion to describe young girls as fledglings ready to leave the nest. The one thing the fad did do, however, was help to revive the slipping sales of the rubber boot industry.

Boots did, however, remain important for recreation. After the war, polo matches resumed and hunting trips were planned. For Americans, the loss of Europe as a holiday getaway in the immediate post-war period saw them turn westward to find amusement domestically. National parks became holiday destinations and so did 'dude ranches', which allowed the East Coast upper-crust to dally in Western adventure. As part of the experience, guests aimed to dress as ranch hands from head to toe, only fancier. The plain, hard-working cowboy boot was not sufficient; instead, holidayers desired boots lavished with embroidery, leather inlay, tooling and leather appliqué like the boots worn by heroes in the movies. These were the boots of rugged romance and 'drugstore cowboys' – a term that as early as 1918 was used to mock people who simply played cowboy rather than lived it. As *Vogue* put it in 1928, dude ranching combined 'the healthfulness of a cure with the amusement of being part of a gaily colored "movie" cast'.[39] The article also commented that while many of the garments worn on dude ranches 'would look impossibly garish at home . . . how attractive they are in the right setting'. The cost of elaborate cowboy boots was, 'anything one is extravagant enough to pay for them'.[40] Indeed rather than being work wear they had become costly costume.

The wearer of these well-worn boots had once been a cowboy and continued to dress like one after becoming a farmer; the romance of the open range echoes in the boot's heels and spurs. American, 1940.

In the 1930s the American love affair with the cowboy and his regalia coincided with the larger interest in folk culture and nationalism that would figure in the Second World War. In Europe, national identities were being linked to the 'traditional' agrarian dress of the peasantry, but in North America, having no national costume, the 'picturesque' cowboy with his unwavering individualism and deep connection to the land was a compelling and distinctly American symbol. The movies of the 1920s and '30s abounded with his increasingly glamorized and idealized image. The genre of the 'singing cowboy' radiated morality, patriotism, duty and clean living.[41] The cowboy boot was an essential aspect of the 'horse operas', which appealed to both rural and urban audiences.

Another booted American icon that came into prominence in the 1930s was the comic book hero. From Buck Rogers to Superman, these heroes were updated nineteenth-century strongmen who saved the day wearing primary-coloured outfits with mid-calf-high boots, commanding admiration and respect. But despite the popularity of these booted idols, men's fashion continued to reject the boot. Boots were also of limited importance in 1930s women's fashion, although the ankle boot made a brief return in the work of the French shoe designer André Perugia and the Italian Salvatore Ferragamo. Their fashion-forward designs caught people's attention but were not widely adopted.

Boots did, however, become a prominent accessory in 1930s pornography, where high, tight-laced boots played a dominant role in fetish imagery. Depictions of female 'dominatrixes' in skin-tight thigh-high boots buttoned or laced in decidedly nineteenth-century fashion were featured in specialist publications such as *London Life* magazine. Most often, these women were also tight-laced into corsets that, like the boots, were suggestive of a bygone era. The common accessory of a riding crop or whip also spoke of a different time. This confusing pastiche of motifs – objectified dominatrixes wielding the lash in decidedly non-equestrian boots – grew in popularity and would eventually influence popular fashion at the end of the century.

These boots, with their high, curvaceous heels and plethora of buttons suggestive of Edwardian footwear, were probably intended for fetish or sex-worker use. Possibly German, late 1920–'30s.

From comic books to pornography, it is clear that boots were present in 1930s popular culture and were used to convey an image of power. This was precisely the impact sought in the design of the infamous Nazi uniforms. With memories of the jackbooted German army of the First World War still fresh in the public imagination, the Nazi Party set out to build upon this image and to once again place the boot front and centre. Their most notorious uniforms were those worn by the ss, Hitler's elite guard, in charge of internal security and the enforcement of racial purity. The all-black uniform was created by the graphic designer Walter Heck and artist Karl Diebitsch. Employing a silhouette that spoke of a military attire from earlier in the century, ss officers were outfitted in jodhpurs and high, sleek butcher boots. The boots created a strong visual punctuation in the black-and-white photography of the day. At the start of the war, German infantry were also outfitted in boots. But, rather than being given sleek riding boots, they were issued *Marschstiefel*, literally 'marching boots', which were the heavy, hobnailed, black jack boots that marched across Europe. These were worn with the trouser legs tucked in, giving the booted army a unified and threatening appearance that was accentuated by ritualistic 'goose-stepping'. The *New York Times* reported on an unsettling Nazi march in Austria that included storm troopers singing 'Today We Have Conquered Germany, Tomorrow We Conquer the World' with a 'blazing fanaticism . . . written on every face . . . one saw it in the taut facial muscles, blazing eyes, clenched fists and rigid stamping legs of the goose-stepping Storm Troop lads.'[42] The booted German military harked back to both the nineteenth century and the First World War and conjured up ideas of empire building. The boots they wore became a symbol of oppression in Allied propaganda. Even after the *Marschstiefel* were abandoned by the Germans in 1942 due to lack of funds and the laced ankle boot came into use, fear-inspiring propaganda images of the jack boot were used to motivate the Allies.

When the United States entered the war in 1941 following the bombing of Pearl Harbor, the new recruits who joined the Marines were called 'boots' and were trained at 'boot camp'. After training, combatants were sent to the Pacific, the China Burma India Theater

(CBI) or Europe. British fighters were engaged on the Continent as well as in North Africa, Southeast Asia and China. France, too, sent troops far and wide. Each of these climes required different types of footwear and, as during the First World War, manufacturers once again focused on military boot production. Everything from leather to rubber was rationed as factories turned out the requisite military footwear, leaving civilian populations mainly with shoes made of non-traditional materials such as vegetable fibre and textile. The development of the combat boot by the U.S. military near the end of the war would influence the footwear of future engagements as well as counter-culture dress as the century wore on.

The German army was well shod at the beginning of the Second World War, as this pair of sturdy 'jack boots' attest. German, 1939–42.

When the war ended in 1945, Europe turned to the task of rebuilding, and Americans once again looked west for inspiration. The swagger of the cowboy fitted the victorious mood of the country. Dude ranches were now a destination for even the middle class. Hopalong Cassidy and the puppet cowboy Howdy Doody kept children glued to their televisions, and Nashville's country music industry produced one 'rhinestone cowboy' after another. Westerns were also one of the most popular film genres. As the movie director Dore Schary noted, 'the American movie screen was dominated by strong, rugged males – the "one punch, one [gun] shot variety".'[43] In this milieu, cowboy boots became increasingly glamorous. Exaggeratedly pointed toes, high-keyed coloured leathers, elaborate appliqué and even actual rhinestone embellishments were not considered excessive. This period has been called the golden age of cowboy boots, and the artistry and imagination expressed in late 1940s and 1950s boot-making is staggering. The cowboy boot was becoming part of costume, a means of dressing up, of playing type. This point was made clear by the popularity of dress-up cowboy clothes, including boots, for children. Indeed, this transformation into costume was becoming the fate of many boots in fashion.

Although most boot styles fell out of fashion in the 1950s, in the immediate post-war period a particular form of military footwear did pass into men's stylish casual dress: the chukka boot, said to have come from India, and its variant, the desert boot. Designed as a low ankle boot with a two to three eyelet closure, chukkas were said to have been worn for comfort by British polo players both on and off the field in India.[44] The simple desert boot was based on the traditional chukka but in Cairo during the war it was given a crepe sole and soft suede upper. Nathan Clark of the British shoe-manufacturing Clark family translated the desert boot for civilian use. Both the desert boot and the chukka had become accessories of casual male elegance by the 1950s, being particularly popular with young men.

For some men, however, relaxation was not to be had lounging in khakis and shod in desert boots; instead they sought to embrace the freedoms for which they had so recently fought and the close male

The high-heeled cowboy symbolized unfettered freedoms and self-reliance in the 20th century. This pair of Tony Lama boots reflects the fashion for finery, from the use of lizard skin at the toe to the high stacked leather heel. American, mid-20th century.

The engineer's boot became popular with bikers after the Second World War. The biker offered an updated version of the cowboy, and his sartorial codes likewise spoke to unfettered freedom. American, mid-20th century.

camaraderie that they had experienced. Groups of ex-military men began to gather together, drawn by their love of motorcycles, and by the late 1940s biker clubs were being established throughout the United States.[45] Often described as mid-century cowboys, American bikers took to the open road astride their motorized mounts wearing a new type of riding boot, the engineer boot.

The first engineer boots were created by the American shoe manufacturer Chippewa. The company had established itself in Chippewa Falls, Wisconsin, making rugged boots for loggers at the turn of the century. By 1937 they had begun to make engineer boots for land surveyors based on the English riding boot, designed to present a neat, professional appearance in the field.[46] These rugged yet elegant boots featured adjustable straps at the knee and across the instep and were soon adopted by other professions. The introduction of the mid-calf-high shaft in 1940 only increased their popularity and they became the footwear of choice for dock workers during the war years.

Bikers began to wear engineer boots immediately following the war. When paired with denim and worn with leather jackets, engineer boots became a central accessory to the 'outlaw biker' look cultivated by members of biker clubs ousted from the American Motorcycle Association. The Hollister riot of 1947 seared this image into the American imagination. The 'riot' occurred when bikers from across the United States descended on the small California town of Hollister on Independence Day 1947. Hollister had hosted gypsy motorcycle races since the 1930s but the Second World War had put an end to them, until 1947, when an attempt was made to re-establish the tradition. Biker culture had dramatically grown in popularity and Hollister was unprepared for the large numbers that arrived in the town. Drunken and disorderly conduct defined the event, but in reality little damage was actually done. Sensationalized news coverage of the event captured America's attention. A staged photo of a boozing and booted biker published in *Life* magazine's 21 July issue helped to convey the idea that bikers were outlaws and rebels. The movie *The Wild One* (1953), inspired by the event and starring Marlon Brando, disseminated this image of the malcontent biker to an even wider audience. The look was further glamorized by James Dean in 1955 when he starred in *Rebel Without a Cause*, and soon the impression of motorcycle boots commingled with ideas of youth alienation and social degeneracy.

The extremely macho and homosocial nature of American biker culture also offered an appealing model of masculinity that spoke to many gay men. Rejecting the stereotype of effete male homosexuals, 'leathermen' began to form their own biker clubs in the 1950s wearing leather outfits – fetishized versions of biker clothing or military attire – from head to toe. The artist Touko Laaksonen, better known as Tom of Finland, captured this in the men's erotica that he started producing in the late 1950s. Leatherman groups, like other biker groups, were drawn to the often militaristic order of clubs. Some included BDSM erotic elements such as bootblacking, in which boots played an important role: the relationship between bootblacks and boot-wearing customers had faded from daily life by the middle of the twentieth century, but the power dynamics inherent in the service were eroticized and moved underground, becoming an important part of leatherman culture.

The romance surrounding American biker culture was also central to the development of the British motorcycle gangs known as rockers, who likewise rode large motorcycles and wore leather jackets and engineer boots. Their rivals were the mods, who preferred pristine scooters and dressed in more Continental fashion, with the exception of their footwear. They favoured the very English desert boot as well as the more refined Chelsea boot. The rockers and the mods shared similar working-class backgrounds and engaged in similar hooligan behaviour, but their sartorial differences were pronounced, the clothing of each group being worn like uniforms. In summer 1964 the two groups clashed at a number of British seaside towns and a 'moral panic' ensued across the UK.[47] As the 1960s progressed the leather-boy attire of the rockers ossified. The suit-wearing mods fractured into two main groups: those who were mainly interested in fashion, and the so-called 'hard mods' who began to sport

shaved heads and wore lace-up work boots, eventually leading to skinhead culture.

In men's fashion, mod style became very influential as the 1960s progressed:

> The new 'Mod look' for men – which could become the hottest thing that ever happened to men's wear fashion, is a controversial subject among the cognoscenti . . . typical of the Mod look – Tom Jones ruffled shirts, corduroy jeans, high-heeled Chelsea boots and similar styles are causing much comment.[48]

The English rock band the Beatles, who took the world by storm, are often credited with disseminating the fashion for mod-inspired suits and 'Beatle boots'. These updated congress or Chelsea boots often featured higher heels, in emulation of the Beatles member

The presence of gleaming boots was often central to the charged eroticism of Tom of Finland's artworks. Tom of Finland, *#82.08*, 1982.

John Lennon had this typical Chelsea boot altered. The heel was replaced with a higher, wooden heel of the kind worn by male flamenco dancers. British, early 1960s.

John Lennon, who had his customized with higher wooden heels taken from men's flamenco footwear. The mod look was part of the larger 'peacock revolution', which argued that males of other species, from peacocks to lions, were the more adorned of the sexes and which looked to fashion from the past for inspiration, including the ankle boot for men. 'At the beginning of the 1960s "fashion" was a feminine gender. By the end of the decade, the male had taken over the world of clothes – the dreariness of his postwar clothing disappeared . . . all in a flamboyant rebellion against the Wall Street Uniform.'[49]

Clothing was at the centre of the ensuing 'battle of the sexes'. An article on Britain's new booted age wrote that 'men and women all over . . . are vying with each other in a semi-sexual competition to prove who wears the boots best.'[50] The article explained that 'The men, of course, claim that they've always worn boots – and their stylish, calf-length, elastic-sided boots with three inch Cuban heels are merely a development from their days in the army or riding the range.' But,

> Rigged out in this 'fab gear' . . . British girls began to emerge from their mouseholes and reveal themselves as pert, poised and brazen creatures ready to battle with any man . . . All they lack, as they strut the streets of Chelsea, is a sword and buckler. In their eyes is a cocksure glare, a challenge to every man to prove he's not a heel . . . At first this jackbooted apparition over-awed the male. It still startles newcomers.[51]

Indeed, boots were in fashion for women and were part of growing discontent with the status quo. Women wanted a brighter future, and this was reflected in the decidedly forward-looking boots which stood in contrast to the nostalgia popular in women's fashions. These space-age boots also stood in stark contrast to the nostalgia for boot styles of the past that defined men's boot choices. English designers from John Bates to Mary Quant, and French designers such as André Courrèges and Yves Saint Laurent, created boots inspired by space-age fantasies. In her minimalist white leather 'go-go' boots, the Courrèges woman was described in *Vogue* in 1964 as being as 'modern as the year after next . . . she lives in the present and a little beyond it'.[52]

*Vogue* also declared the new boots appropriate for heroines.[53] They were certainly a feature in the costuming of Jane Fonda as *Barbarella* in the 1968 film. Likewise, boots were central to the costuming of Dr Cathy Gale and Emma Peel, the female protagonists in the British 'spy-fi' television show *The Avengers*. Their skin-tight outfits and boots carried strong fetish overtones that were rivalled only by the outfits worn by the villainous Cat Woman on the American television show *Batman*. Even Chief Communications Officer Nyota Uhura wore knee-high boots with her miniskirt uniform in *Star Trek*'s TV debut in 1966. The men on the show were also booted. Captain Kirk periodically wore knee-high officer boots, while the other men wore mod ankle boots with cropped trousers. It was clear that 'Space: the final frontier' would be conquered in boots. As it happened, the actual boots worn on the lunar missions, starting with *Apollo 11* in 1969, would go on to inspire a terrestrial fashion for moon boots in the 1970s – one of the few times that winter boots would become a notable part of fashion.

Fetish-inspired thigh-high boots, such as those sported in *Barbarella*, also entered mainstream fashion. The American shoe designer Beth Levine, in addition to making the boots worn in publicity shots by Nancy Sinatra for her hit single 'These Boots Were Made for Walking', created the first thigh-high leg-hugging stocking boots fabricated with Lycra. The famed French shoe de-signer Roger Vivier also turned to making boots in the 1960s. The thigh-high boots he designed for Yves Saint Laurent were made famous by Brigitte Bardot when she wore them astride a Harley-Davidson motorcycle. They may have been reminiscent of seventeenth-century riding boots, but they also suggested dominatrix boots.

The connections between boots and domination became central to subculture dress in the 1960s and it was in this milieu that Dr Martens, or DMs, became the footwear of rebellion and disaffection. Dr Martens were invented by the Second World War German

In 1964, André Courrèges introduced white boots, including this pair, as part of his 'Space Age' collection, sparking a trend for 'go-go' boots that helped define the 1960s fashion look. French, 1964.

Army physician Klaus Märtens after he injured his ankle skiing. Basing his design on the army boots given to German soldiers at the end of the war, Märtens, with the assistance of Dr Hebert Funck, created rubber soles comprised of two separate pieces with hollow compartments that when heat-sealed together formed air pockets, bringing increased cushioning to the feet. Although these boots did well with German housewives in the 1950s, they did not have broad appeal until a contract was signed with the British shoe manufacturer R. Griggs in 1959. Griggs had been looking for an innovation that would give their company an edge over the competition's work boot and the air sole, eventually dubbed AirWair by the Griggs company, proved interesting. On 1 April 1960 the first eight-eyelet Dr Martens boot was made, named the 1460 after the date of its manufacture. It was immediately embraced by postal workers, factory workers and policemen, but it was only after the hard mods and then the skinheads added DMs to their arsenal of steel-toed work boots that they became the symbols of defiance often associated with violence. The American photographer and former skinhead Gavin Watson recalls, 'we cut off the leather at the front to reveal the steel caps – those boots were seen as weaponry and you felt safe wearing them.'[54]

In the late 1960s, hard mods and skinheads were part of a larger climate of social unrest that found expression in a multitude of subcultures, each with its own uniform:

> He doesn't mind the word 'skinhead' at all, or the slightly menacing overtone that it has for many Britons . . . In a city swarming with long-haired young men wrapped in passivity, the sight of skinheads in brutally short hair-cuts and big boots often startles passers-by.[55]

Skinheads used their booted fashions to distinguish themselves from hippies, whom they saw as effeminate, and they proclaimed their hypermasculinity through branded working men's dress. The skinhead costume was also very nationalistic, constructed from local

The classic British Dr Martens 1460 is named after the date of its inception,
1 April 1960. The British shoe manufacturer R. Griggs & Co. had acquired the
exclusive rights to the Dr Martens sole and the resulting work boot went on to
become a counter-culture classic. British, 1995.

components. Dr Martens were seen as expressly English, a point that linked them to nationalist sentiments. Hippies, in contrast, were very global in their attire; worn while protesting against war, hippies' Native American moccasins and Jesus sandals said 'citizen of the world'. Skinheads reportedly christened new pairs of DMs 'by kicking someone with them. It didn't matter who, and if you got some blood on them that was even better.'[56] This connection between costume and political view was taken to an extreme by a small subset of skinheads who became increasingly xenophobic and embracing of neo-Nazi ideology. Their affiliation with Dr Martens risked tainting the brand. Nonetheless, the brand's wider reputation as reliable work boots and their rugged authenticity tempered such associations and allowed them to have a wider currency as the century progressed.

In the 1970s another type of boot, the high-heeled, platform-soled boot, also came to be used by men to proclaim their masculinity. The heel had been rising in men's footwear during the 1960s, as the heeled Beatle boot attested, but in the early 1970s heels for men reached unprecedented heights. On the street most men interested in this new fashion wore heeled shoes, but larger-than-life rock stars strode across the stage in knee-high boots sporting thick platforms and exaggeratedly high heels. David Bowie, perhaps the most truly gender-bending star of the glam rock scene, wore high platforms as well as make-up, but even as his sexuality was called into question he was adored, and understood to be adored in the popular media. *The Rocky Horror Picture Show* (1975) further illustrates this sexual dynamic. The character Dr Frank N. Furter, played by Tim Curry, is dressed in a costume of corset, ripped fishnets and high-heeled lace-up fetish boots, which burlesqued rather than adopted notions of traditional feminine clothing; the character's bisexuality did nothing to diminish his dominant and domineering masculine presence in the film. Indeed, the majority of glam rock performers did not have their sexuality or gender called into question as their acts established them as both hypersexual and masculine, despite their flamboyant

Skinheads continue to wear Dr Martens as part of their uniform of discontent. This photograph by Mark Henderson was taken in Dublin in 2012.

The Toronto shoemaker Master John made this men's platform-sole boot
complete with five-and-a-half-inch high heels, appliquéd stars and veritable
landscape in leather. In the 1970s, some men followed the lead of rock stars in
adopting lavish personal adornment including knee-high boots. Canadian, 1973.

costumes. This point was carried into street fashions, where some men wore knee-high boots in public as part of their aggressively masculine personas. One young man relayed how he wore a pair of extravagantly embellished and exaggerated high-heeled boots made by Master John specifically to 'kick the shit out of other guys'. This combination of glam and tough found expression in the rock opera *Tommy* (1975) by the English band The Who when Elton John as the Pinball Wizard wore a cartoonishly oversized pair of Dr Martens.

Although men's fashion had dismissed high boots by the end of the 1970s, boots remained important within various subcultures and were central to their image. Dr Martens continued to suggest disgruntled and disenfranchised masculinity, motorcycle boots continued to be linked to outlaws and rugged escapism, and cowboy boots remained signifiers of hard-working and authentic individualism. In effect, boots were central to the costuming of these subcultures. This was both celebrated and burlesqued by the exceptionally popular American musical group Village People. Members of the band dressed in costumes that referenced booted hypermasculine stereotypes, including a cop, a leatherman, a GI, a construction worker and a cowboy; even the 'Indian chief' often wore knee-high moccasin boots and in doing so clearly illustrated that variant constructions of masculinity were significantly costume-dependent. The Village People's disco songs, such as 'Macho Man' and 'Y.M.C.A.', became international hits and further helped to sear these masculine stereotypes into the collective imagination. The blatant suggestion that costume was central to performative maleness reflected dramatic shifts that were on the verge of happening in men's fashion. The uniform of authority – the business suit and brogues – that had become normative masculine attire was set to be revealed as a costume itself, and as men increasingly stepped into the fashion system, all kinds of footwear from cowboy boots to sneakers would be used to construct more individualized and often performative expressions of the masculine self.

Punk also coalesced in the 1970s. Splintering off from skinheads, punks were less political and more individualistic. Originally democratic and heterogeneous, early punk centred around DIY music and fashion, borrowing wildly from a wide variety of inspirations. At its centre was the British band manager and entrepreneur Malcolm McLaren who, along with his girlfriend Vivienne Westwood, ran the London clothing shop SEX. The pair had originally provided costumes for the New York Dolls, but by 1975 they were looking for another band. McLaren solved the problem when he assembled the infamous Sex Pistols from customers who frequented the shop: Johnny Rotten, Steve Jones, Paul Cook and Glen Matlock, who was replaced by Sid Vicious in 1977. Their look incorporated Teddy Boy, BDSM, rocker and mod references, all shredded and reassembled in ways that spoke of anarchy and rebellion. This riot of coexisting elements did not require a specific type of footwear, yet Dr Martens eventually emerged as the premier form of punk footwear. One scholar suggests that with punk shops being limited to London, as punk spread, followers in other parts of the country had to create their own costumes.[57] Dr Martens were readily available across Britain and became a means of establishing group cohesion through brand identity. The relatively high price of DMs also played a role in establishing group allegiance, as the boots represented an actual monetary investment that reflected a commitment to the lifestyle.

In the 1970s, boots still figured in women's fashion but the trend had shifted from a space-age future to reclamations of a romanticized past. As one newspaper article declared, 'the 1970 boots are grand-motherly in concept and reek of "good old days" nostalgia.'[58] When asked about the shift, shoe designer Beth Levine opined:

> Boots moved into prominence about the same time the pill did. Both were symbols of a woman's new freedom and emancipation. But inwardly women cowered at the idea of total independence, and the theory of 'equal footing' terrified her.

This pair of Yves Saint Laurent boots with their Russian-inspired appliqué date to 1974, two years before the designer's famed Russian Collection. French, 1974.

The article summed up her view by remarking that 'One of the reasons for the granny look is that it tones down a boot's rough-tough qualities and still allows a woman to look semi-helpless.'[59] The 'Cossack boots' in Yves Saint Laurent's famous Russian collection of 1976, the same year as Diana Vreeland's exhibition 'The Glory of Russian Costume', at the New York Metropolitan Museum of Art's Costume Institute, were likewise celebrated for being part of a romantic look that 'men and women (at least before the women's liberation movement) regard as feminine'.[60] This desire to return to a more 'ideal' period when men were men and women were women renewed interest in the cowboy boot. The movie *Urban Cowboy*, which came out in 1980, added fuel to the fire, and although the pointed-toe boots that urban cowboys wore would 'never feel a stirrup or a rattlesnake's fang', they functioned as a 'badge associated with an ideal'.[61] The popularity of the cowboy boot coincided with a resurgence of American conservative values and a longing for traditional American heroes in the aftermath of the divisive and humiliating Vietnam War as well as the economic pain of the oil crisis and years of social unrest. Texas oil men may have attempted to redefine the look of business, but it was U.S. president Ronald Reagan – who ranched, wore cowboy boots and, perhaps most importantly, had played cowboys in the movies – who captured the spirit of the age. A *Washington Post* article titled 'Tailored for President?', written years before Reagan's election, described his mien as 'Western, television-cowboy look, carefully rumpled' and said he came across as 'all man. No mincing frills. Out-doors-y, athletic, earnest, he's the Marlboro Man.'[62] In his western costuming, Reagan represented exactly what many conservative Americans sought to preserve: an 'authentic', hyper-masculine persona as well as a culturally and economically hegemonic nation.

The return of the English equestrian look in women's fashion in the 1980s likewise reflected a desire for a bygone era. Vreeland's influential exhibition 'Man and the Horse' at the Costume Institute in 1984 returned equestrianism to the forefront of fashion's imagination. It was no coincidence that it was sponsored by Ralph Lauren, who, as the *New York Times* had pointed out in the late 1970s, had made a polo player his logo as a symbol of 'breaking away from the 60s: an image of the polo player, [was] the ultimate symbol of privilege and elitism'. Indeed, the American designer was famous for his ability to construct fantasies of entitlement, and his use of the riding boot, which he paired with equally elegant and evocative fashions, spoke of tradition and advantage. The 'Me' generation of the 1970s may have set the stage for a return of conspicuous consumption, but it was in the 1980s that the trend really took off. *Vogue* reported in 1988: 'riding clothes still seem to elevate the wearer's status.'[63] The fashion reflected the aspirations of many during the status-hungry 1980s but, just like other boots that were increasingly being worn as costume, riding boots in women's fashion were about playing dress-up. Like little girls in princess costumes, equestrian-inspired fashions did not fool anybody that the wearers were part of the horsey set. As the *New York Times* quipped, 'horses are almost as rare in midtown Manhattan as free cabs.'[64] The use of equestrian boots and their insinuation of moneyed privilege also suggested that the wealth, real or imagined, exhibited by the wearer was inherited rather than earned. That in the 1980s women were making inroads into white-collar professions in droves discomforted many. Fashions such as dominatrix-referencing heels and equestrian-style riding boots complicated the high-fashion look of success for women by visually implying that the women's wealth had been acquired through alternative means, rather than as straightforward compensation for professional work well done.

Vreeland's exhibition on equestrianism also included a homage to the Wild West, and she recounted in the press having been given a pony by Buffalo Bill himself when she went to Wyoming at the age of twelve to escape a polio epidemic. Ralph Lauren capitalized on this nostalgia as well. His windswept models wrapped in Navaho blankets and wearing long prairie skirts and cowboy boots counter-balanced the romance of English equestrianism with the romance of the American West, while simultaneously updating the bohemian prairie dress and granny boot look of the 1970s.

Heavy-soled boots such as these were often paired with more delicate 'Gothic' attire. The look drew upon a number of sources that ranged from 19th-century dress to Japanese anime. This pair by Buffalo was worn by Spice Girl Geri Halliwell. British, 1997–8.

Other major trends in women's boots in the 1980s included low-heeled ankle boots in bright or pastel colours and with a slouchy appearance to complement the postmodern aesthetic and New Wave music of the era, while Japanese designers paired combat-referencing boots with deconstructed fashions that spoke to both tradition and the idea of a post-apocalyptic future. It was a look that goth fashion would take even further in the last decade of the twentieth century, when black lace-up boots, be they Dr Martens or 'granny boots', were worn in ways that combined Victoriana, fetish and punk with millennial anxiety. Many of the looks, such as Gothic Lolita, originated in Japan, influenced by Japanese manga and anime in which characters were often drawn in outsized boots with thick black soles. In fashion, this look was achieved by the wearing of high black platform boots, often called monster boots, that simultaneously repelled and attracted.

The use of hypersexualized items of dress that specifically referenced fetish and the sex trade were also becoming increasingly prevalent in women's mainstream fashion. The publicity material for the hit Hollywood movie *Pretty Woman* (1990) pictured Julia Roberts in shiny black vinyl thigh-high boots with stiletto heels as a means of immediately identifying her character as that of a prostitute. This relationship between boot and profession was also promoted in fashion. 'If you want a quick update for your wardrobe this season, your best investment may be a simple boot', wrote Jane Thompson in the *National Post*. 'For those seeking to make a statement' she suggested boots like those worn by 'Julia Roberts' hooker in *Pretty Lady* [sic] . . . that crawl above and beyond the knee'.[65] In a way similar to the fashion for equestrian boots, 'hooker boots' were worn as a type of costume. Yet, unlike equestrian boots, which suggested upper-class privilege, and if pushed further could connote mastery over a powerful beast, sex-worker-inspired boots were linked to those considered by broader society to be exploited and motivated by socioeconomic distress. Despite ideas of 'power' related to the domination and manipulation of male sexual desire for female economic benefit, itself a rather unsettling response to women's recent ascent in the white-collar workplace, this 'slut-style', like 1990s 'heroin chic', also functioned as a disturbing kind of poverty chic charade for 'good girls' and found expression in many areas of women's fashion well into the twenty-first century.

Grunge, which started in Seattle in the late 1980s, gained popularity in the early 1990s and also embraced boots, but the genre was not as driven by brand-consciousness. Grunge style consisted of second-hand (thrift store) clothing worn with either hiking boots or Converse All Stars; Dr Martens were worn by some, but their cost, which had dramatically increased over the decades, was often prohibitive. Kurt Cobain, lead singer of the band Nirvana, often wore hiking boots with thrift store clothes, but few men emulated him. When worn by women, however, that pairing transitioned into a style called 'kinderwhore'. Courtney Love, Cobain's wife and a successful musician in her own right, popularized a version of the look. She wore dresses or slips in states of disarray and the look suggested a range of scenarios from rumbled romps to outright victimization through the tension created by the public revealing of intimate lingerie paired with either childlike Mary Janes or rugged footwear.[66]

Despite the anti-consumption stance of grunge, in 1992 the American fashion designer Marc Jacobs, while working for Perry Ellis, brought the look to the mainstream and upped the ante by sending models down the runway wearing brand-name Dr Martens. *Vogue* declared 1993 'the year of the boot'; that same year, the *enfant terrible* of the fashion world, Jean Paul Gaultier, debuted his Hasidic-inspired line, complemented by combat boots. As the fashion of Dr Martens grew, the brand met the new market with increased offerings. Colour and patterns from pastel to floral became popular among young women and DMs were even made available in children's sizes. The impact on business was good but it brought the gritty authenticity of Dr Martens into question. Soon, Timberland boots,

The thigh-high boots popular in turn-of-the-21st-century fashion made direct reference to sex-worker footwear. This pair came from a manufacturer in Toronto specializing in erotic footwear. Canadian, 1998.

which were simultaneously outdoorsy and urban, began to rival Dr Martens, particularly in the United States:

> No longer do sneakers have a firm hold on the top spot in the shoe wear market as outdoor shoes and hiking boots – whether they are worn on a mountain hike [or] to the mall – are gaining ground . . . One of the biggest beneficiaries of this new trend is Hampton-based Timberland Company, which saw a 47 per cent increase in second-quarter sales of its outdoor footwear this year.[67]

This article from 1993 reflects the rapid embrace of 'Timbs' in the early 1990s. Like Dr Martens, Timberlands were solid work boots that had been in production since 1952 and likewise spoke to ideas of working-class reliability. Timberland, as the name implies, also suggested an American aesthetic that combined physical labour with the great outdoors. In urban culture, where brand was paramount, they were linked to authenticity. They also did not carry the taint of racism that patronage by skinheads had imparted to Dr Martens. Timberlands came in black but, perhaps as a mark of distinction, the most popular colour was yellow. Timbs were first worn in urban centres as popular winter boots, unlaced and with the legs of the wearer's baggy jeans caught in the open shaft, and paired with large, puffy down jackets. They offered status sneakers a winter break, but by the 1990s many men were wearing them instead of sneakers, regardless of weather. Drug dealers began to wear them as part of their 'work' uniform and that cachet carried them into broader fashion. Soon many of the most prominent rappers, such as Notorious B.I.G., Tupac Shakur and Jay Z, were sporting Timbs, and they spread the fashion worldwide. The popularity of Timberlands grew so quickly among urban men in the 1990s that they even challenged Nike Air Jordans for style supremacy and market share. Given the prescience of fashion, perhaps this particular trend was announcing the fact that jobs requiring physical labour were disappearing and that the work boot was on the verge of becoming costume, like the cowboy boot.

But Timbs were not central to women's dress, urban or otherwise. Instead it was the polarizing ugg that swept into prominence in the early 2000s. Uggs, as with slides in men's dress, allowed the wearer to appear fashionably nonchalant. They were the casual footwear of choice for celebrities from Oprah Winfrey to Gwyneth Paltrow and retailers faced an unexpected demand for the sheepskin boots. Traditionally, uggs were a form of footwear from Australia and New Zealand worn by sheep shearers to keep their feet warm. By the 1960s, male surfers were wearing them on the beach after spending hours in the cold ocean. The term ugg, short for 'ugly boot', had been in use since the 1920s but only became branded in the 1970s. In 1978, when

The UGG Classic Short became a fixture in the wardrobe of many young women in the 1990s and early 2000s. Although ugg boots were originally Australian, the brand UGG is now American. This pair are Classic Short II, 2016.

American surfer Brian Smith returned to southern California from Australia with the idea of selling uggs locally, he trademarked the name UGG and his boots sold well, with girls wearing their surfer boyfriends' UGGs 'like letterman [varsity] jackets'.[68] The fashion lingered on the West Coast until 2000, when it exploded, becoming the fashion of choice for many young women across the U.S. Like Air Jordan sneakers, branded UGGs were in such demand that one retailer reported answering thousands of phone calls requesting the boots, ultimately deciding 'to sell the few pairs it received from [the manufacturer] Deckers under strict conditions, one pair per customer, and people often lined up outside stores as early as 6 a.m. to get them'.[69]

Paired with tracksuit trousers (sweatpants) and loose tops, and worn with the hair tied up in a dishevelled topknot, the look was highly contentious. Some saw UGGs as slovenly, especially since they were frequently worn to shreds, while others felt they were attractive and comfortable alternatives to the hypersexualized high heel. In many ways, UGGs were an update to grunge fashion, but instead of pairing lingerie and boots, the clothes young women wore with UGGs were suggestive of what they might have actually worn to bed. Yet others saw them as signifiers of privilege, a judgement justified not only by the branded UGGs high price point but also by their seemingly exclusive use by so-called 'basic bitches'[70] – young white women who were characterized as overly brand-conscious and exceedingly bland.

The 2000s also saw the popularization of the rubber Wellington among young women – specifically those made by Hunter, the supplier to the British royal family. Unlike the UGG, which was worn to create a very casual appearance, Hunters represented a more elegant look. In part this was related to the brand's long association with privilege. Green rubber Wellingtons were part of the uniform of upper-middle-class leisure in Britain and were associated with country pastimes and pleasures such as gardening, hence the phrase 'green welly brigade' to refer to the demographic. This suggestion of British privilege made it a desirable fashion in both Europe and America; when worn in urban environments, the Hunter Wellington, like the equestrian riding boot, suggested a privileged private life. The cost of Hunters also made them a signifier of status. In short order, luxury brands such as Burberry and Gucci were offering their own rain boots. In North America, Hunter and other brands of Wellingtons were considered distinctly feminine, but another type of boot, the classic American L.L.Bean, with its distinctive waterproof foot, found itself revived in men's fashion. Like Hunters, L.L.Bean boots spoke of privilege but in this case practical Yankee traditionalism and Boston Brahmin breeding. The reinvigorated interest in the Clarks desert boot was also part of this trend in men's fashion, which saw the revival of a number of classic styles, such as the laced ankle boot and the Chelsea boot, as part of a larger trend which included the return of the full beard in the hipster costume of nostalgia.

In the early 2000s boots in the domain of play found an eager audience among young girls, whose preferences turned from high-heel-wearing Barbie to booted Bratz dolls. These dolls wore heavy make-up and streaks of bright colour in their hair, and were outfitted in short skirts and chunky lace-up boots in a nod to counter-culture goth style. Like Mattel's Barbie, Bratz were fashionable and sexy, but they projected a kind of sexiness more aligned with the sex trade than fashion. The dolls made some parents nervous. 'Not every parent . . . thinks it's ok that Bratz look as though they might be at home on any street corner where prostitutes ply their trade,' reported the *Pittsburgh Post* in 2003.[71] The links between high boots and hypersexuality would only get stronger, particularly in cyberspace.

In the first decades of the 2000s digital experiences proliferated; regardless of whether or not boots are actually worn in fashion, they are staples in the virtual world. Online dress-up games for children are replete with boot choices while video games for older players incorporate 'customizing' – or, perhaps more accurately, costumizing – one's avatar as part of the amusement. Often the access to clothing in gaming is progressive and based on success in the game, which makes the function of fashion in multiplayer games a direct expression of status. The types of clothing, including footwear, that players select to construct their identities, however, is varied and often relies on established if exaggerated tropes that commonly exist in the culture. In some versions of the game *Grand Theft Auto* a great deal of work and thought is put into how one's character is presented. Sneakers and boots vie for the player's attention and money just as they do in actual contemporary life, and style and expense reflect achievement. Other games invite players into imaginary realms where both the environment and fashions may be extremely fantastical and the wardrobes of players' characters include boots of all sorts, including thigh-high boots used to connote sexiness. Boots are also a prominent feature of superhero costuming. In the current age of incessant conflict and fear of enemies without uniforms, the superhero seems to provide escapist relief and the boots they wear serve to perpetuate long-standing associations between boots and domination, in addition to action, adventure and heroism. Ultimately though, the boots superheroes wear are costume, just like the majority of the real-life boots worn for fashion.

III   High Heels: Instability

To wear high heels, then, sweet traveller, is to hobble, to be insecure and to be unable to stand erect. I know how pretty they look in the shop windows. They are delicately made and dexterously curved, and sharpen to such a point, and they are so red and bright! But what a price to pay for delicacy, and pretty curves, and high color!

An Old Bachelor, 'Of High Heels', 1871

One of the biggest misconceptions that a woman has is that a man has to accept her the way she is. No, we don't. I don't know who told you that. We like the bright and shiny. If you stop wearing the makeup, stop putting on nail polish, stop wearing high heels, you'll lose us.[1]

Steve Harvey, 2009

High heels are remarkably impractical. They may have originated as a feature of equestrian footwear but off the horse they are hobbling, counter-intuitive; their function lies elsewhere. For centuries, heels have been an aspect of women's dress, both dictated and decried as accessories of seduction. Despite the fact that privileged men wore them for the first 130 years of their use in Western fashion, they have become icons, albeit complicated ones, of feminine desirability.

In contrast to sandals and boots, which were innovated independently by numerous cultures in prehistoric times, heels are a more recent and localized invention. Exactly when they were created remains to be discovered; however, a tenth-century Nishapur bowl from what is now Iran held in the collection of the Museum of Fine Arts, Boston, provides evidence of heeled footwear from at least as early as the tenth century CE.[2] At the centre of the bowl a rider is depicted astride a beautiful steed. Poised for battle or perhaps the hunt, he holds the reins in one hand, arrows in the other, and his

Beth Levine, one of the few female shoe designers of the 20th century, was inspired by the world around her and often translated her observations into footwear infused with a unique sense of wit. This shimmery pair seems to be decorated with golden fish scales. American, 1960s.

heeled footwear is slipped into a stirrup. The stirrup, the origin of which also remains to be determined definitively, profoundly changed horseback riding, making military campaigns more effective by allowing riders to steady themselves and wield their weapons with greater accuracy.[3] The heel seems to have been a further development of this technology, allowing the wearer to hook his foot firmly in the stirrup. Over the following six centuries heels spread across Western Asia to the edges of Europe. By the sixteenth century, heels were being worn by Persians, Mughals, Ottomans, Crimean Tatars, Polish and Ukrainian Cossacks and Hungarians.[4] Surprisingly, Western Europeans did not wear heels, though they were aware of them, as military incursions, pilgrimages and trading ventures put them in contact with heel-wearing cultures. Even though Europeans had adopted the stirrup by the ninth century and had long found inspiration in Near Eastern attire for a wide variety of European fashions, there is no evidence of heel-wearing until the turn of the seventeenth century, when heels became a part of Western dress.

(*above*) This textile shows Safavid courtiers leading captured Georgian nobles defeated during military campaigns between 1540 and 1553. Both the Persians and the Georgians are depicted wearing heeled footwear. Persian, mid-16th century.

(*right*) This heeled Persian riding boot is made from shagreen leather. The pebbled appearance is made by pressing wet horsehide into mustard seeds. Persian, 17th century.

The reasons for the heel's abrupt appearance are complex. In the sixteenth century, Europe was undergoing dramatic changes. Ottoman imperialism and the opportunities offered by an expanding seafaring trade were destabilizing traditional trade networks and creating new alliances. The Spanish and the Portuguese sought to bypass the Ottoman stranglehold on Indian and East Asian trade via the circumnavigation of the oceans, while the English, followed by the Dutch, sought inland routes to India around Ottoman strongholds via Poland and Persia.[5] Although establishing trade relations with India at first proved difficult, Persia was open and towards the end of the century relations between England and Iran grew stronger when the new ruler, Shāh 'Abbās I, rose to power. Like his European counterparts, 'Abbās was concerned about the increasingly powerful Ottoman Empire and was eager to make alliances with European powers. Knowledge of the shah's military might – one of the largest mounted militaries in the world – preceded him. It was precisely at the time that European and Persian political interests aligned that the heel debuted in European fashion.

There is scant mention in contemporary commentary of the sudden appearance of heeled footwear in Western European dress – a lacuna, along with discussions of imbibing tobacco and coffee, and other previously unseen and unknown customs and fashions newly imported by explorers and traders – but there are abundant images from the period depicting the new fashion. Many of the earliest representations of heeled footwear in Western art can be found in pictures of men on horseback or in equestrian attire, suggesting the continued association between heels and riding in the European context. By the 1610s, men began to be depicted wearing heels for formal dress as well as equestrian attire, suggesting that the meaning of the heel was transforming to meet specifically European interests. A portrait from the 1630s by Anthony van Dyck of James Stuart, 1st Duke of Richmond, provides a striking image of the heel as an item of fashion and status. The early years of the fashion for heels in Western attire resulted in a number of interesting innovations, including the wearing of heels and mules, together. This short-lived

James Stuart may be posed with a hunting greyhound but everything about his outfit speaks of more formal attire, including his shoes with their large roses and self-covered heels. Anthony van Dyck, *James Stuart, Duke of Richmond and Lennox*, *c.* 1633–5, oil on canvas.

trend is clearly depicted in a 1630s print by Abraham Bosse showing a man playing a lute. The earliest 'slap-soles', as the style came to be called, were a combination of heeled footwear slipped into flat-soled mules, worn as a means of preventing one's heels from sinking into the mud – but here the gallant simply doubles his stylishness by donning not one but two pairs of heels. It was precisely the promise of impracticality that would give the heel such enduring cultural value.

It was not the heel's impracticality, however, that first attracted women; it was its associations with exoticism, equestrianism and masculinity that made it an appealing accessory. Early seventeenth-century women's fashion borrowed heavily from the male wardrobe and the heel was an additional feature that could be used to masculinize women's dress,[6] a point remarked upon by the chaplain to the Venetian Ambassador in London, who noted in 1618 that women 'all wear men's shoes'.[7] The notable trend also attracted criticism. In 1620 the English pamphlet *Hic Mulier; or, The Man-woman:*

This gentleman is the height of fashion in his slap-soled boots. Abraham Bosse, *Man Singing and Playing the Lute*, 1630s, etching.

*Being a Medicine to Cure the Coltish Disease of the Staggers in the Masculine-feminines of Our Times* declared that women 'swimme in the excesse of these vanities, and will be man-like not only from the head to the waste, but to the very foot'.[8] Despite the assimilation of heels into female fashion in the early years of the century, they remained central to expressions of masculine privilege until the eighteenth century, although the types of heels worn by men and women began to take on gendered shapes and, with that, gendered meanings.

The earliest European heels were typically made of wood covered in leather – the so-called 'self-covered heel' – and bore formal resemblance to Persian examples. Stacked leather heels, made by stacking thin pieces of leather to create a heel, came in to fashion a bit later and likewise were inspired by Western Asian models.[9] Both forms of heel were worn by men and women in the early decades of the seventeenth century, but as the century wore on women's footwear

This shoe was most likely made for a well-to-do boy. The fact that the wearer was male is suggested by the shape and stacked-leather heel, which is painted red in keeping with the fashion of the day. French or English, mid-17th century.

tended to favour self-covered heels while men's fashion included both types, albeit worn in different settings. Leather-covered heels came to be used on men's footwear for wear in the home or in more formal settings, while stacked leather heels became the type worn for horse riding and outdoor activity. The distinction between these two types of heel and the settings in which they were appropriate for men was epitomized by the footwear choices of the French king Louis XIV later in the century. In regal or domestic settings he is depicted wearing self-covered heels, while in images of action he wears stacked leather heels. In both situations, Louis XIV often made use of either red leather or red paint on the heel, to attract the eye. The political significance of heels in men's fashion increased when Louis XIV made the wearing of red heels a sartorial statement of political privilege: although the fashion for red pre-dated the king, during his rule those granted access to the French court were permitted to wear red-heeled footwear.[10]

High attenuated heels and pointed toes were a hallmark of feminine footwear at the end of the 17th century. This pair was made of exceptionally soft kid embroidered with silk thread. Italian, 1690–1700.

As the century wore on, structural differences between men's and women's heels also developed – men's grew high but were thick and sturdy, while women's likewise increased in height but also grew more attenuated. Foot size itself also became a greater marker of gender. The lines 'Her feet, beneath her petticoat,/Like little mice stole in and out,/As if they feared the light', from the poem 'A Ballad Upon a Wedding' by Sir John Suckling (1609–1641),[11] capture the feeling of the day. Beauty ideals emphasized a preference for dainty feet, and heeled shoes became a useful means of creating the illusion of small feet as they lifted the majority of the foot up under skirts. It should come as no surprise that Charles Perrault penned both 'Cinderella' and 'Puss in Boots' at the end of the century.[12] As these gender differences in footwear became more pronounced, leather-covered heels, with their associations of domesticity, began to smack of effeminate refinement and in the eighteenth century they would be almost completely abandoned in men's fashion.

Sensitivity to men in heels began in England when rising nationalism brought male dress into focus. Charles II's declaration in 1666 that he was setting a new fashion 'after the Persian mode',[13] in an attempt to declare British independence from French fashion, ushered in what has been termed the Great Male Renunciation. This adoption of Persian-inspired clothing marked the origin of the vest and three-piece suit, but it also tolled the bell for that other Persian borrowing, the heel. The irrationality of the heel in addition to its importance in French fashion caused it to lose its footing in British men's dress, and by the turn of the eighteenth century the term 'red heels' implied effeminacy and unpatriotic affectation. Judith Drake's book *An Essay in Defence of the Female Sex: In Which Are Inserted the Characters of a Pedant, a Squire, a Beau, a Virtuoso, a Poetaster, a City-critick, &c.* articulated this prejudice clearly:

> the first rank of these is the *Beau*, who is one that has more Learning in his Heels than his Head . . . He is One that has travell'd to see Fashions, and brought over with him the newest cut suit, and the prettiest Fancy'd Ribbands for Sword Knots.

His best Acquaintance at Paris was his Dancing Master, whom he calls the Marquiss, and his chief Visits, to the Opera. He has seen the *French* King once, and knows the name of his chief Minister, and is by this sufficiently convinc'd that there are no Politicians in any other Part of the World. His improvements are a nice Skill in the Mode, and a high Contempt of his own Country.[14]

Religious thinkers also added to the argument by suggesting that artificially augmenting the body was an offence to God. In 1714 the 'noted wrestler, and author of a treatise on that manly and athletic science'[15] Thomas Parkins advised, 'let us leave off aiming at the outdoing [of] our Maker in our true symmetry and proportion; let us likewise, for our own ease, secure treading and upright walking, as he designed we should, and shorten our heels'.[16] The stacked leather heel, albeit lower, remained a feature of men's equestrian footwear, and seventeenth- and early eighteenth-century images of heroic leaders mounted for battle wearing high-heeled jackboots continued to feature prominently in state propaganda. By the 1730s, however, the majority of men had abandoned high, self-covered heels for formal and domestic wear and would not sport them again for another two centuries, leaving them to become an exclusively feminine form of footwear.

The gendering of the high heel also coincided with the rationalist philosophy of the Enlightenment that was developing across Europe. Women were portrayed as being guided by instinct, sensuality and irrational passions, while men were seen as regulated by reason. Interest in dress was presented as an innately feminine trait and indulging in fashion's foolish artifices was seen to be a prime measure of female weakness and even vice.[17] Heels, which had become the focus of cultural criticism, with charges ranging from unpatriotic feeling to ungodly pride, were now positioned as essentially female trappings.

The feminization of heels increased their erotic associations. But their erotic value did not rest on the fact that heels elongated the leg or drew the eye to it: women's legs were not only hidden from view,

they were not even yet a focus of attention, as this quote from 1724 attests:

> it will never be the Fashion to shew the Lower-parts, for there women are Ugly, Ill-shaped, Nasty Creatures, or else they would have brought up the Fashion of shewing them long ago. Don't think 'tis let alone one of Modesty: no, they are only afraid Men will despise and hate them for it.[18]

Instead, the specifically erotic value of heels lay more in the type of shoes worn. High-heeled mules, for example, were worn when a woman was in her boudoir and connoted intimacy. When mules were worn in the more public spaces of a home or even outdoors for casual walks, they signified a relaxed informality infused with erotic undertones.

Mules – footwear with no back quarters – have long been worn indoors. The addition of high heels infuses this domestic shoe with increased eroticism. This pair is embellished with elaborate silver thread embroidery and the ruched ribbon that decorated the throat was originally pink. French, 1700–1730s.

The thought that some women might exploit such erotic undertones troubled many in the eighteenth century. Enlightenment thinking may have declared men uniquely rational, but there remained a deep-seated cultural concern that women might use dress as a means of seducing men and usurping power. It was as though Cinderella's stepsisters haunted the collective imagination. Cinderella's nobility and virtue may only have come to light through the power of fashion, but her sisters' attempts to use fashion to conceal rather than reveal their true selves suggested that devious minds might use dress as a form of subterfuge to gain advantage. The message was clear: the high heel's ability to suggest a diminutive foot, real or imagined, threatened to trifle with men's sexual desires and could lead to dire consequences for any ensnared by such wiles.

More common was the argument that wearing impractical high heels proved women's innate lack of sense. The line 'in ran the lively Harriott, tottering on her French heels and with her head as unsteady as her feet',[19] penned in 1781, captured the essence of the empty-headed yet alluring female. High heels had become complex and contradictory emblems of desirable femininity and were used as evidence of women's vapid intellect as well as their cunning deceit. It was a set of meanings that would stay with the high heel for centuries to come.

By the end of the eighteenth century, high heels, among other accoutrements of the aristocracy, were becoming objects of scorn. The revolutions in the United States, Haiti and France had spurred fashion to reject aristocratic dress, including women's heels, and after reaching unprecedented heights in the 1780s, the heel was reduced to only a few millimetres at the end of the century. These democratic leanings, coupled with an enthusiasm for Greek and Roman antiquities, marked the banishment of the high heel in women's fashion for more than half a century. The early years of the nineteenth century saw fashion-forward women don flat-soled sandals in emulation of Grecian models from antiquity, while more conservative women wore delicate and demure flat-soled slippers of silk or leather that featured ribbons to lace up the leg, Roman-sandal style.

(*top*) Pink and black high heels. By the 1780s, high, thin heels were often covered in contrasting fabric that drew the eye. Probably English, 1780–85.

(*bottom*) As the 18th century drew to a close, high heels and shoe buckles, among other accoutrements of the aristocracy, became objects of scorn. The acceptance of leather as an alternative to silk for upper-class footwear was another signifier of impending cultural change. This pink pair was made using roller-printed leather; all the dots were originally silver. English, 1790–1800.

Though this rejection of aristocratic fashion caused the heel to be discarded in women's dress, it also led to the temporary reintroduction of the heel into men's fashion. Breeches, like the high heel, smacked of eighteenth-century privilege and were hence abandoned. Ankle-length pantaloons spoke to a new era, yet they also presented a challenge. Commonly knitted, pantaloons were designed to be worn long and lean, free of any sagging. This look was achieved by a strap that was attached to the hem of the trouser leg and wrapped under the foot. The pantaloons could be worn inside a boot, typically a Hessian, or they could be worn with the strap slipped under the sole of a shoe or boot. This latter style required a heel to prevent the strap from slipping off the back of the shoe. Fashion plates of the day depict men in heels of significant height and advice books suggest that men of shorter stature should take advantage of this new opportunity to augment their height, as long as it is done discreetly.[20] Eventually, pantaloons gave way to looser trousers that did not require straps in order to hang correctly. The loss of pantaloons did away with the excuse for wearing heels in daily fashion, and in urban settings men in heels were ridiculed.

For women, the loss of the heel was not simply a rejection of aristocratic excess; it signalled a profound shift in the construction of idealized femininity. The new cult of domesticity limited 'respectable' women's interactions with the greater community outside their homes, and their delicate, flat-soled footwear, unfit for sustained wear, reflected this lack of participation in the public realm.

Motherhood was to be a woman's vocation and those who wished to have their say in the world were admonished to exert influence over society strictly through the raising of morally upright citizens. Many women were uncomfortable with these limitations and by the middle of the century they began to use the power invested in them as stewards of familial morality to engage with ethical issues in the public sphere – first the abolition of slavery and then women's suffrage.

When pantaloons were worn over a pair of boots, the boot leg needed to be slim and the sole required a heel to prevent the foot strap from slipping. This elegant boot would have worked well with pantaloons as well as trousers, and would have also provided a lift. Viennese, 1846.

As if in reaction to women's increased participation in the public realm, the heel, with all its eighteenth-century associations, was re-inserted into fashion. It was a set of meanings clearly illustrated in this quote from 1852, just before the heel was reintroduced:

> the high-heel was truly both a bad and grotesque extravagance – a useless and uncomfortable vanity – a very break-ancle [sic] fashion – and only a 'fashion' because the 'lady' of the former age ... wanted to be 'Something' and yet was really 'Nothing' – a piece of ballon-becrowned – patched-faced – peacock-necked – and heel-lifted pomposity.[21]

The reintroduction of the heel was part of a larger fashion trend that revived and reinforced negative female stereotypes through the use of clothing that blatantly referenced eighteenth-century dress, recasting women in clothing that carried the taint of aristocratic excess and female frivolity. By the 1860s the new heel, Rococo in form and meaning, was dubbed the Louis heel, in honour of the eighteenth-century French king Louis XV, thus making clear its connections to the aristocratic past.

The reintroduction of the heel was immediately noted by champions of the burgeoning women's rights and dress reform movements, who condemned it as destabilizing to women both physically and politically. Their cries, however, were unheeded, for, as the *Christian Inquirer* reported in 1859, advocates for dress reform faced opposition from 'fashion, taste, education, dry goods dealers, undertakers ... [despite that] in its favor could be urged health, economy and commonsense'.[22] Even though heels were promoted as fashionable, they were also predictably the focus of condemnation, even by those not interested in dress reform. Predictably, heels and their associations with imprudence were also targeted. Some ridiculed the stance of women in heels. In contrast to claims made today that high heels create an alluring posture that men are biologically programmed to be unable to resist, women in heels in the 1860s were criticized for the ugliness of their silhouette, which was mockingly termed

The heel was reintroduced into women's fashion by the mid-1850s on a wave of nostalgia for 18th-century dress. The term 'Louis heel' was coined at this time. This pair of chestnut-brown Adelaides features a modest heel and was worn by the Contessa Fravineti di Ferrari. French, *c.* 1860s.

the Grecian bend. Heels were deemed responsible for disfiguring the body and the effects were ridiculed as a malady brought on by vanity:

> One of those calamities which makes whole communities feel particularly uncomfortable is the prevalence of a contagious disease, especially one which will not yield readily to medical treatment. The first I heard of the distemper called the Grecian Bend was from a minister who told me of one of his parishioners that had hitherto borne an irreproachable character.

The story continues, and the minister tells of having warned his wife and daughters to steer clear of the patient whose illness had already caused her to look like a lame kangaroo.[23] Others focused on the stilted gait effected by wearing heels. High heels were even used as evidence that women were unfit to vote. An editorial article in the *New York Times* dated 1871 stated,

> [When the heel] first came into fashion, the ladies were told by a few sensible men that . . . a heel three inches high . . . would insure suffering and deformity . . . No degree of sense, or independence, or stability of character seems to absolve any woman who had the charm of womanhood about her from slavery to fashion, at whatever sacrifice of time, comfort, money or health. Suffrage! Right to hold office! Show us first the woman who has independence and sense . . . enough to dress attractively . . . in shoes which do not destroy both her comfort and her gait.[24]

That links could be drawn between women's high heels and women's right to vote and hold office might seem overwrought, yet in coming years, especially as women stepped into the public realm, these ideas would resurface time and again.

## "THE GRECIAN BEND"
### FIFTH AVENUE STYLE.

PUBLISHED BY CURRIER & IVES 152 NASSAU ST NEW YORK

In stark contrast to the sombre business suits and sensible shoes worn by men, the revival of 18th-century-inspired fashion, including the heel, reinforced negative notions about women as 'slaves to fashion'. This caricature mocks the posture women were accused of adopting when wearing the new heel. Thomas Worth, *The Grecian Bend: Fifth Avenue Style*, c. 1868, lithograph.

The forays of privileged women into the civic arena during the nineteenth century were fraught. The cult of domesticity had suggested that respectable women need not be part of the larger world, and those women who did move about in the public realm were imagined as having been driven there by economic need; their morality was suspect and their interactions with men outside their families were laden with suggestions of sexual impropriety. One acceptable response to the new call for increased freedom of movement among sheltered women was to couch their public activity in terms of non-productive leisure and conspicuous consumption that served to display familial wealth.[25] The newly created urban boulevards and recently invented department stores became spaces where women of leisure could walk in their delicately embroidered heeled boots, advertising the wealth and influence of their households through the fashions they wore and consumed. This new engagement with conspicuous consumption came at a critical moment in the history of footwear production, ultimately giving birth to the phenomenon of the acclaimed shoe designer.

Over the course of the nineteenth century, shoemaking shifted from artisan craft to industrialized manufacturing. Brand identity became a principal means of establishing quality, and the idea of the designer as arbiter of taste and style was established. François Pinet, the French shoe manufacturer, is often pointed to as the first celebrated shoe designer. The footwear he made straddled the pre-industrial world of handcraftsmanship and cutting-edge industrial practices and featured exquisite hand-embroidered uppers paired with elegant 'Pinet heels'. They quickly became objects of desire and the Pinet name became associated with luxury. As always, the consumption of luxury goods presented an opportunity to accuse women of avarice and to caution them against imprudence or even more disastrous loss of virtue.

Situated between bespoke and mass-produced, Pinet boots offered consistently high quality with expensive and time-consuming hand embellishment and finishes, at a price point only the well-off could afford. An eager innovator, Pinet created a machine to make the curvy Louis XV heel that came in to fashion in the 1860s. French, c. 1880s.

'If a woman paints her cheeks, dyes her hair, draws in her waist, and wears too high heels, she may not be morally bad, but she will be sure to be mistaken for quite another person than the lady she is.'[26] These words of caution from the *Ladies' Home Journal* in 1888 are just one example among many that appeared in the second half of the nineteenth century advising women on how to dress so as not to be mistaken for 'women of little virtue'. Questions of female vice were the topics of the day. The idea of the courtesan, itself an eighteenth-century revival, engaged the public imagination. Intellectuals and artists obsessed over the subject, while the popular media endlessly played with the trope of men inadvertently soliciting 'honest' women:

> But there is cause for sorrow when we have no means, so far as dress is concerned, of discriminating between a respectable but fashionably attired woman and a courtesan: since the one has assumed all the trappings and the meretricious adornments and the tricks in dress for showing off her person, and drawing attention to it on the street, which, a few years ago, were considered the exclusive property of the other.[27]

The courtesan was characterized, like upper-class women, as a lover of luxury, and like upper-class women she also wore eighteenth-century-referencing clothing, including heels, albeit ones that were a bit too high. Furthermore, she was painted as a supreme manipulator whose duplicity was perhaps shared by many of the well-dressed wives and daughters of respectable men.

The eroticization of women's heels in their association with sex work was not only promoted by the fantasy image of the courtesan. The invention of the camera and its immediate adoption by pornographers led to the practice of photographing women in little more than their shoes, a convention that continues to this day. In formal terms, the shoes, and in early photographs stockings as well, were used, as Valerie Steele has put it, to frame the genitals. On a more conceptual level, the presence of shoes heightened the voyeuristic appeal of the

pornographic image through their quotidian associations. The inclusion of contemporary shoes in these 'French postcards' rescued the images from drifting into metaphor or allegory; the shoes pinned the body in time and space and established the women as naked and real. The widespread distribution of these pornographic images infused the everyday footwear worn by women with increased erotic value, and as the century wore on high heels became increasingly suggestive of both the private and public realms.

As the erotic value of heels increased, so did their height. Higher heels were suggestive of excess and impracticality in the extreme, and their consistent labelling in English-speaking media as 'French heels' carried with it the age-old cultural bias linking things French to looser morals and/or more seductive wiles. By the 1890s these 'French heels'

This classic 'French postcard' from the turn of the 20th century is typical of the type of erotic image that used the high heel to heighten the allure of the image. French, late 19th century.

These fetish shoes offered the wearer no support and were clearly not designed for outdoor wear. European, early 20th century.

could often be found on footwear that was specifically designed to be suggestive. Boots designed to look like stockinged legs slipped into high-heeled shoes gave onlookers a thrill but were also harbingers of change. In only a few decades' time, hemlines would rise and women's legs – and the heels they wore – would be fully visible. The ramifications of this increase in the high heel's erotic currency was evidenced by the debut of fetish footwear with exaggeratedly high heels at the end of the century, as well as by the growing sense that heels were no longer appropriate for young girls.

At the same time as fashionable high heels were becoming emblems of sexualized femininity, in the American West high heels of a different sort were becoming icons of rugged individualism with their own type of allure. The 'opening' of the West coincided with the rising dominance of manliness over refinement in the United States. This trend had begun earlier in the eighteenth century, when the 'active' man – a man engaged in the workings of his estate or embroiled in the military actions of his country – started to supersede the courtly man, whose refinements began to be seen as effeminate. It was an essentialist concept of masculinity that crossed socioeconomic boundaries, linking gender to one's exploits and thus enfranchising more men.

Manliness spoke to nation building, and it was this image of masculinity that helped to lay the foundation for 'American values', which included a profound reverence for rugged individualism in contrast to Old World elegance and inherited position. Some of those who in time came to symbolize the manliest of them all were cowboys, a heterogeneous and rough lot made up of new immigrants from Europe, recently emancipated African American slaves, Mexicans and ex-military men, who were allowed a level of flamboyance that would have drawn scorn in urban settings but was tolerated given the hardships of their job. George W. Wingate in his book *Through the Yellowstone Park on Horseback* (1886) was struck by the fashion for heels among cowboys: 'some of them are as much the slaves of fashion as anyone . . . Boots with high French heels are very popular.'[28] And the book *Our Great West: A Study of the Present Conditions and Future*

*Possibilities of the New Commonwealths and Capitals of the United States* (1893) included this quote: 'You can't walk in a cowboy's shoes; they fit too much. You see, we wear high-heeled boots, and get 'em as small as we can . . . Cowboys are very particular about the look of their feet and have a right to be, because they pay $15 for a pair of boots.'[29] These comments seem to be the perfect set-up for mocking the cowboy, but it was in fact city slickers who were mocked; the high-heeled cowboy boot was considered a necessary adjunct for the active man, a tool of the trade rather than simply a fashionable frivolity.[30] The cowboy, as dime novels and Buffalo Bill's Wild West shows demonstrated, personified dreams of individual freedom and self-reliance held dear by Americans, and their heels were central to their image.

Heels in women's fashion, however, carried no such heroic associations. As women attempted to gain a political foothold, suffragettes were negatively stereotyped in the media, whatever shoes they wore. The sandal-wearing frump and the high-heeled flirt were both pressed into the service of anti-suffragists. Some critics denigrated women's rights activists for their slovenly dress and unattractive footwear, while other anti-suffragists took the opposite tack, arguing that the suffragettes' acquiescence to fashion, such as the wearing of 'French heels', was a sure sign of their lack of reason. To counter these extremes, suffragettes themselves attempted to walk the tightrope between these two caricatures by pounding the pavements in *moderately* high-heeled button boots. Eventually, women won the right to vote, but entrenched ideas about the relationship between heel height and character persisted.

The right to vote came just after the conclusion of the First World War. Although young women of the post-war period benefited from the hard-won freedoms gained for them by the suffragettes, they were coming of age when the war and the subsequent Spanish flu pandemic of 1918–19 had decimated the population of eligible young men, thereby increasing homosocial competition among women. To many, the previous and now ageing generation of suffragettes looked like

High-heeled button boots such as this example by Bally were popular with fashionable suffragettes. Menswear influence gave them the right amount of seriousness, while the high heels infused it with femininity. Swiss, 1916.

the de-feminized old crones depicted in anti-suffragette caricatures, 'the old school of fighting feminists who wore flat heels and had very little feminine charm', as one young woman wrote.[31] The new age seemed to call for a new model of femininity.

The shifts in women's lives during this period were stunning. Not only had women gained the right to vote, but they had gained increased mobility both physically and socially. They travelled, went to university and drove cars, and 'racy', with all its connotations, became a descriptor of fashionable modern women. The symbol of this new fast-paced world was the media darling, the young flapper, whose style and morals were seemingly unfettered. Her boyish silhouette seemed to deny female morphology and her shockingly short hair flew in the face of tradition, while her scandalous flaunting of skin and use of

Much of the flapper's shocking behaviour was a media construct, as seen in this publicity image. *Latest Thing in Flasks: Mlle. Rhea, Dainty Dancer Who Is Now in the City as Part of the Keiths Program Inaugurates the Garter Flask Fad in Washington*, 26 January 1926.

make-up – previously the purview of the 'wanton woman' – were used to create an aura of hypersexualization. The one thing that was not abandoned was the high heel, which was brought into greater focus as hemlines were lifted. Now fully exposed, the erotic value of high heels only grew stronger and the archetype of the posed, naked female body adorned only in heels was established as a staple of pornographic photography during the 1920s.

The connection between eroticism and heels in the 1920s was still not linked to posture, however. The current assessment that heels force the body into a position that men find irresistible – with the chest thrust forward and the buttocks forced out – was not yet part of heels' allure, as the ramrod-straight silhouettes of the 1920s clearly affirm. Heels were exploited to visually lengthen the leg – a function given to women's heels for the first time by short skirts in the 1920s. But their real importance lay in the perpetuation of centuries-old ideas of illogical femininity. For all her modernity, the flapper in her heels was in actuality simply an updated version of the irrational and

The gold starburst that explodes across the uppers of these shoes made by Th. J. de Bont is a translation of dynamic Art Deco into fashion. Dutch, 1922–5.

delectably desirable female whose ludicrous choice of footwear provided evidence of her fundamental frivolity as well as a source of criticism.

'Animated with a holy zeal for the preservation of both health and morality, he denounced the vile thing in every mood and tense . . . being wishful to send to the penitentiary all manufacturers of high heels on the ground of mayhem and mutilation.'[32] This report in the *Washington Post* in 1920 on a presentation against the high heel to three hundred women by one of the city's best-known surgeons was one of many. As doctors decried the heel's effects on posture and foot health, the media repeatedly bemoaned women's unreasonable reluctance to abandon the fashion. Just as the flapper revamped the image of the irrational female, the physician replaced the preacher as the voice of moral outrage concerning women's footwear choices. These medical concerns soon combined with moral concerns and led to calls to prohibit heels altogether. James H. Kirby sought nomination to the U.S. Senate with a platform that included banning high heels. 'Hooch and high heels . . . are driving the nation to perdition,' he was quoted as saying in the *New York Times* in 1930.[33] Headlines from across the United States proclaimed the submission of bills in many state legislatures aimed at banning high heels. But when Texas representative J. B. Gates introduced a law in the legislature to ban heels higher than an inch and a half in the interest of public health, he was reminded that in Texas not only women but also cowboys would be impacted by such an edict.[34] The attempt to ban high heels was not limited to the United States. In France, the Paris Police Office also banned heels, but the motivation was different. Rather than being focused on morality, the rule was meant to encourage frugality among workers. Not surprisingly, shoe manufacturers decried the proposed laws, arguing that since 60 per cent of women wore high-heeled footwear, a law limiting their shoe sales to heels only an inch and a half high would have dire financial consequences.[35] Indeed, the shoe industry was enjoying the 'awakening of what they termed "shoe consciousness"',[36] by which it was meant that more and more women were thinking of the role of shoes in their ensembles and in turn were buying more shoes, the majority of which had spiked

heels.[37] Reports such as this and claims made by pop psychologists that women were somehow genetically programmed to be shoe-obsessed emerged at this time and gave rise to the cultural conceit that 'women just love shoes'. This focus on high heels also gave increasing importance to the idea of high-end shoe designers as arbiters of fashion.

The most famous of these designers during the 1920s was André Perugia, who was one of the most innovative shoe designers of the twentieth century. Born into an Italian family of shoemakers, he followed in his family's trade and by the age of sixteen had opened his own shop in Nice offering elegant handmade shoes. He was discovered by the famed fashion designer Paul Poiret at the exclusive resort hotel Negresco in Nice in the 1910s. By the 1920s, Perugia's shoes were being worn by international movie stars as well as

André Perugia designed imaginative footwear, as this pair of silver and teal shoes attest. This pair features an 'Aladdin toe', one of his favourite toe shapes, while the exquisitely appliquéd black stripes draw the eye to the heel. French, 1920s, possibly early 1930s.

members of Paris high society. His avant-garde designs pushed the boundaries of heel architecture. When asked in 1936 to muse about footwear of the future he responded, 'In a world governed by a perfect economic condition, including a 2-hour working day, there will be no sensible shoes. Metal (gold, silver, steel, aluminum) will be used, not because they are more durable than leather but because they are more flattering to the foot.'[38] His words were prescient, as he would later go on to create some of the most innovative heels of the twentieth century.

If heeled footwear was non-negotiable in women's fashion in the 1920s, male height was emerging as an issue of cultural concern that in turn increased cultural sensitivity to the idea of men wearing heels. The devastation and global destabilization of the First World War had led to the unprecedented loss of life among men and in turn increased competition for eligible bachelors and encouraged overtly sexualizing fashion for women, but it also drew greater attention to men's physical fitness. More troubling, it made ideas of racial superiority based on physical traits a topic of interest, specifically in relation to fears over the mixing of 'the races' and the resultant contamination of 'old stock' citizenry brought about by increased immigration. In 1918 the book *Applied Eugenics* included the predictions of Edward A. Ross, a sociology professor at the University of Wisconsin, that the new waves of immigrants to the United States were 'in many cases inferior in average ability to the earlier immigrant races' and that the result would be a lessening of 'American good looks', which would result in a more 'diminutive stature, a depreciation of morality, an increase in gross fecundity, and a considerable lowering of the level of average natural ability'.[39]

While sentiments like this had been developing in Western thought since the nineteenth century when the Darwinian concept of survival of the fittest was employed to link factors such as height to sexual attractiveness, by the 1920s self-help books were disseminating them to large audiences and provoking increased anxiety in connection to male height. The book *Personal Beauty and Racial Betterment* from 1920 stated:

concerning the handsomeness of a man who has a general combination of desirable and undesirable characteristics, but who is a trifle below medium height [women offer] a criticism of his stature . . . This preference for stature undoubtedly harks back to more primitive times, when it was above all important that man should be a fighter and hunter in order to secure food for his wife and children, and protect them against wild beasts and against the designs of other males.[40]

By the early 1930s, global tensions were rising and male stature became further embroiled in the racial politics of the day. Height became linked to the idea of natural superiority, and men who dared to wear footwear with height-augmenting heels were ridiculed for needing them. As with much-mocked toupees, heels served only to highlight natural shortcomings. But all was not lost. Lifts – shoe inserts that could be worn invisibly slipped inside a pair of business shoes to subtly increase height – became widely available.[41]

Just as sensitivity about men's natural height was increasing, platform footwear came into fashion for women. It had first appeared in the 1920s as part of women's beachwear. As war began to brew, the popularity of these elevating shoes only grew, in spite of the fact that this fixture in the wardrobes of fashionable women was dismissed by men as unattractive. An Associated Press article from 1940 states, 'Right now, men are almost unanimous in disliking the wedge. Those delicate high insteps pattering along on spindle heels were a sight that brightened their day, they say.'[42] The *New York Times*, meanwhile, proclaimed, 'To please the men, there is an extremely feminine shoe with a regulation high heel.' Platforms were also sparsely represented in men's erotica. *Esquire* magazine, which debuted in 1933, was directed towards the upper-middle-class male consumer and employed the 'artistic' pin-up among its pages of advertisements for high-end clothing, tobacco products and liquor. The renowned 'Petty Girls' created by the artist George Petty and, later, the 'Varga Girls' by Alberto Vargas, were full-page colour fantasy cheesecake drawings or paintings based on the standard scantily clad pornographic model

Scantily clad women with long legs in high heels became a staple of both men's erotica and advertisements in the 1930s and '40s. Swiss, 1928.

in high heels. Although there is some variation in footwear on these pin-ups, exaggeratedly high and often extremely slender heels predominate. In fact, the majority of the shoes depicted on 1930s and '40s pin-up girls existed, like the women wearing them, only in the imaginations of the artists and their audience. Pencil-thin heels would have to wait until after the Second World War to be invented.

At the outbreak of hostilities and throughout the war, the high heel on shapely movie stars and on glamour girls in photographs or drawings was employed to arouse the fighting spirit of the troops. Tacitly endorsed by governments, images of scantily clad spike-heeled beauties decorated aeroplane cockpits and army barracks, and were even painted by the enlisted men themselves on planes and other military equipment. Of the many Hollywood stars of the time, the most famous American pin-up of all was the photo of Betty Grable in a one-piece swimsuit with her million-dollar legs clad in high heels. Even barefoot pin-up girls' feet were often arched unnaturally, as though in invisible heels. What is markedly missing are sexually charged images of women in work shoes or fashionable platforms. Sex appeal was supposed to inspire the troops to victory, and high heels were directly linked to the construction of the desirable female.

Close inspection of the pin-up painted on this plane reveals that she is wearing a pair of high-heeled mules. Nose Art on a B24 Liberator, *c.* 1945.

Back on the home front, it was women's hard efforts working in jobs that had been vacated by men, not their feminine allure, that was championed. Millions of women answered the call in low-heeled, practical footwear. Rosie the Riveter had no time for sexy shoes. The girlfriends and wives left behind were not supposed to be generating inappropriate attention, though they longed for a bit of glamour on their off hours. Women were offered stylish platforms and wedges fabricated from cork, raffia and bits of other materials not rationed for the war effort. These fashionable yet non-erotic shoes provided a remedy for wartime deprivation and helped to keep shoe manufacturers in business. As the war was concluding, the discrepancy between the no-nonsense supporter of the war effort and the voluptuous plaything of soldiers' dreams was becoming evident. As a returning soldier put it in 1945,

In contrast to pin-ups, during the war effort the majority of women wore sensible shoes with low heels. Perhaps the bomber plane these women worked on went on to be emblazoned with an image of a woman in heels. *Women at Work on Bomber*, October 1942.

The pin-up is the only feminine companion a man has . . . and after a while a man comes to believe that all women are like his pin-up girl. Imagine his disappointment when he comes home to discover that his wife or sweetheart does not measure up to his ideal. Pin-up photographs are bad enough, but the Petty and Varga girls are worse. Women simply aren't constructed like that.[43]

After the war, then, a new model of femininity, a kind of domesticated pin-up girl, became the cultural ideal. Just like Disney's Cinderella, who appeared on screen in 1950 as a virginal Varga girl discarding her brown work scuffs for a pair of heels, women put away their workplace lace-ups and clunky platforms and made way for the invention of the stiletto heel.

The invention of the very high, thin stiletto in the early years of the 1950s made the fantasy shoes pin-ups had been wearing available in the real world. The origin of the stiletto is complicated and difficult to pin down, but it is clear that with the advent of Christian Dior's New Look, heels began to grow higher and more slender. The slimness of these immediately post-war heels was relative, however. The heels designed by Ferragamo to complement Dior's New Look were elegant and curvaceous but far from attenuated. An image of an Andrew Geller shoe described as a stiletto heel in an issue of American *Vogue* from 1952 appears quite thick to modern eyes, but for the period it represented a striking and stylish slenderness. The use of the word stiletto to describe Geller's heel was not specific to that heel. Instead, the word was used to describe all manner of sleek, modern, elegant design in the early 1950s, from the U.S. Air Force's new research plane, the x-3 Flying Stiletto, to the new narrow fashion silhouettes coming into vogue as Dior's New Look became dated.[44] Dior's Eiffel Tower line of 1953 and his H line the following year epitomized 'stiletto slimness', a slender silhouette that called for an equally 'stiletto' heel. That the very high, thin heel appeared at a moment when women's curves were being suppressed is a reminder that a woman's posture while in heels is as reliant on cultural practice as it is biomechanics. Although fashion was calling for one look, Hollywood was promoting another. The 1955 film *The Seven Year Itch* featured the buxom Marilyn Monroe, whose figure-hugging outfits accentuated rather than restrained her curves; she wore high, thin heels as a means of accentuating these curves as she moved.

The vogue for slim heels required shoemakers to explore new materials, ones that could be exceptionally fine yet still support a woman's weight. The answer was steel. The first thin steel heel was Perugia's 1951 evening sandal created for Christian Dior. A newspaper article titled 'Steel Heel Holds up New Shoe' proclaimed it a 'style first'.[45] The shape of Perugia's steel heel was a long, flattened stem that proved too minimal for the period, but his innovative use of steel as structural support in heels proved to be revolutionary, with many designers quickly going on to offer their own interpretations of stiletto heels.

Roger Vivier, the shoe designer Dior chose to bring into the House of Dior, in 1953 created some of the most coveted stilettos of the decade. Vivier came to Dior's attention while contracted to Herman Delman in New York. He had created designs for Delman since the 1930s and in the early 1950s caught the attention of Dior.[46] Vivier was charged with designing the shoes for soon-to-be Queen Elizabeth II's coronation by means of a convoluted partnership between Rayne, the shoemaker to the Queen, and Delman in 1953; after that commission was completed Delman and Dior entered into their own contract, giving Dior the right to use Vivier. He became the only designer working for Dior to have his name added to Dior products.

As designers such as Vivier and Ferragamo refined the stiletto, it quickly became an almost obligatory feminine accoutrement and was represented in the media as appropriate for a wide range of activities, from house cleaning to entertaining to, of course, seduction. They were clearly out of place, however, in work environments such as munitions factories, where women had so recently been employed. Stilettos, like high heels in previous eras, were useful tools in

This high *aiguille* heel made of steel was designed by Roger Vivier for Delman-Dior and matched the new streamlined silhouette being promoted by Christian Dior. French, mid-1950s.

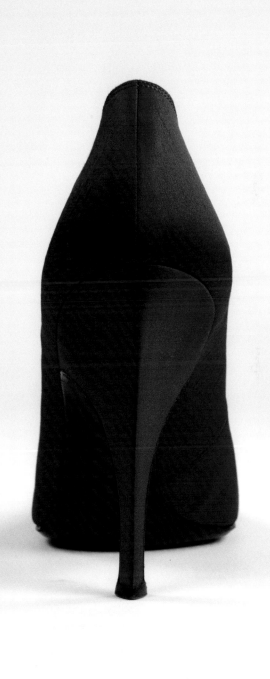

perpetuating stereotypes about women; they were central to images ranging from depictions of voluptuous women wiggling while they walked to photo documentaries showing women with their heels caught in escalators or manhole covers, suggesting that their choice of footwear reflected their irrational submission to fashion. Stilettos were also a supremely eroticized form of footwear and their place in men's pornography quickly became unrivalled. Throughout the 1950s, high-heel-wearing women graced the pages of men's magazines from *Playboy* to *Bizarre* and infused the everyday stilettos women wore with even greater erotic value. These associations also gave heel height greater sexual significance: very high stilettos seemed to suggest a kind of aggressive sexuality. The term stiletto, meaning little knife in Italian, although generally used to convey a sense of sleekness, could also imply danger and possible menace. Exaggeratedly high heels had been an important part of erotic BDSM imagery since the 1930s, and the popularization of pin-ups such as Betty Page gave even slightly higher heels an edgier feel. In contrast, lower kitten heels were deemed more appropriate for the modest wife or youthful teen. By the end of the decade, the high heel had become so naturalized that the new Barbie doll, a 'wholesome' American interpretation of the bawdy German Bild Lilli doll, came with feet posed to wear only high-heeled footwear, and in photos taken on the beach or other places where real women might be found *sans* shoes, they would pose on tiptoe as though they were wearing invisible heels.

Despite the ubiquity of the high heel in women's fashion and men's erotica, its ascendency was challenged in the 1960s when the 'youthquake' movement ushered in a new look. Young designers centred in London's prêt-à-porter boutiques began to offer fashions inspired by children's clothing. Slender and leggy models were dressed in little-girl-inspired outfits, including short skirts, tights or knee-high socks, and childish, low-heeled footwear. Once again, many men were not fans. In Thomas Meehan's article 'Where Did

The psychedelic fabric, large rhinestone-encrusted buckle and low heel of these shoes designed by Roger Vivier are all hallmarks of 1960s fashion. French, mid-1960s.

All the Women Go', he lamented that 'the Little Girl-look clothes leave almost no room for bosoms, bottoms, etc., and are distinctly un-feminine from the point of view of the American man.'[47] The loss of the heel was noted as being 'tough on girl watchers',[48] but its rejection was more than simply a shift in style: it reflected the brewing discontent that baby boomers had with the post-war status quo. The short miniskirts popularized by the London fashion designer Mary Quant were proclaimed as 'the final word in the emancipation of women – improving her economic independence . . . Long, hampering skirts were fetters to keep a woman at home. The very short ones scream: "I am stepping out."'[49] Likewise, heels were rejected as objects of oppression by women's liberation activists as well as back-to-nature hippies. The only place where women's high heels remained important was in men's erotica. In men's fashion, however, it was a different story.

As cultural norms came under scrutiny, men also questioned the status quo and fashion offered the opportunity to break away from the strait-laced dress codes of the 1950s. The increasingly extravagant attire being promoted for men as part of the 'peacock revolution' suggested that men should by rights be the more decorative of the sexes; the animal kingdom and men's dress in other cultures and times offering examples. Among the many new styles that were offered to men as part of the peacock revolution were shoes with slightly higher heels. As *Time* magazine reported, 'somewhat alarmingly, teen-age boys are taking to high heels.'[50] John Lennon's high-heeled Beatle boots helped to set the trend.

By the early 1970s, 'the peacock . . . tucked in its tail feathers – a victim of what one fashion leader [called] "too muchism".'[51] The return of greater conformity in men's fashion was mitigated by choosing individualist accessories and retaining the heels that were continuing to rise in men's footwear. The *Washington Post* reported, 'some feel that much fashion expression will turn up in accessories such as shoes . . . Men's shoes sport higher heels – in conservative styles, as well as wild five-color suede styles with a three-inch lift.' More interesting perhaps is that these higher heels for men were being advertised as a way of increasing one's stature, 'masculinity and confidence'[52] by means that all could see. Often self-covered rather than stacked, these blocky heels harked back to the footwear worn by court fops from the turn of the eighteenth century. This was often promoted in the media, dismissing plainly any ideas that they were borrowing from the female wardrobe.

One of these heel-wearing types was the blaxploitation pimp, a problematic yet popular character in much 1970s media. In the movie *The Mack* (1973) he was 'a trendsetter in the male peacock world of fashion. The pimp, along with the rest of the black hustler world (con men, numbers bankers and dope dealers), was among the first to wear lavender and pink suits, billowy shirts and two-toned perforated shoes with super-stacked heels.'[53] This racist observation does not obscure the fact that despite bigoted stereotyping, the fantasy role of the pimp in popular culture was related to societal challenges to male hegemony that sought to establish that black men

In the early 1970s, men were encouraged to use accessories, such as high-heeled shoes, to express their individuality. The most popular form of footwear remained traditional lace-ups but like the traditional lace-ups was updated by the addition of high heels, platform soles and a wide variety of non-traditional colours and patterns. American, early 1970s.

In the 1970s, Elton John strutted on stage in outrageous outfits and glittering high heels, including this pair by Ferradini. Italian, 1972–5.

were first and foremost men. The hypermasculine Italian was likewise a stereotype whose presence in films such as *Saturday Night Fever* (1977) helped to put a heteronormative stamp on disco and disco fashions, including high stacked heels for men.

Yet another prominent cultural icon of hypermasculinity who donned heeled footwear in the 1970s was the male glam or glitter rock star, who likewise reaffirmed the male/female binary. Glam rock started in the UK at the end of the 1960s and was characterized by male singers who wore outrageous stage outfits that often burlesqued aspects of foppish dress. In Britain, David Bowie wore high platforms, as did Gary Glitter, Elton John and Marc Bolan. In the U.S. the band KISS rose to fame as much for their make-up and costumes as for their music, with their high-heeled footwear reaching seven or more inches in height. Like the dress of blaxploitation pimps, the outrageous attire of glam rock musicians was central to the reaffirmation, rather than challenging, of concepts of masculinity and were often portrayed in the media as being the focus of female adoration, even while some such as David Bowie earnestly engaged with the topic of gender fluidity. These stars gave commanding performances and were portrayed in the media as being the focus of female adoration. Fee Waybill of the band The Tubes parodied the effeminate fop by way of glam rock, but in no way came off as feminine. As his character Quay Lewd, he wore high, fetish-referencing heels 'designed from an image in a bondage catalog with the curved toe and long stiletto heel',[54] make-up, and a wig that suggested specifically male eighteenth-century debauchery; his gender was masculine, his privilege declared by his domineering actions, while his sex was clearly displayed through his attire, which aside from his heels consisted of a pair of small briefs from which jutted a seemingly aroused penis. The function of such extreme costumes in glam rock as well as the more flamboyant dress of disco and blaxploitation stereotypes was to project an aura of hypermasculinity and hegemony in a period of actual social flux, as women strove to gain more equality, and served to reaffirm the idea that white or black, straight or gay, more than anything, men were still men.[55] The heels worn by these models of masculinity did not, in any way, reflect an earnest incorporation of feminine styles and their meanings.

At this time, women also wore platform heels and, like men's heels, they too referenced the past, in this case the 1940s. Vivier reintroduced the platform in 1967 and by the 1970s platforms were seen as a playful female fashion by some but, as in the 1940s, unattractive by others. These 'great, galumphing, paralyzingly ugly, monsters are nonetheless the most visible shoes around today', was how *Time* described them in 1970.[56] And as with platforms in the 1940s, they were markedly absent from men's erotica, which continued to favour the high heel.

In the middle of the decade, women's fashion turned once again to the stiletto. Fashion was dramatically influenced by pornography and the high, slender heel, as an established part of the lexicon of erotic imagery, returned as an important accessory in fashion. In the pages of *Vogue* and *Harper's Bazaar*, Helmut Newton's spike-heeled ice princesses reflected this conflation of the pornographic and fashionable image, as did Guy Bourdin's work for the Charles Jourdan shoe company. The reintroduction of the high heel was concomitant with the articulated fashion goal of looking sexy; throughout the 1970s, the stiletto remained the most highly sexualized form of high heel. 'If shoes can be termed sexy, these certainly are. They're the kind of shoes women want when they're feeling festive . . . They are as provocative as a low-necked dress.'[57] Stilettos were deemed appropriate for evening wear; few imagined the role they would play in women's work attire in the following century. Manolo Blahnik, whose high stilettos would define luxury, privilege and femininity at the end of the twentieth century, began designing shoes at this time.

> Do low necklines, slit skirts, and stiletto heels make sense in an era when women are asking not only for equality but for respect? . . . Perhaps now that women in America have made such gains and are struggling to improve their own self-esteem, they do not fear sexism as they once did and no longer feel they have to dress somberly, or drably, to achieve what they want.[58]

This heavily sequined platform heel by Loris Azzaro might have seemed utterly contemporary in the 1970s but its form referenced the 1940s and the use of a Harlequin pattern linked it to a patchwork pattern codified in the 15th century. Italian, early 1970s.

By the end of the 1970s conservative values had crept back into society and men abandoned heeled footwear in favour of a more traditional signifier of male success, the low-heeled business brogue. The more sartorially daring wore cowboy boots, which saw a resurgence in fashion as part of the return to tradition and romantic remembrances of American rugged self-reliance. Ronald Reagan embodied these ideals. Famous for wearing cowboy boots, his fundraising gift given out during his second term in office was a little ceramic boot decorated with the presidential seal and 'Ronald Reagan 1984'.[59] As the 1970s came to a close, for professional women conservative fashions were also the order of the day for professional women. Margaret Thatcher, the UK's first female prime minister, came to power in 1979, and her skirted suits and low-heeled pumps reflected the uniform of white-collar women everywhere, who despite growing conservatism were entering the business workplace in unprecedented numbers. Nevertheless, as women attempted to adopt and adapt men's business wear to meet their professional needs, their choices were roundly criticized as lacking in sex appeal. The now infamous *Newsweek* article 'Too Late for Prince Charming?' suggested that women's intense focus on climbing the corporate ladder had made them profoundly unattractive and unmarriageable.[60] High fashion's solution was to insinuate the pornographic into dressing for success. In fashion layout after fashion layout, female success was pictured as aggressive, even predatory, both financially and sexually. 'Killer heels', invariably stilettos, transformed the power-dressing fashion model into a dominatrix from pornographic fantasy and complicated the image of professional women.

The linking of female success and sexual commodification also expressed itself in the new luxury market that emerged in the 1980s specializing in expensive undergarments suggestive of Edwardian bordellos. If the fashionable female executive of the 1980s was represented as having a hard, cold exterior, in lingerie ads she was stripped of this facade and exposed on her high stilettos wearing silky evidence of her more compliant femininity. The romanticization

This shoe, with its very high heel and fetish-referencing high-gloss finish, reflects the insertion of eroticism into 1980s 'power dressing'. French, designed by Givenchy, 1985-8.

These brightly hued pumps by Bally have a postmodernist aesthetic. Their low heels would have been appropriate for the office in the 1980s but they were probably worn outside of the workplace. Swiss, late 1980s.

of sexual commodification mirrored the obsession with the courtesan in the mid-nineteenth century, which arose as a similar reaction to tensions concerning female social and economic advances.

A year after the *Newsweek* article, the stock market crashed, bringing an end to confidence in 1980s prosperity. The economic downswing that had begun on Black Monday was followed by corporate downsizing and increased instability in the workplace. The computer age had also fully arrived and the traditional image of masculine success, the suited businessman, suddenly seemed old-fashioned and behind the times in comparison to sneaker-wearing Silicon Valley tycoons. In this age of uncertainty, reinforcing gender binaries became a focus of high fashion. These trappings of gender, such as the high heel, also became a focus for third-wave feminists and some suggested that the power associated with them should be harnessed and used to individual advantage. In many ways, however, it was traditional meanings of these hypersexualized accessories that won out, transforming the 'New Girl Order' as some called it into second-wave flapperism. Like the flappers of the roaring twenties, 1990s 'pro-fashion choice' women self-consciously sought to distance themselves from the image of the sexually unfulfilled and overworked 1980s 'superwoman'. They sought empowerment by co-opting men's construction of femininity. In 1999, Debbie Stoller, editor of *Bust* magazine, wrote: 'From lipstick lesbians to rouge-wearing riot grrls, today's vampy visionaries believe that it is possible to make a feminist fashion statement without resorting to wearing Birkenstocks 24/7.' By referencing the unisex Birkenstock sandal Stoller conjures up the stodgy 'woman's libber', whom she characterizes as being devoid of femininity, just as the 'low-heeled fighting feminists' had been characterized earlier in the century.

This 'reclamation' of exaggerated femininity in the 1990s suddenly elevated shoe designers to the level of cultural icons. Manolo Blahnik and Christian Louboutin, famous for their toweringly high heels, became celebrities. Blahnik was already an established master when his name became synonymous with luxury at the end of the twentieth century, but Louboutin was a rising star when his trademark red soles captured international attention. He opened his first boutique in Paris in 1991 and his red-soled high heels quickly became cultural icons.

The hit TV show *Sex and the City* made designer shoes symbols of independence, status, sexuality and a commodifiable expression of 'girl power'. The flip-side of this conspicuous consumption of distinctly not-sensible shoes was that they also served to perpetuate long-standing stereotypes concerning women, such as their misuse of money. Designer heels came with astonishingly high price tags and the media was filled with articles not only about exorbitantly priced footwear but also women's seeming inability to control their lust for shoes. It was reported that women spent thousands on shoes in a lifetime, that many hid their purchases from their partners, and that the most coveted shoes of all were high heels. This point was made in *Sex and the City* by the characters' seemingly insatiable obsession with designer high heels, as well as the line stated by the character Carrie Bradshaw: 'I've spent $40,000 on shoes and I have no place to live? I will literally be the old woman who lived in her shoes!'[61]

The shoes that threatened to bankrupt women often referenced the footwear associated with strippers and sex workers. Soaring high heels balanced by high platform soles first originated in fetish in the 1930s and had become the footwear of choice in strip clubs by the turn of the century. By the early 2000s, luxury shoe designers translated these styles for their eager clientele:

> Dominatrix heels studded with spikes. Stilettos with bondage-inspired ankle straps. Over-the-knee, skin-tight boots with five-inch heels . . . No, this is not the set of a pornographic video. These are shoes that ordinary women wear today. They are so open and revealing, with heels so high, it's difficult to imagine that anyone other than strippers and sex workers could wear them without irony.[62]

Indeed, mainstream culture such as the 1996 film *Striptease* and the trend for activities like pole-dancing aerobics classes and Brazilian

Christian Louboutin fused features of 1920s shoe design, such as geometric patterning and the instep strap, with the modern stiletto heel when he created his Cathedral shoe. Louboutin's revival of flapper fashion seems appropriate to the age of 'girl power'. French, 2007.

bikini waxes in addition to sky-high stripper fashion footwear served to make the pornographic pedestrian. As in the 1920s, actual strides made by women in the preceding decades were countered by a focus on female desirability and sexual attractiveness above all other attributes.

In spite of this, or maybe because of it, heels became increasingly associated with concepts of power in the 2000s. It was the same tale, repeated since the eighteenth century: that women gained power chiefly through the sexual manipulation of men. Many asserted that women were embracing towering heels as a means of gaining a foothold at work through the exploitation of their erotic currency – which, it was argued by some, women not only possessed, but should spend.

High heels were positioned in the media as female 'power tools', accessories of seduction that women should use to their advantage. Nobody, however, offered information concerning the exact value of this currency and its exchange rate remained at the whims of those agreeing to the exchange, be they employer or barista, and resulted in few actual quantifiable advances such as pay equity. This 'power' associated with heels was also inherently limited only to those within a certain age range, as demonstrated when the actor Helen Mirren dared to wear 'stripper' heels on the red carpet at the age of 67, setting the Internet ablaze. Although many celebrated her choice, the fact that it was considered 'bold' simply reinforced the idea that in reality she, and other women of a similarly 'advanced age', no longer had access to the 'power' attributed to the wearing of heels. The outcry caused when Suri Cruise, the young daughter of actors Katie Holmes and Tom Cruise, was seen dressed in a pair of heels deemed too high for a toddler, and by the popular outrage against Heelarious, a line of soft-heeled shoes for girls aged zero to six months old, modelled after iconic high heels, also reminded the public that heels, and the power associated with them, were specifically sexual in nature. The limited access many had to 'power' heels, either because of age

Sex-worker shoes from the 1990s often featured 'aggressive' embellishment and strapping suggestive of bondage wear. It was a look that inspired mainstream fashion footwear design. American, 1995.

or finances, led to an explosion of high-heel-referencing merchandise in the early 2000s. From high-heel-emblazoned tote bags to *objets d'art*, high-heel merchandise provided opportunities for all females, from the very young to the old, to signal their support of ideas related to 'empowerment' through sexualization, despite their own marginalization.

The symbolic value of high heels also increased during this period. Images and reports of women with bloody feet carrying their shoes or having abandoned their heels as they attempted to escape the World Trade Center attacks in New York City in September 2001 spoke to the vulnerability of the female victims. A bloodied high heel worn by Linda Raisch-Lopez, an office worker in the South Tower, is a poignant artefact in the 9/11 Memorial Museum, symbolizing 'the widespread panic, confusion and numbness that characterize the events of that unfathomable Tuesday'.[63] Immediately after the event, some suggested that heels would go out of fashion in response to the new age of terrorism. Yet if anything, heels increased in importance within fashion. The Taliban was widely reported to have banned high heels in Afghanistan, not only because women were not to be heard while walking but also because the shoes had become symbols of Western decadence. Thus ironically, high heels became signifiers of Western freedoms and female autonomy.

As the first decade of the 2000s came to a conclusion, heels also came to the fore for many fashion designers, who began to challenge their architecture, arguably transforming them into works of art. Alexander McQueen's 'Armadillo' shoes designed by Georgina Goodman from his 2010 Plato's Atlantis collection is perhaps the most famous example, with its height and shape referencing the fetish heels worn on stage by The Tubes' Quay Lewd; they were 'incontestably the strangest and most amazing thing that had been created in fashion for a long while'.[64] The shoes were a highlighted artefact in the Metropolitan Museum of Art's exhibition 'Alexander McQueen: Savage Beauty' of 2011, and in 2015 three pairs sold at Christie's to the highest bidder, the American pop singer Lady Gaga, for $295,000, confirming their status as fine art.[65] The trend for extremely high fashion-forward heels at the end of the decade coincided with the Great Recession and in many ways mirrored the incredible burst of creative energy in relation to footwear design seen during the Great Depression, when sheer height rather than erotic associations became the focus of shoe design.

In this moment of economic distress, some pointed to research that suggested that a person's height was directly correlated to their earnings.[66] The message became a simple equation: greater height equals higher income, career advancement and increased desirability. As Joel Waldfogel wrote in the *National Post*,

> It is well-documented that short people earn less money than tall people do . . . if you compare two large groups of people who are similar in every respect but height, the average pay for the taller group will be higher. Each additional inch of height adds roughly 2% to average annual earnings, for both men and women.[67]

What those advocating high heels neglected to note is that the study was discussing actual height. Heels on women, like heels on men, did more to highlight lack of natural height than function as contrivances to deceive. It should also be noted that the majority of women in positions of actual power, such as former U.S. Secretary of State and presidential nominee Hillary Clinton and German Chancellor Angela Merkel, who are both under 5 foot 7 inches tall, eschewed such footwear. Their lack of sex appeal was a constant point of discussion in the media, yet they were in fact very powerful.

For men, the artifice of high heels offered no help. Reports listing the heights of U.S. presidents, CEOs and other male leaders proved that those in positions of power were rarely under 6 feet in height and that the majority were 6 foot 2 inches and over. Online social media discussions recorded men desperate to increase their stature without resorting to heels. Thick-soled basketball shoes and boots such as the urban fashion staple Timberlands were touted as means of enhancing stature, and of course, lifts inserted into shoes remained an option for men, as long as they watched their step: even slight disparities in height could attract unwanted attention. The actor Tom Cruise has been a frequent victim of media speculation about his use of lifts and the footwear choices of former French president Nicolas Sarkozy were a constant source of amusement in both the French media and abroad. The British tabloid the *Daily Mail* quipped in 2009, 'When you're lacking in the height department, it can be hard to come across as a politician of great stature. So it is only natural to give yourself a little artificial lift.'[68] Marco Rubio, the u.s. senator who sought to be the 2016 Republican presidential nominee, likewise attracted ridicule because he sported boots with 'three-inch' Cuban heels and earned the derisive nickname Lil' Marco.

Reaction to men in heels was extreme in the early decades of the twenty-first century, although a number of celebrities made them their on-stage and off-stage trademarks. The American superstar Prince began wearing heels in 1981, just as they were being abandoned in men's fashion.[69] Lenny Kravitz, another American musical performer, frequently wears them, yet his choices do not escape criticism, as seen for example in the *Daily Mail* article 'Lenny Kravitz Dresses Like an American Woman and Strolls Around New York', penned in reaction to Kravitz being photographed in tight leather trousers and a pair of wedged heels.[70] Similarly, when the rapper Kanye West wore heeled velvet boots for the Paris Givenchy fashion show in 2015, comments on the Internet accused him of raiding his wife's closet. The American fashion designers Rick Owens and Marc Jacobs have made and worn high-heeled footwear for several years, and Christian Louboutin introduced heels into his 2015 line of shoes for men. The work of the Canadian-Jordanian designer Rad Hourani, who launched his first unisex collection at Paris Haute Couture Fashion Week in 2012, prominently features high-heeled footwear. However, all these examples involve footwear with thick, blocky heels that remain borrowings from the male, rather than female, wardrobe, despite the fact that any degree of heel on a man's shoes seems to bring instantaneous condemnation as too feminine.

Rad Hourani was the first designer to offer a unisex collection at Fashion Week. Although he often puts his models in high heels, the heels themselves are often traditionally male in design. French, 2015.

Today, the sinuous, narrow high heel is both *the* icon of femininity and a potent signifier of the binary construction of gender; but it is also a form of footwear that is increasingly being worn in a variety of situations by men. The International Men's March to Stop Rape, Sexual Assault and Gender Violence asks men to walk a mile in red high heels to raise awareness of sexualized violence. Walk a Mile in Her Shoes is promoted as a fun, non-threatening activity for fundraising and stimulating conversation – the event being usually perceived as highly comical though well-meaning. A number of male dancers have worn high heels while performing, garnering responses that celebrate their strength and endurance rather than provoking the largely negative commentary reserved for males wearing high heels as fashion. Lady Gaga's award-winning music video for her song 'Alejandro' (2010) included fetish-referencing fashion and male dancers wearing stilettos in a way that was not traditionally feminizing. Similarly, Madonna's male backing dancers for her *MDNA* tour in 2012, from the dance troupe Kazaky, performed in an un-ironic way wearing heels designed by Prada. Yanis Marshall has likewise become famous for his choreography and performances in very high stilettos. The online magazine and newspaper *Queerty* puts it this way: 'There's something about men in heels. And it's nothing against the ladies, but men in heels just look so damn fierce.'[71]

The increasing awareness and tolerance of gender fluidity in the twenty-first century seem to suggest that in the future heels will be permitted in more people's wardrobes. Yet currently, high heels remain central to expressions of femininity and are an expected and naturalized form of footwear for women. The American transgender celebrity Caitlyn Jenner's very public transition to wearing female attire often focused on her new love of heels. Using misgendering pronouns when referring to the retired Olympic athlete's previous public identity, *People* magazine reported on Jenner, 'He's so excited about everything female . . . He loves wearing high heels, he loves doing his hair. He's just really having a lot of fun.'[72] Male cross-dressers also make high heels central to their performance of femininity – indeed, their desire for heels is the focus of the plot of the 2005 film and subsequent 2012 family musical *Kinky Boots*. Although it could be argued that such examples point to increasing freedom concerning who may wear heels, heels are so central to present-day constructions of femininity that they are non-negotiable in many instances. In 2015 the Cannes Film Festival turned away female attendees on the grounds of inappropriate attire if they were not in heels, including women in bejewelled flats as well as the film producer Valeria Richter, whose partially amputated foot made wearing high heels an impossibility.[73] In 2016 a British receptionist lost a day's pay when she was sent home

In 2014 French choreographer Yanis Marshall and his dancers became Internet sensations for wearing women's boots with high, slender heels when they danced.

from work for not wearing heels, and a Canadian waitress posted pictures online of her bloodied feet after being required to wear high heels for her entire shift.[74] These stories illustrate the fact that in this day and age the heel remains such an essential emblem of femininity that for many women, refusing to wear them can result in actual retribution. The fact that these stories were newsworthy also suggests that times may be changing. Sneakers are becoming a staple in women's fashion and their increasing presence in men's erotica suggests that perhaps change is on the horizon.

# IV Sneakers: Exclusivity

Collecting sneakers is like scrapbooking. It's about preserving memories, marking a place and time. When I ask my son what he's going to do with his sneakers when he doesn't wear them anymore, he tells me he's going to keep them. He says that even now, he just likes to open the boxes and remember where he was and what he was doing when he wore his prized purchases.

Annette John-Hall, 'Sneaker-collecting Trend Gains Traction, Sneaker Collecting: Scrapbooking for the Feet', *Philadelphia Inquirer*, 26 July 2006

A sneakerhead has knowledge of releases, material, history, and availability that runs deeper than the box they come in. A regular person may compliment you on your blue and white Nikes; a sneakerhead will stop you in your tracks to learn how you acquired the Nike Air Jordan 1 High 'North Carolina' like a dying man asking for an antidote.

Keith Nelson Jr, '#SneakerHeads: How a New Generation of Sneaker Fans Are Taking over the Internet', *Digital Trends*, 24 October 2015

The eminently modern sneaker is an innovation of the industrial age. From their origins in the nineteenth century, the history of sneakers has been intertwined with the pursuit of technological innovation as well as the politics of consumption. Today, sneakers are worn around the world and in many ways could be considered the most democratic form of footwear, yet commodification and branding have transformed some into highly coveted objects of desire that are increasingly central to men's fashion. Under the broad category of 'sneaker' lies a wide range of nuanced meanings linked to exclusivity, social aspiration, athletic prowess and shifting constructions of idealized masculinity.[1]

Pierre Hardy was inspired by the artwork of Roy Lichtenstein when designing this pair of Poworamas, translating the artist's graphic appeal into wearable art. French, 2011.

The story of the sneaker starts in the forests of South and Central America, where the indigenous people had used the milky sap of the 'weeping wood' tree (*Hevea brasiliensis*, or rubber tree) to make everything from rubber balls to waterproof footwear for centuries. Europeans became aware of this unusual substance in the sixteenth century but it did not arouse much interest until the middle of the eighteenth century, when the remarkable elasticity and waterproof qualities of the gum began to fascinate Western scientists. By the early nineteenth century inventors as well as the public were becoming enamoured with the substance, and the introduction of rubber overshoes made in Brazil for export to the U.S. and Europe in the 1820s created a rubber craze.[2] The price for these remarkably stretchy and waterproof overshoes was five times that of leather footwear, marking them as luxury goods that reflected the high cost of rubber due to its relative scarcity.[3] Rubber tree cultivation was extremely labour-intensive and trees could only be tapped every other day, with each tapping yielding about one cup of latex, as the sap came to be called. Despite this challenge there were high hopes for the new type of waterproof overshoe, including health considerations, which would go on to become a core motivation for the acquisition of sneakers:

> What a crowd of painful recollections are conjured up in the mind of the physician, of any age and experience, by the words *wet feet* . . . The child which had been playing about in the morning in all its infantile loveliness and vivacity, is seized at night with croup from wet feet, and in a day or two is a corpse.[4]

This lament in the *Journal of Health* in 1829 promoted rubber overshoes as a means of keeping illness at bay, but despite the potential health benefits sought by doctors and hopes for quick profits envisioned

Stretchy, waterproof overshoes made in Brazil for the Western market captured the imagination of consumers but proved to be unstable in both hot and cold temperatures. Brazilian, 1830s.

by importers, Brazilian-made overshoes proved to be unstable. They melted in the heat of summer and cracked in the bitter cold of winter, and the market collapsed.[5]

Notwithstanding the ensuing 'rubber panic', many continued to strive to make rubber a stable and useful material. Charles Goodyear was one of many focused on the task. His dedication to the potential of rubber verged on mania, and he saw a future in which almost everything, from dishes and jewellery to clothing and footwear, would be made of the material.[6] Goodyear began his experiments in 1834, during one of his repeated stints in debtors' prison, with a batch of raw rubber and his wife's rolling pin. He finally hit upon the solution in 1839. Building on the experiments of Nathaniel Hayward, he began adding sulphur to boiling latex and eventually created a material that retained its elasticity while remaining impervious to heat or cold. The British scientist Thomas Hancock, inspired by Goodyear's experiments, further developed the process in England, where, according to his book on his work, a friend dubbed it 'vulcanization' after the ancient Roman god of fire, Vulcan.[7] The ability to transform raw latex into durable rubber paved the way for many revolutionary consumer items, including sneakers.

Early sneakers were canvas or leather shoes with rubber soles, and despite their humble appearance they began as costly luxuries with social implications, like their overshoe predecessors. The nineteenth century was a period of booming industrialization, which gave rise to an upwardly mobile middle class, and leisure time, long a privilege of the rich, was eagerly pursued as a means of proclaiming one's new-found status. This in turn led to a demand for specialized equipment and clothing designed specifically for these amusements. Enterprising manufacturers began to offer rubber-soled athletic shoes at prices reflecting not only the high cost of rubber but also the financial success of their intended clientele.

Establishing exactly when the first sneaker was made and for exactly what purpose remains elusive. Wait Webster was granted a United States patent for his process of attaching India rubber soles to shoes in 1832, but there is no indication that he intended this process to be used specifically for athletic footwear.[8] A mention is made in the 1835 *Public Documents of Massachusetts*, a few years in advance of

Many 19th-century women's sport shoes were appropriate for a range of activities, including tennis. The brogue detailing is a nod to the male wardrobe. Italian, late 19th century.

Goodyear's breakthrough, concerning the adhesion of rubber soles to sports shoes. Although the material used for the uppers is not disclosed, it is noteworthy that rubber-soled footwear was being designed for sports.[9] The frequently touted claim that the British Liverpool Rubber Company introduced sneakers in the 1830s is disproved by the fact that the company did not appear until 1861. The other common theory, that John Boyd Dunlop, the inventor of the pneumatic bicycle tyre and founder of the Dunlop Pneumatic Tyre Company, later the Dunlop Rubber Company, was the inventor of the sneaker in the 1830s is also put to rest as he was not born until 1840 and his company was not established until 1890. There is no question that the Dunlop company did go on to produce sneakers, including the famous Dunlop Green Flash, but that was not until the late 1920s. In the United States, the Candee Rubber Company has been posited as the originator of sneakers. They certainly made croquet shoes, but it is difficult to establish what a croquet shoe was exactly. In 1868 *Gentleman's Magazine* advised, 'In wet weather, if anxious mammas forbid thin shoes, shoes may be cast away altogether, and India-rubbers substituted, not over the shoe, but over the sock or stocking.'[10] Other period sources suggest that croquet shoes, also called croquet sandals, were simply rubber overshoes.[11] Similarly, sandshoes are described for seaside wear, but what constituted a sandshoe is challenging to determine. Period descriptions often suggest that the soles were made of cork. There can be no argument, however, as proved by mid-nineteenth century advertisements and newspaper articles, that tennis shoes were made with rubber soles.[12] An article from *Harper's Bazaar* in 1881 on the appropriate dress for lawn tennis includes the advice to women to wear bright-coloured stockings with low canvas shoes without heels. It goes on to praise these flat shoes for offering a reprieve from high heels and allowing 'the female foot for once to touch mother earth', saying that this alone is worth the rest of the game.[13] Despite advice like this, many women's tennis shoes were made with heels. The article also discusses men's tennis outfits, noting that they too wore a 'cool canvas shoe ... with corrugated India rubber soles'. In their specialized tennis garb both men and women enjoyed the game and often played it together. The game of doubles infused the sport with the air of romance. The writer R. K. Munkittrick's (1853–1911) fond recollection of his first pair of tennis shoes reflects these cultural ideas about the game, but also suggests that sentimentality and nostalgic longing have been a part of sneaker culture from its origin:

> I note my first pair of tennis-shoes . . . I was told I needed the exercise to reduce my weight and keep me in good condition. Various young ladies offered to teach me to play, and make me acquainted with all the mysteries of the game. Of course I yielded. What else could I do? So I purchased the shoes . . . It was also pleasant . . . talking airy nonsense to the dear little specimen of sweet seventeenity . . . I suppose many of these bucolic pleasantries have melted into the rubber soles of these canvas shoes.[14]

Tennis was the perfect sport for the upwardly mobile. It had a very long association with the aristocracy. Henry VIII had been an enthusiastic player, Queen Elizabeth I an avid fan, and a book from 1660 listing petitions from people connected to Charles II's household includes an entry for a Robert Long who, seeking to be a Groom of the Great Chamber to the King or Duke of York, had as part of his credentials that he had been the keeper of 'tennis shoes and ancle socks' to the previous king.[15] The game of lawn tennis, a less complicated version of the 'ancient game', was re-emerging in popularity in the middle of the century, as advertisements for tennis shoes from the 1860s show. Major Walter Clopton Wingfield codified the game in England in 1874 and promoted this simpler version of tennis as the perfect pastime for the wealthy. The game required specially manicured lawns, and soon those with means added courts to their estates, where rubber-soled tennis shoes were preferred over those with spikes as they left the grass undamaged. Before long, however, the popularity of the game led to the creation of public courts. The *New York Times*, reporting in 1884 on the great demand for access to public tennis courts in the Brooklyn parks system, stated that the Park Commissioners required all players 'to wear tennis shoes, to avoid injury to the turf',[16] providing evidence of the widespread embrace of the game and the concomitant use of rubber-soled footwear.

The early sneakers were offered in a range of colours; an advertisement from 1888 lists black, brown, drab and slate as well as white and brown check. Many also featured brown or red rubber soles. Uppers were frequently textile but they could be in leather, and many were trimmed with leather. Both the two-tone spectator shoe and the white buck came into being at this time. The spectator shoe is often credited to the British shoemaker John Lobb, who is said in 1868 to have added dark leather pieces to white leather cricket shoes at the points typically soiled during play; yet the use of overlays of leather for both decorative and protective purposes pre-dates this. What is

This page from the *Deutsche Shuhmacher Zeitung* depicts a range of athletic footwear styles from sandals to sneakers. German, *c.* 1890.

clear is that two-toned shoes become associated with participating in sports as well as watching them, and by the twentieth century the spectator shoe was a part of the wardrobe of many style-conscious men. The white buck developed out of tennis shoes. When worn spotless with summer whites like tennis shoes they were declarations of status that would be echoed in the urban fashion for pristine white sneakers later in the twentieth century.

Although play and leisure attire were important means of flaunting success in the mid-nineteenth century, exercise for the health of mind and body was increasingly being seen as an antidote to the 'diseases of affluence'.[17] As populations shifted from rural to urban, concerns grew that the disruptive effects of industrialization were corrupting the moral and physical fibre of society. Sedentary office jobs held by the middle classes as well as the repetitive factory tasks now required of the working classes taxed rather than strengthened the body. The flood of people with unknowable backgrounds to cities in search of work also posed challenges in the assessment of character and led to concerns about the morality of strangers. In addition, the squalid living conditions in which the poorest urban workers lived led to fears of contagion both physical and moral and increased anxiety about urban criminality. It was an age of upward mobility but also of anxiety. Charles Darwin's theories on natural selection and survival of the fittest spoke not only to science but to society, and exercise and fresh air came to be seen as antidotes to the afflictions and uncertainties of the modern age as well as means of ensuring fitness and longevity.

The relationship between morality and physical activity found its most emphatic expression in the Muscular Christian movement, which preached that physical health and godliness went hand in hand. The Young Men's Christian Association (YMCA) was the epicentre of the movement. Established in London in 1844 by the 22-year-old George Williams, the YMCA sought to offer young men flocking to the city diversions that were enriching both physically and spiritually. The concept was compelling in the rapidly changing mid-century world, and the idea spread first across England and then to

North America, where Associations were opened in both Canada and the United States in 1851. In contrast to leisurely activities such as croquet and lawn tennis that were enjoyed by men and women together, the YMCA offered a highly gendered place for men to engage in strenuous exercise as a means of uniting them across varying, albeit mostly middling, economic backgrounds and professions in the pursuit of idealized masculinity, guided by Protestant faith. The exercises advocated by the YMCA as well as other proponents of physical culture included various gymnastics and calisthenics, which had been innovated earlier in the century, as well as the use of Indian clubs and medicine balls. These activities were pursued inside specially built gymnasiums with wooden floors, which required footwear that did not scratch or mar the finish. In the 1860s Archibald MacLaren, a physical culture proponent who opened a gymnasium at the University of Oxford, included in his book *Physical Education: Theoretical and Practical* the 'Rules and Regulations for the Gymnasium', the first being that 'no pupil shall do any exercise without his gymnastic belt and shoes.'[18] It is not known if MacLaren was specifying rubber-soled footwear, but later in the century manufacturers began to

Each of the male students in this photo is wearing sneakers for exercise. *Male Students Exercising, Some with Equipment, Western High School, Washington, DC*, late 19th century.

advertise gymnasium shoes, which were similar to tennis shoes but generally without added decoration. The market for sports shoes was diversifying.

By the middle of the nineteenth century it was clear that organized exercise was a way of helping to bring order to the social chaos created by industrialization. It was seen as a means of tempering ambition and upward mobility through connection to Christian reverence and devotion:

> Self-reliance is the element which prompts us to great physical conquests . . . makes a man nobly mighty in himself . . . Reverence is the element which promotes a man to recognize the worth and power of something besides himself . . . something greater and better than himself.[19]

As sports enabled disparate individuals to become united towards a similar goal, team sports exploded. Furthermore, as work hours began to be reduced, team sports and exercise were opened up to people from across the socioeconomic spectrum. Baseball, American football, cricket and tennis began to be enjoyed by increasing numbers of people. In the United States, large urban parks, inspired by European examples, offered both the wealthy and the poor access to places where games could be played, teams organized and fresh air inhaled.

Like other men's clubs, criminal gangs sprang up in the increasingly dense urban centres as a means of creating group identity. In an article on gangs in America in *Harper's New Monthly Magazine*, Josiah Flynt relays how they were formed. A ruffian

> comes to see that his world is a large one – so large, in fact, that he can never understand it all – he chooses as he can those particular 'pals' with whom he can get on the easiest. Out of this choice there develops . . . the outcast's club . . . and his clubhouse a hangout.

These low-cut, lace-up sneakers would have been worn for a variety of athletic and leisurely pursuits at the end of the 19th century. American, made by Goodyear Rubber and Metallic Company, late 19th century.

The Rapper's clubhouse by the Brooklyn Bridge had 'two rooms – one fronting the street, and used as a bar-room; the other, in the rear, was the gambling and "practisin'" room. Here they came every night, played cards . . . and exercised themselves in fisticuffing and "scrappin'".'[20] Whether criminal or Christian, these associations helped men create new identities through physical exertion and homosocial bonding, establishing patterns of behaviour that would inform the cultural importance of sneakers well into the future.

Gymnasium or club-based exercise was just one of the activities recommended for health in the nineteenth century. Walking and running were also promoted. Walking had been encouraged as a means of increasing health and vitality since the eighteenth century, and by the middle of the century races attracted quite a few spectators, and champions became celebrities of a sort. One of these was the famous pedestrian Charles Westhall. In 1863 he wrote *The Modern Method of Training for Running, Walking, Rowing and Boxing, Including Hints on Exercise, Diet, Clothing, and Advice to Trainers*, in which he advocated the wearing of light lace-up shoes, the forerunners of specialized running shoes. As with other emerging sports, running too called for specialized footwear. he oldest extant running shoes are a pair of spiked shoes from 1860–65 made by the British maker Dutton & Thorowgood and held in the Northampton Museum and Art Gallery. Like the shoes Westhall advocated, they lace up and are lightweight, but they do not feature rubber soles. Track and field sports often required footwear with spikes and featured sturdy leather soles and uppers. Many of these sports did not embrace rubber-soled footwear until well into the twentieth century. Long-distance running was perhaps the first to do so. Images from the numerous races and marathons held at the turn of the twentieth century suggest that some runners were indeed wearing sneakers. The Canadian Onondaga runner Thomas Longboat from the Six Nations of the Grand River reserve won the Boston Marathon in 1907 and became one of the most celebrated runners of the day. In studio shots promoting his achievements he clearly wears sneakers and seems to have worn them to compete. The achievements of Longboat and other

Most serious running shoes were made of leather in the mid-19th century. Thought to be the oldest extant running spikes, this pair features leather uppers and small heels similar to men's dress shoes of the period. The broad band of leather across the instep was added to increase stability. British, made by Dutton & Thorowgood, 1860–65.

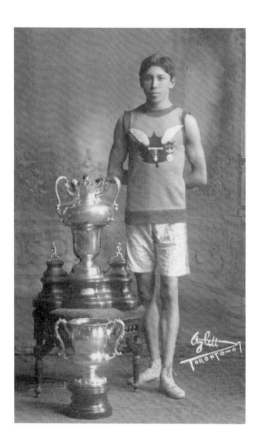

non-Anglo-Saxon runners, such as Spyridon Louis, a Greek water-carrier who won the first modern Olympic marathon in 1896, and Dorando Pietri, an Italian baker who was the first across the finish line during the 1908 Olympic marathon, challenged prejudiced notions of Anglo-Saxon racial superiority.

The increased interest in exercise led to greater demand for special athletic footwear and manufacturing stepped up to meet these needs. Production methods improved and the cost of rubber began to drop. Brutal labour conditions in Brazil increased the supply of rubber. When rubber tree seeds were secreted out of Brazil in 1876 to British tropical colonial holdings, the availability of rubber increased, as did the misery of those enslaved to collect it. The horrors playing

Celebrated Canadian runner Tom Longboat was photographed wearing his running shoes, which appear to be canvas high-tops with rubber soles. Canadian, 1906.

out in places such as the Belgian Congo under the leadership of King Leopold II shocked many and shined a spotlight on abusive labour practices – a concern that would return to haunt sneaker manufacturers at the turn of the twenty-first century. Despite these abuses, rubber collection continued unabated, reducing the cost of sneakers and transforming them into signifiers of inclusive enfranchisement rather than exclusive privilege. As the century drew to a close, sneakers were being integrated into millions of wardrobes for a wide range of activities, as reported in an article from 1887 in the *Shoe and Leather Reporter*:

> The very qualities that make it useful to the tennis player recommend it for wear other than a sporting shoe. The farmer in the fresh-cut meadow or walking the stubble of the harvest field, the yachtsman on the deck of his boat, the pleasure seeker by the sea coast, or in the woods, on the rural highways – all quickly realize the ease and comfort of the soft canvas shoe with a rubber sole. As a matter of name, these are called tennis shoes, but, as a matter of fact, while one pair is worn at the game, hundreds are on feet that never tread a tennis court. They have come into general use as a summer, and more especially as a vacation shoe.[21]

In the United States, in addition to being called a tennis shoe, this increasingly ubiquitous form of footwear also came to be called the sneaker. The term 'sneak' was used as early as 1862 in England to refer to rubber galoshes, in relation to the fact that rubber soles let one pad around noiselessly: a notation in the book *Female Life in Prison* notes, 'The night-officer is generally accustomed to wear a species of India-rubber shoes or goloshes. These are termed "sneaks" by the women.'[22] Sneaks are mentioned again in the British reporter James Greenwood's book *In Strange Company: Being the Experiences of a Roving Correspondent* (1873). As with the earlier reference, the footwear is found on the feet of a prison worker, but they are here more fully described as canvas shoes with India rubber soles, which in 'criminal phraseology, are known as "sneaks".'[23] However, it was only in the U.S. that the term sneaker became commonplace to identify rubber-soled athletic footwear, and it was fully a part of East Coast American slang by the 1870s. Like sneak, sneaker also suggested nefarious behaviour and, even if used humorously, implied a kind of criminality. Sneakers were clearly shoes that could be worn to accomplish things on the sly. A rather curious interview with a Chicago criminal named Patrick Kent from 1887 included his recommendation that to be a successful criminal, 'you must wear rubber shoes, then you can sneak up when [the victim's] back is turned and do him.'[24] In an effort to distance sneakers from these connections with ne'er-do-wells, Guyer's Shoe Store in Cambridge, Massachusetts, addressed the issue in an advertisement reading, 'A man is not necessarily a sneak because he wears sneakers. That is a name applied to rubber sole tennis shoes.'[25] The advert copy was remarkably similar to the lyrics 'I wore my sneakers but I'm not a sneak', written by Run-DMC a hundred years later for their song 'My Adidas', illustrating the long history of linking sneakers to delinquency.

In Britain, in addition to sandshoe and tennis shoe, the term plimsoll came into general use at the end of the 1870s. In 1876 Samuel Plimsoll's Act requiring that load lines be painted on the hulls of boats to prevent dangerous overloading came into effect. These new load lines reminded people of the lines created by the foxing that bonded rubber soles of sports shoes to the canvas uppers, and people playfully pointed out that if one's foot was submerged above this line, the foot would become waterlogged.

Near the end of the century, basketball, one of the most important sports in the history of sneakers, was invented by James Naismith in Springfield, Massachusetts, the same town in which Charles Goodyear had established his rubber business fifty years earlier. As Naismith recounted, 'During the summer of 1891, the need for some new game became imperative . . . members of the gymnasium classes were losing interest in the type of work that had been introduced by R. J. Roberts, at one time a circus performer.'[26] Regardless of their rather interesting provenance, the gymnastics promoted by Roberts were stodgy

and the young men with whom Naismith was working sought daring competition rather than repetitive calisthenics. In particular, Naismith's students needed an outlet for their energy during the winter, when games such as football and baseball could not be played outdoors. So, in keeping with the Christian ideals of the YMCA, Naismith devised basketball as a wintertime diversion that encouraged camaraderie, dispelled boredom and limited aggression. The game required only a small amount of space in which to be played, indoors or out, and did not necessitate specialized equipment.

Enthusiasm for the new sport was almost instantaneous. Universities and secondary schools incorporated it into their athletic programmes and it took off in city playgrounds and empty lots. From the very beginning, basketball was played in urban settings and the game would go on to be dominated by urban players from diverse ethnic backgrounds. It was a sport also enjoyed by women.[27] The image of the strong, athletic young woman was even glamorized by the American artist Charles Dana Gibson. The statuesque Gibson Girl's

Children playing the newly invented game of basketball in New York City. *Carnegie Playground, 5th Ave,* 1911.

self-possessed demeanour and eager engagement with the world was helping to redefine femininity to include athleticism, and many embraced her as a role model. Basketball was perfect for this so-called New Woman. It did not require the coquetries of lawn tennis and offered an outlet for the competitive spirit. A first-time observer of basketball reported to the *New York Times* that the enthusiastic players at Vassar College in New York State were 'a fine-looking lot . . . light-footed, lithe, alert, and graceful . . . the ringing cheer echoed . . . Hippity bus! Hippity bus! What in the world is the matter with us? Nothing at all! Nothing at all! We are the girls who play basket ball!'[28] Despite praise like this, many were uncomfortable with the idea of women in competitive sports. A defender of women's participation wrote that the game offered the athletic girl a chance 'to display her wit, courage, grace and strength', and noted that in spite of this there was a storm of protest from 'those who think that the women of the future should be nothing but a brain box of Greek verbs, eye glasses and a body fit for nothing but corsets and high heels'.[29]

The popularity of the new sport ensured that, in short order, a basketball sneaker would be invented. But which company created the first basketball shoe and when it became a standard part of the uniform are points of contention. The Colchester Rubber Company based in Connecticut has been posited as offering in 1893 the first specially designed basketball shoe, but there is no evidence of them tailoring their rubber-soled athletic shoes expressly for basketball. A *New York Times* article stated in 1896 that the Vassar players wore tennis shoes. An advertisement for A. G. Spalding & Brothers in the following year promoted a special offer to YMCA members of a 'complete' outfit, presumably for gym activities, that included tights, a shirt, trunks, a towel, bathing trunks and one pair of 'strong canvas rubber sole shoes'. At the bottom of the advertisement, it is noted that basketball and football suits are also available, but there is no mention of specialized footwear to complete the outfits. In his book *Basketball: Its Origin and Development*, Naismith wrote that in 1903 the Spalding Company offered the first suction-sole basketball shoe,

which suggests that basketball shoes without suction had been worn prior to 1903.[30] Photographs of the Buffalo Germans YMCA basketball team, which won the demonstration tournament at the 1904 Olympics in St Louis, show all the players in canvas high-tops, but such sneakers were common and not limited to basketball. Images of university teams from around the same time show players wearing high-tops and low-tops of different types. An advertisement for Spalding's basketball shoes from 1907, however, shows only high-tops including their 'old favorite Spalding no. BB shoe' with the suction sole, priced at a significant $4.50. Even more interesting are the Spalding no. BBR shoes for the expert, priced at $8, which suggests that there was already a hierarchy being established within the basketball shoe market and that some players deemed it important to pay top dollar for their athletic footwear.

The history of the basketball shoe was changed when the Converse Rubber Shoe Company introduced the Converse All Star and the

Women eagerly played basketball and many high schools and colleges added basketball to women's athletics. *Unidentified American Basketball Team, c. 1910.*

No. BB

Converse Non-Skid in 1917. All Stars featured brown canvas uppers, while the Non-Skid was the same shoe in white canvas and with a slightly different tread. Both featured what would go on to become enduring visual identifiers of the brand, including the toe cap, licence plate on the heel, and the ankle patch placed over the inner ankle for protection. Although marketed as general indoor gym shoes, they were specifically advocated for basketball. By 1920 it was clear that there was confusion because the two styles of sneaker were so similar, and eventually the Non-Skid was abandoned, leaving the Converse All Star to become one of the most important sneakers of all time.

In the same year that the All Star came out, the u.s. entered the First World War, a full three years after the start of hostilities. America had been hesitant to send its citizens overseas, but once committed, the physical fitness of American men became a patriotic issue. Battle readiness had long been a focus of fitness across Europe: much of

Spalding advertised this high-top sneaker with suction sole in 1907 in their *Spalding's Athletic Library Official Collegiate Basket Ball Guide.*

the nineteenth-century focus on gymnasium exercise in France, England and Germany had clear militaristic overtones. The revival of the Olympics in 1896 had provided an outlet for the increasingly competitive spirit of the age. An article in the *Telegraph Herald* discussed the role of sports to prepare men for battle:

> there is a saying in the British Isles that 'England's battles were won on the cricket fields.' America's coming victories in the cause of democracy and humanity can be attributed to the baseball diamond, the football field, the tennis court, track, field and water, for the ten million young men who have answered the registration call of the president have received a preliminary training in the great American army of sport.[31]

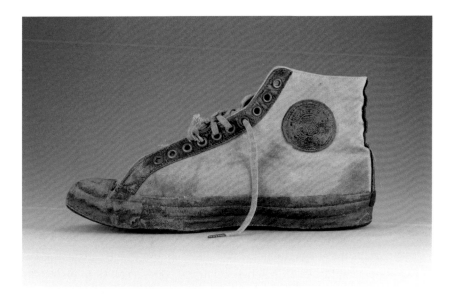

The Converse Rubber Shoe Company debuted one of the most enduring sneaker styles in 1917. Brown canvas models were marketed as All Stars while the same shoes in white canvas with a slightly different tread were called Non-Skids. Eventually the Non-Skid name was removed, leaving the All Star to become an icon. Converse All Star/Non-Skid, American, 1924.

The article promotes physical education not only as a means to victory but also as a means of preventing the U.S. from being disgraced on the world stage. While the article might have been a bit hyperbolic, the fears seem to have been well founded. *Physical Culture Magazine* reported, perhaps also with exaggeration, that 'only two million men out of ten million are physically available for military service.'[32] The lack of physical fitness among those called to arms was unsettling. Even more disturbing was the cost of war on those who did fight. Science had innovated weaponry that created unimaginable carnage and medical advances had saved many of the profoundly wounded. The social impact of the visible vulnerabilities represented in their wounded bodies and the fragile peace that followed the conclusion of the war made exercise and fitness a central cultural concern in the 1920s.

The bodily perfection of the ancient Greeks was promoted as the ideal and infused the 1920 and 1924 Summer Olympics with new energy. Exercising out of doors and suntanning became means of creating bodies that rivalled the bronzed 'gods' of antiquity in their gleaming perfection. In women's fashion, the statuesque Gibson Girl gave way to the lithe Hollywood flapper, and women began to worry about 'excess' weight. In a kind of cruel irony, fasting, so recently a tool of protest used by hunger-striking suffragettes, came into vogue and exercise was sought not so much to display 'wit, courage, grace and strength' but as a means of weight reduction. 'The chief methods in vogue for reducing', Dr Brooks said in 1926 in the *New York Times*, 'were overexercise . . . starvation diet, going without water, and the use of thyroid, iodine and smoking to excess, all of which he declared injurious.'[33] Despite the new emphasis on exercise, athleticism and femininity remained opposing ideals. Some women continued to play competitive sports and a few, such as the French tennis great Suzanne Lenglen, even reached celebrity status. Yet, despite *Vogue*'s declaration that although 'the general public of the metropolis totters to its work in high-heeled slippers or sandals . . . it is beginning to admit that low heels for sports are "correct" (that awful word), and it knows that for games like tennis and squash almost none are worn,[34] many women continued to wear sports shoes that featured high heels. Heels were even advocated for wear with bathing suits:

> Bathers and vacation campers who stand around barefooted or in flat-soled sneakers are not taking the right course if they want to preserve their foot arches, according to the Reconstruction Hospital, which says that girls who wear high-heeled pumps with beach suits have the right idea for avoiding weak or flat feet.[35]

While tennis whites continued to be used to flaunt wealth in luxury resort towns, the majority of sneakers on offer were low-cost and worn by people from across all socioeconomic strata. The *New York Times* reported in 1923 that sales of canvas and rubber shoes and other sports shoes with rubber soles were doing particularly well because of the technological innovations in materials and production.[36] That same year the newspaper also reported on the potential in France for a market in American-made sneakers, despite the

Despite women's increased participation in sports, concerns remained that athleticism would detract from their femininity. This pair of Fleet Foot sneakers featured high heels to promote the femininity of the wearer. Canadian, made by Dominion Rubber, *c.* 1925.

already thriving industry in that country. The opportunity was linked to the fact that

> the market for the sale of footwear of all classes has increased with the higher standard of living since the war, as mechanics, laborers and farmhands are no longer content to wear the heavy and clumsy articles of the last generation . . . working people who formerly wore canvas shoes with rope soles now wore similar shoes with rubber soles. School children, especially during the vacation period, are wearing footwear of the latter type more and more. The market is also increased by the fact that sports and outdoor games have grown in favor since the war.[37]

As more and more people began to wear sneakers, more manufacturers got into the game, production increased to meet demand and the price of sneakers fell even further. Sneaker manufacturers now had to fight for market share by seeking new ways of marketing their products, including receiving endorsements. The University of Chicago coach Harlan 'Pat' Page endorsed the Converse All Star in 1920, while Keds received an endorsement from the Original Celtics in 1925. These accolades were vaunted in ads placed in magazines such as *Boy's Life* and *Popular Mechanics*. It was also at this time that the young basketball player and coach Chuck Taylor began to work with Converse.

The Great Depression further propelled the ascendancy of the sneaker. 'Leisure time' increased for the under-employed and unemployed, and frugality was of utmost importance. Less expensive sneakers were substituted for leather shoes and wearing them for non-athletic purposes became common. It was a trend that sneaker manufacturers capitalized on. In 1934 an article about the fourth annual National Sport Shoe Week at Macy's wrote, 'again America takes to the out-of-doors. Everybody – men, women and children – planning to be out in the open as much as possible, and most of them having more time than ever to loaf or play! It's up to the shoe merchants to emphasize and dramatize sports shoes!'[38] One way that

companies sought to 'dramatize' sports shoes was through the debut of signature shoes. More than simple endorsements, signature shoes promised that consultation with sports heroes or at least their approval had figured in the actual design of the sneaker. The first signature shoe was the Converse Chuck Taylor All Star, which came out in 1934. The following year, the Canadian division of B. F. Goodrich created the Jack Purcell, endorsed by the famed Canadian badminton player, and which, like the Chuck Taylor All Star, would go on to become an enduring style. The Dunlop Green Flash, which Dunlop had debuted only a few years earlier, received a boost when the unstoppable British tennis player Fred Perry wore them to win three consecutive Wimbledon titles from 1934 to 1936. However, while Dunlop profited from this association, Perry was forbidden from seeking compensation through official endorsement, as doing so would have nullified his amateur status. The prohibition against amateur athletes benefiting financially from their success in sports was particularly irritating to

Basketball coach Chuck Taylor began working for Converse in the 1920s and by 1934 his name was added to the famous Converse All Star. American, 1920s.

Jesse Owens, one of America's greatest athletes, whose four gold medals at the 1936 Summer Olympics garnered him fame but not fortunes.

The story of Owens's Olympic victories and the footwear he wore went on to become part of sneaker lore. Before the start of the Olympics, the Dassler brothers, Adi and Rudi, who would eventually go on to create Adidas and Puma respectively, were working together at their company Gebrüder Dassler Schuhfabrik making athletic footwear. One of their principal goals was to have Olympians wear their shoes. They had managed to outfit athletes in previous Olympics, and in 1936 they were working with the German track coach Josef Waitzer to develop sprinting shoes. One of the athletes whom Adi was eyeing was Jesse Owens, and he asked Waitzer to assist him in getting some running spikes to the athlete. Waitzer was hesitant due to the highly charged Nazi climate – Owens was not only American, he was African American and his achievements offered a strong rebuttal to Nazi ideology – but eventually a few pairs got to Owens and he wore them during practice. Although Owens never wore them for competition, pride in the association reverberates in Adidas even to this day.[39] It is interesting to speculate what might have happened if Owens had been able to do an endorsement deal with Gebrüder Dassler Schuhfabrik. The politics of the Second World War swept the Dasslers up into the Nazi movement and after the war the brothers separated, establishing their independent companies in the same small German town of Herzogenaurach and becoming bitter rivals.

Despite Owens's individual Olympic success the Germans took home the most medals overall, and the myth of the physical supremacy of the Aryan race remained at the heart of Nazi ideology. As during the First World War, men's physical fitness and battle readiness became a concern worldwide. Hitler declared in *Mein Kampf* that

> If the German nation were presented with a body of young men who had been perfectly trained in athletic sports, who were imbued with an ardent love for their country and a readiness to take the initiative in a fight, then the national State could make an army out of that body in less than two years . . . They must

Jesse Owens won four gold medals in the Berlin Summer Olympic Games in 1936. He is said to have trained at the Olympics in shoes provided by Adi and Rudi Dassler. *Jesse Owens at the Start of His Record-breaking 200-meter Race*, 1936.

also develop that athletic agility which can be employed as a defensive weapon in the service of the Movement.[40]

Physical perfection became touted as the outward evidence of social and racial superiority and the Germans, Japanese and Italians all held mass fitness rallies. Benito Mussolini reportedly put his leaders, including those who were 'fat and fifty plus', to a four-day physical fitness test in 1939.[41] The Allies likewise sought to increase the fitness of their citizens through health awareness campaigns that linked personal health to national security: 'Every day more people are realizing the importance of physical culture. In many overseas countries it has become a national affair – with the Governments doing everything possible to encourage the youth of the country to become physically perfect.'[42] In this period of the 'politics of perfection', sneakers became a mandatory part of many people's wardrobes. Sneaker production improved further, the availability of rubber increased and the sneaker industry boomed. By the outbreak of war, sneakers were being manufactured and worn worldwide. The Czech shoe manufacturer Bata, one of the largest producers of footwear, including sneakers, in the world, established a factory in India in the early 1930s and started producing the Bata tennis shoe there in 1936, becoming one of the first Western shoe companies to move production to Asia.[43] The rise of fascism and fears of it had made sneakers the most democratic form of footwear in the world.

At the outset of the war, the fate of sneakers was called into question. The Japanese quickly gained control over many of the largest rubber-producing regions of the world in the Pacific Ocean theatre, and the subsequent rubber shortages threatened Allied military success; rubber was essential to everything from tyres and life rafts to gas masks and pontoon bridges.[44] The Rubber Survey Committee created by u.s. president Franklin D. Roosevelt declared that lack of rubber posed 'the greatest threat to the safety of our Nation

By the 1930s, sneaker production and sneaker wearing had gone global, in part due to the Bata innovation of the CENEL press. This poster promotes India-made Bata sneakers. Czech, 1930s.

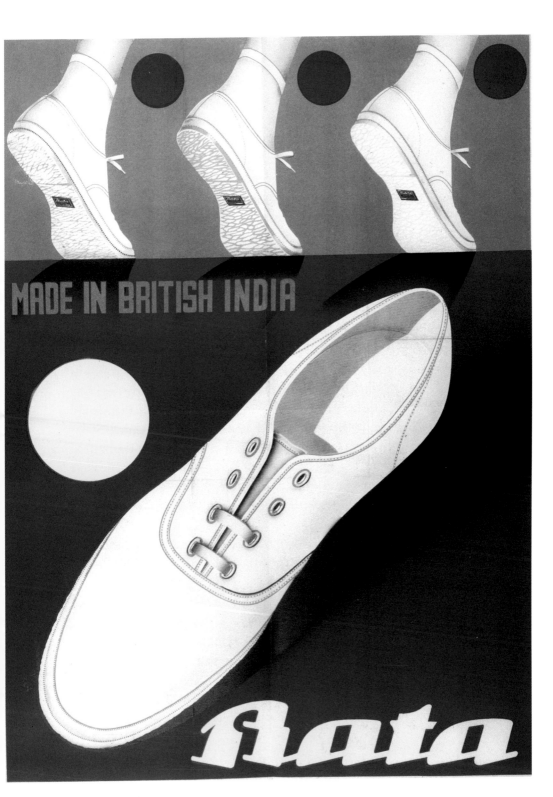

and success of the Allied cause . . . if we fail to secure quickly a large new rubber supply, our war effort and our domestic economy will collapse.'[45] As a result, rubber was one of the first things to be rationed and the production of sneakers stopped. In the United States, sneaker manufacturers tried a range of marketing techniques to remain in the public eye:

> 'Keds' was one of the first casualties of war . . . Under the compulsion of war, these 'shoe-makers' began thinking, creating, meeting war needs that they alone could meet . . . It is these 'shoe-makers' who build rubber life rafts, the life vests, the bullet sealing gasoline tanks, the jungle boots – dozens on dozens of products.

Through advertising copy like this, Keds and other companies sought to stay at the forefront of people's minds. The distribution of mail-order booklets directed at boys with advice from sports heroes was another method used by sneaker manufacturers. This early targeting of the teenage market presaged the focus on youth culture that would grip marketing in the post-war era.[46] Early in the war, the United States Army had tried outfitting troops in high-top sneakers, but the limited availability of rubber and the inferior construction of the sneakers created for military purposes proved it impractical, although for combat in tropical places sneakers were deemed more desirable than leather boots.

The Japanese control of the rubber-producing regions in the Pacific not only led to rubber rationing worldwide, it also fuelled the race to develop alternatives. Almost since the discovery of vulcanization, scientists had sought to create synthetic rubber. The First World War, which had similarly experienced rubber shortages, had moved the field forward, but the most important discoveries had to wait until the middle of the twentieth century. During the war years the development of synthetic rubber became a focus for both Axis and Allied nations. German chemists at IG Farben combined butadiene with styrene, creating Buna, a relatively pliant synthetic rubber, and

in the U.S. synthetic rubber that came to be called Neoprene was developed by DuPont in 1931.[47] American manufacturers focused on petroleum-based materials, with B. F. Goodrich becoming the largest producer of synthetic rubber while also laying the groundwork for the creation of plastics, which would revolutionize the industry.[48] These developments, in addition to the innovation of other synthetics such as DuPont nylon, transformed sneaker production in the subsequent decades.

Once the war was over, sneaker manufacturing began again, although recovery of the industry was challenged in many countries where rationing remained in place. In the U.S. sneaker production swiftly returned to normal; Converse, Keds and B. F. Goodrich all resumed production. Family vacations recommenced and sneakers with canvas uppers and rubber soles were once again the footwear of summertime for all family members. Post-war production capabilities reduced the cost of sneakers to an all-time low, and the baby boom pushed sneaker consumption to new heights, transforming

These aptly named Garrison high-tops were designed for military wear. Unfortunately, their construction was so poor that they were quickly abandoned. Canadian, 1940.

inexpensive canvas high-tops and low-cut 'skippies' into the footwear of childhood. Television, one of the most culturally significant technologies of the post-war period, pitched sneakers to American kids on weekends in the 1950s. Kedso the Clown was featured in animated spots promoting Keds sneakers on Saturday morning cartoons. The popular family TV shows *Dennis the Menace* and *Leave It to Beaver*, *Lassie* and *Father Knows Best* featured boys and girls invariably clad in sneakers. In this era of suburban sameness, sneakers temporarily lost all associations with status. Nonetheless, television would later prove to be instrumental in the reinstatement of sneakers as an accessory of status and exclusivity.

As American sneaker companies focused on producing sneakers for wear in physical education (gym) class and summertime, manufacturers in other countries, including those defeated in the war, began producing sneakers for elite athletes. Japan's Onitsuka Tiger debuted in 1949 and concentrated on the niche market of long-distance running and track and field. Germany's Puma, established by Rudi Dassler in 1948, and Adidas, established by Adi Dassler in 1949, both excelled in the elite athletic footwear market. Adidas shoes were designed for serious competitors but many of the company's models, such as the Samba, an all-round training shoe first issued in 1950, proved to be an instant success with amateur athletes. The graphically strong three stripes found on Adidas shoes helped to establish the brand. When the German football (soccer) team wore Adidas football boots to beat the Hungarians and take the FIFA World Cup in 1954, the brand became a household name in Europe. In 1965 Adidas broke into the American basketball market with the introduction of the leather Pro Model. By the 1968 Mexico City Olympics, Adidas was the unrivalled supplier of elite athletic footwear: 85 per cent of all competitors wore Adidas.[49] The following year, Adidas introduced the Superstar, the first low-cut leather basketball shoe with a stitched shell sole construction – one of the most important shoes in sneaker history.

'Keds are always all play and no work!' proclaimed this post-war advertisement, which touted play shoes for all family members. American, c. 1950s.

PATIO COOL for women

BOOSTER-AIR for men

DRESS 'N PLAY KEDS for men and boys

## Wish You Were Here!

GLADIATOR KEDS for men and boys

CHAMPION BLUCHER for kiddies

Something wonderful happens all summer—with Keds along to share the fun!
Your feet feel young and gay, hardly ever tire. Even Dad's a cool guy in
Keds Casuals, so relaxed 'n ready to go! His Booster® Keds are floating-light,
"breathe" when he walks. Keds are always all play and no work!
They hop, skip, jump with the kids, rarely show wear.
Just tub Keds clean. Economical shoes—for a stylish family!

KEDS ARE GOOD FOR YOUR FEET

### Natural Support

1. HEEL-TO-TOE CUSHIONED INSOLE
2. SHOCKPROOF ARCH CUSHION
3. CUSHIONED SHOCKPROOF HEEL

- **BOOSTER-AIR**—Claret, Brown, Blue, Timber Brown.
- **DRESS 'N PLAY KEDS**—Brown, Blue, Maroon; Jeans Blue Denim, Brown Denim.
- **CHAMPION BLUCHER**—Red, Blue, Brown; Faded Blue Denim, Brown Denim.
- **GLADIATOR KEDS**—Anti-slip soles. Slant-cut tops won't bind. Jeans Blue Denim; Black.
- **PATIO COOL**—Skyline Blue, Yachting Blue, Resort Red, Havana Suntan.

## U.S. Keds®
### *The Shoes of Champions—They Wash*

MADE ON FOOT-CONFORMING LASTS

Lets Toes Lie Straight and Free, for Action

US RUBBER

# UNITED STATES RUBBER COMPANY • Rockefeller Center, New York

Puma also excelled during these years, making football boots as well as track shoes. They succeeded in having medallists wear their footwear in the 1960 and 1964 Summer Olympics.[50] At the 1968 Olympics, although the majority of athletes wore Adidas, Puma was given the spotlight when American Olympic Gold medallist Tommie Smith and his bronze medal-winning teammate John Carlos removed their Puma Suedes and mounted the podiums in stockinged feet, lowered their heads and raised their black-leather-gloved fists at the playing of 'The Star-Spangled Banner'. It was the height of the Civil Rights movement and the athletes used their moment of fame to highlight the hypocrisy in America which valorized their achievements yet maintained a racist society.

It was not just Olympic prominence that was catching people's attention. The streamlined and colourful leather shoes on offer from Adidas, Puma and Onitsuka Tiger were markedly different from

The original Adidas Samba was launched in 1950 and was designed for wear in icy conditions. By the 1960s, the shoe was gaining in popularity and in the '70s it was remodelled for indoor football practice and went on to become the second best-selling sneaker in the history of Adidas. German, 1965.

the sneakers produced in the United States. Converse All Stars and P. F. Flyers had changed little over the decades and their appeal was fading. Some companies, such as New Balance, quickly adapted; the company's two-tone leather Trackster from 1960 featured a somewhat aerodynamic design and was the first running shoe to feature an innovative ripple sole. Running shoes became increasingly import-ant in the 1960s, when jogging emerged as a popular recreation. Jogging for fun and fitness was first popularized in New Zealand by Arthur Lydiard in the early 1960s and was brought to the u.s. by Bill Bowerman, a track and field coach at the University of Oregon. Enthusiastic about this new form of eercise, Bowerman published the book *Jogging* in 1966, and by 1973 6.5 million Americans were jogging.[51]

The rapid embrace of jogging coincided with the self-focused interests of members of the so-called 'Me' generation, who sought to beautify their bodies and flaunt success through conspicuous con-sumption. By the late 1960s, ideas of perfecting the body in service of one's nation had long been abandoned and in their place came in-creased emphasis on expressions of individual success. This interest in the self drove a dramatic increase in solitary exercises such as jogging and running. Even group exercise shifted from amateur team sports to exercise classes led by an instructor, with each participant focused on improving his or her own performance. When competition was sought it was often in sports such as marathon running that pitted individual against individual. These trends were a boon for sneaker companies. Consumers were willing to invest in footwear that they thought would give them an edge, whether competing for attention on the track or in the disco. It was in this milieu that one of the most important companies in the history of the sneaker, Nike, was founded.

Nike came about out of a partnership between the Oregon coach Bill Bowerman and one of his middle-distance runners, Phil Knight. In the 1960s at the start of the jogging craze, Knight, as part of his MA in business at Stanford University, wrote a paper on Japanese versus German sneaker brands in their competition for American market share. He was convinced that Japanese brands could outpace the Germans. After graduating, Knight convinced Onitsuka Tiger to make him a U.S. distributor. Bowerman had been tinkering with ways of making running shoes lighter, and rather than simply buying a few pairs he offered to become Knight's partner and to provide design ideas to Onitsuka.[52] They named their company Blue Ribbon Sports and Phil Knight sold the first shipment of Tigers out of his green Plymouth Valiant. By 1970 the two had become interested in making their own sneakers based on Bowerman's designs. They chose the name Nike, after the Greek goddess of victory, and paid Carolyn Davidson, a young graphic design student at Portland State University, $35 to create their logo – the now iconic Swoosh.[53]

In 1972 the first Nike sneaker, the Cortez, became an instant classic. Bowerman's first iteration had debuted as the Onitsuka Cortez, but after Nike's bitter break-up with the Japanese company, they tweaked the design slightly, added the Nike Swoosh and issued it as the Nike Cortez. Onitsuka eventually made their own changes and renamed their version of the shoe the Corsair. Nike's instantly recognizable trademark and high quality quickly attracted the attention of amateur runners as well as the track and field elite. The success of the Cortez was followed by the Waffle Trainer in 1974. The sole was famously inspired by experiments Bowerman undertook using rubber poured into his family's waffle iron to create a sole with high tread but using very little rubber. This sneaker also featured an eye-catching and exceptionally lightweight nylon upper in bright blue with a bold yellow swoosh that allowed the sneaker to move effortlessly between fitness and fashion.

As high-end brands combined costliness with flashiness, top-of-the-line running shoes were transformed into aspirational objects of desire and signifiers of conspicuous consumption. *Vogue* proclaimed in 1977, 'real runner's sneakers (the hottest status symbol around)' and indeed sneakers had become a ten-billion-dollar industry meeting the needs of the 'me decade' and its 'rampant narcissism resulting from new-found wealth and the time in which to spend it'.[54] The increasing variety of sneakers also allowed them to be used to create

One of Bill Bowerman's lifelong goals was to make the lightest running shoes possible. His quest led to the development of the waffle sole, which was lightweight with a high tread. Nike Waffle Trainer, American, 1974.

individualized fashion statements: 'Normally, if you had 30 million people doing the same thing at the same time it would seem like conformity, as if everyone were being stamped out of the same mold. But with sneakers it's different, as if everyone simply had decided to show some independence *en masse*.'[55]

Expensive, high-end sneakers were not embraced by everyone, however, and many bemoaned the need to have specific shoes for each and every sport. It was an oft-repeated lament. One father recounted his shock in the article 'Sneaker Plague Threatens to Sap the Strength of This Great Nation': eager to have his son play sports, he was soon made to realize just how many sneakers he would need to purchase. He wrote,

> So I was glad that my son became interested in this charac-ter-building sport, until he announced that he needed new sneakers. This troubled me, because he had new sneakers . . . but my wife and my son gently informed me that I am a total idiot. It turns out you don't run in pump sneakers . . . for running, you need a completely different kind of sneakers, for which you have to pay a completely different set of U.S. dollars. Not only that, but the sneaker salesperson informed me that, depending on the kind of running my son was going to do, he might need SEVERAL KINDS of sneakers.[56]

While many parents caved in to the desires of their offspring, some kids preferred low-tech, old-school sneakers, as an anti-fashion statement. Punks favoured canvas high-tops similar in form to those other staples of punk fashion, the lace-up combat boot and Dr Martens. Many, such as the punk band the Ramones, also liked low-cut sneakers. West Coast skaters also embraced the low-cut – a classic of California beach life – and morphed it into the skateboard shoe. The Randolph Rubber Company first made the Randy 720 in 1965, but it was the Van Doren Rubber Company's Vans that went on to dominate the market. Skateboarders saw something they liked in Vans and the company reciprocated; their famous black-and-white

checked pattern was inspired by the way some kids decorated the white uppers of Vans slip-ons. This particular style went global after Sean Penn wore a pair in his breakout movie *Fast Times at Ridgemont High* in 1982. Vans spoke to youth, to freedom, to speed – to a forward movement that was propelled by one's own efforts – and by the end of the decade had been embraced by many in hip hop.

It was basketball shoes, however, that would come to define sneaker culture and dominate sneaker fashions. The epicentre was the boroughs of New York City. On its innumerable basketball courts, both official and improvised basketball shoes began to emerge as cultural icons and staples of urban street fashion. Basketball had been an urban sport almost from the moment of its inception and by the 1960s, the courts of New York were places where the inner-city elite could hold audience, establish political alliances, orchestrate rivalries and create stars through the staging of basketball games. The aggressive style of play and audacious braggadocio of these 'street

The iconic skateboarding sneaker, the Vans Checkerboard Slip-on, sports a pattern inspired by designs kids drew on their sneakers. The shoes were immortalized in the film *Fast Times at Ridgemont High* (1982). American, 2014 retro of 1980s.

The Puma Clyde debuted in 1973 as the signature shoe of New York Knicks player Walt 'Clyde' Frazier and quickly became central to urban fashion. This orange example was signed by Walt Frazier across the toe. Clyde, Chase Pack, 2005 retro of 1973.

ball' players was riveting – a point not lost on professional recruiters. This shift towards spectacle was perfect for the age of televised sports and a more street style of play began to seep into professional basketball and transform the game. By the 1970s, 90 per cent of professional players came from urban centres.[57] Although only a few attained celebrity status, those who did became superstars and their fame was quickly commodified. Adidas signed Harlem-born Kareem Abdul-Jabbar in 1971 and released the first basketball shoe to feature the signature of an endorsing celebrity player.[58] Puma signed New York Knicks great Walt 'Clyde' Frazier in 1972, and Converse, in an effort to compete with the European brands, introduced the All Star Pro Model Leather endorsed by Dr J in 1976. Of these three sneakers, it was the Puma Clyde that linked the sports and fashion worlds. Frazier, considered the most flamboyant dresser in the National Basketball Association (NBA), even appeared in a Puma advert wearing his mink coat, marking one of the first times sneakers were pictured with a suit. Within urban fashion, basketball sneakers were becoming a means by which masculine individuality could be flaunted both on and off the court.

The debut of hip hop in 1973 offered another kind of contest for young men, based on equal parts skill and style. Breaking began when DJ Kool Herc began using two turntables so that he could play with the 'break', or instrumental part of a song. His verbal exhortations to the break-boys, or B-boys, who would dance during these breaks, helped lead to the development of rap. B-boying was competitive by nature and the dances were inventive, extremely athletic and, like urban basketball, required footwear that was both functional and 'fresh'. As breaking evolved, group cohesion was often expressed through uniformity of dress, but individuality was established through footwear. Indeed, as Bobbito Garcia, author of *Where'd You Get Those?*, writes about his remembrances of the time,

> From 1970 to 1987, the goal in New York was to assert your individuality within a collective frame. The collectives were playground ballplayers, graffiti writers, B-boys and B-girls,

DJs, MCs and beatboxers. The spirit was competitive and progressive . . . whether it was coming up with a new boogie move on the court or a new freeze on the linoleum, ballplayers and hip-hop heads alike were pushing the creative envelope at all times.[59]

Their interest in specific types and brands of sneakers gave rise to sneaker culture and coincided with the larger cultural trend throughout American society that suggested individual expression could be achieved through brand association. Sneakers, in particular, offered a wide range of possibilities, as each brand, each model, each colourway could be used to construct nuanced social statements. It was not long before connections between masculinity, urban culture and sneakers were understood and popularized to a larger audience. Professional basketball, especially the Slam Dunk Contest televised in 1976 from Denver, Colorado, was one means by which

Breaking was competitive in both form and fashion. These dancers, wearing a variety of sneaker styles and brands, were captured on a street corner in New York City. American, 1981.

status sneakers began to insinuate themselves into the imaginations of Americans across the country. Music was another. The Sugarhill Gang's 'Rapper's Delight' in 1979 was the first rap single to make the Top 40, and the blockbuster movie *Flashdance* (1983), which showcased the B-boying Rock Steady Crew, started a breaking craze that swept the world and brought wide recognition of hip hop fashion, including sneakers. As urban fashions gained popularity, attention shifted from the brightly coloured running shoes of the 1970s to the eye-catching basketball shoes of the 1980s, and companies tried to keep pace. Nike had offered basketball shoes since its early days but as Andrew Pollack of the *New York Times* wrote in 1985, Nike had been 'caught off guard . . . when fashions began changing'.[60] Nike's earnings had dropped by 29 per cent in 1984, the first decline for the company in ten years, the article reported. The one bright spot was that its 'new black and red Air Jordan shoe, endorsed by Chicago Bulls basketball star Michael Jordan, looks like a hit'.[61] The article continues with a quote from Nike spokesperson Douglas S. Herkner: 'We're going back to what we know best, athletic wear with a little fashion thrown in.'[62] What neither Pollack nor Herkner could foresee was the impact of Nike's new venture, the Air Jordan, on both fashion and culture.

The first Air Jordan was designed by Peter Moore. It was a leather high-top in the Chicago Bulls colourway of red and black and featured Nike Air technology – encapsulated air located in the sole, meant to provide cushioning. When Michael Jordan first saw them he supposedly declared them 'devil shoes', and indeed the shoes got him into trouble. When he stepped onto the court in a pair during the 1984–5 season he was immediately reprimanded and fined by the NBA for not conforming to the 'uniformity of uniforms rule'. It was clear that Nike had hit pure advertising gold. Gifted, skilled, daring and hardworking, Michael Jordan personified the valorization of American individualism by defying the rules and wearing his Air Jordans for every game. Nike gladly paid the fine for each infringement.[63]

Just as Air Jordans were allowing millions to ally themselves with the athletic prowess of superstar Michael Jordan, the all-white Nike

(*above*) One of the most pivotal moments in sneaker history occurred in 1984 when Nike began making sneakers for the phenomenal Chicago Bulls rookie Michael Jordan. Original Air Jordan, American, 1984.

(*right*) In 1982, Bruce Kilgore designed the Nike Air Force 1. This first version came in white with a light-grey Swoosh design, but in 1986 the iconic all-white version was released. American, 1982.

Air Force 1 was coming to represent a different kind of individual success. Named after the U.S. presidential plane, the style first debuted in 1982 but was discontinued after only one year. But when it was reintroduced in 1986 in the white-on-white colourway, it quickly gained in popularity, especially in New York City. Colloquially known as Uptowns,[64] they became touted as the sneakers of choice for drug dealers, whose ability to wear unscuffed white sneakers implied untouchability and signified both wealth and status. It was a problematic image whose ambiguity appealed to a broad spectrum of people. In the media, the sneaker-wearing urban drug dealer was positioned as both a hero and villain, to be feared and glamorized. Like an updated version of the complicated icon of the cowboy, the drug dealer was celebrated for his rugged individualism as well as his hypermasculine allure, his violent flouting of the law and self-made wealth further infusing his image with glamour.

Needless to say, not everyone agreed with this portrayal of urban masculinity. The rap group Run-DMC's song 'My Adidas' directly challenged this image. Their signature look included Adidas Superstars, which like the Air Force 1 were central to urban fashion, worn without laces, a style discussed in the media as having started

in prisons to keep inmates from harming themselves or others. But Run-DMC rapped that although they wore their sneakers without laces, their Adidas 'only bring good news and are not used as felon shoes'. Indeed, as the lyrics declared, they had legitimately purchased their sneakers, had gone to university and wore their Superstars to promote goodwill.[65]

The popularity of the song emboldened the group to reach out to Adidas in 1986, asking for a million-dollar endorsement deal. After Adidas executives became enlightened about the market share represented by hip hop, this arrangement, and the numerous deals with musicians that followed, helped to bring urban music and fashion – including sneakers – to an even bigger audience worldwide. The popularization of hip hop fashion put increased pressure on sneaker-heads seeking to proclaim their individuality with unique shoes. Rare vintage footwear found eager buyers while established manufacturers pushed cutting-edge innovation and design.

Another pressure being put on sneaker culture was the fact that older people were turning to sneakers and tracksuits for comfort and ease of wear. Many bought run-of-the-mill unknown names but others were willing to pay more for sneakers that featured cutting-edge innovations such as increased cushioning or Velcro straps that made putting sneakers on and taking them off easier. Industry needed to court both the fashion-conscious consumer and the more practical consumer, who likewise was willing to pay top dollar.

Air technology stands out as the most notable among the innovations introduced in the mid-1980s. Air pumps were used to inflate internal bladders that cushioned and customized fit in models such as the Nike Pressure and the Reebok Pump, and encapsulated air was used to cushion the sole in a number of Nike sneakers. The 1980s also saw the incorporation of wearable computer technology into sneaker design, including the Adidas Micropacer and the Puma RS-Computer Shoe, which helped track runners' progress. Converse, in an effort to remake its image, introduced a number of brightly hued leather basketball shoes, including the Weapon. New sneaker companies also emerged and found eager customers awaiting them as they entered the urban fashion market.

This Adidas promotional postcard dates to the early years of the company's collaboration with the rap group Run-DMC. Each member is wearing a pair of Adidas Superstars, the sneakers they made famous in their song 'My Adidas'. German, 1986.

British Knights, an American company that started in 1983, artic-ulated the strategy shared by many companies. They focused on the urban consumer but their ultimate aim was to reach the larger white, suburban crowd. As one of their press releases stated, 'The only way to get a middle-class suburban high school kid to buy your product is to have an inner-city kid wear it.'[66] The strategy laid out by British Knights was to become an increasing issue with the spread of sneaker culture. The African American superstar athletes who promoted the shoes and the black youths who legitimized them imbued these sneakers with an edgy aura that suggested a gritty authenticity while also being aspirational. Yet inner-city young men were also the focus of ridicule, and their quest for and use of sneakers was widely criticized. This opening paragraph of the *Boston Globe* article 'Sneaker Chic is the Sole Trend for Inner-city Fashion' by Nathan Cobb was just one of many that were blatantly racist and offensive when discussing sneaker culture:

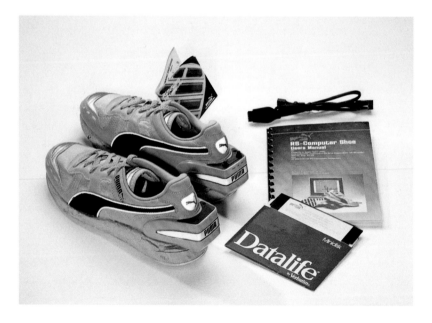

Peter Cavanaugh designed this sneaker with a computer chip in the heel that could record distance and time. The sneakers had a software package, program disk and connector cable that linked to a home computer for analysis. RS-Computer Shoe, American, 1986.

My oh my, don't Shakil Muhammed's shoes look fresh! Check them out as they strut along downtown Washington Street, $109 worth of suede and rubber and polyurethane and anything else that the folks at Nike Inc. care to wrap around a young man's feet. Under Muhammed's arm, inside a box inside a bag, are the $92 Nikes he was wearing 15 minutes ago. Last month's model, dude. Later.[67]

Others wrote with paternalistic concern that black youths were being duped and were in need of guidance in regard to sneaker consumption. The debate on whether or not inner-city youths should be buying expensive sneakers completely missed the point: that African American males were not so much being advertised *to* as much as they were being advertised *through*.[68] Bill Brubaker in the *Washington Post* came close when he wrote: 'The phenomenon is especially remarkable in that black inner city youths . . . set the pace and styles for an industry managed mostly by white businessmen who sell the bulk of these products to white consumers.'[69] Despite observations like this, the rhetoric around sneakers and the urban customer continued to focus on curbing black male appetite, rather than addressing the underlying social issues that made the co-option of urban culture so desirable and highly commodifiable.

The pairing of the film director Spike Lee as his character Mars Blackmon from his film *She's Gotta Have It* (1986) and Michael Jordan in a series of highly successful commercials at the end of the 1980s created intense controversy focused on the inner-city consumer. In 1990 a number of highly publicized murders perpetrated in the course of stealing sneakers prompted Phil Mushnick of the *New York Post* to blame Nike, Michael Jordan and Spike Lee for stoking desires that resulted in criminality. Incensed, Lee responded that Mushnick was being racist and ignorant of the larger social issues at work, and the debate exploded. *Sports Illustrated* fuelled the flames in their 14 May 1990 issue, which featured an illustration on the cover of a pair of sneakers and a young black man's hand holding a gun to the back of an unidentified victim. The accompanying article focused on the fantasy-fueled market for luxury items in the economically blasted inner cities willingly tapping into the flow of drug and gang money. This has led to a frightening outbreak of crimes among poor black kids trying to make their mark by 'busting fresh,' or dressing at the height of fashion.[70]

In response, Ira Brekow wrote in the *New York Times* that Jordan and Lee were

> quintessential role models for inner-city youths, or for anyone else. They work. They work hard. They have attained status by developing their talents to the highest degree they could, by sweat and by brains, and they have done so within the social system, and within the laws of the land. They have kept the faith. They are champions.[71]

In September 1990, Les Payne at *Newsday* added,

> blaming Jordan, even partially, for the street murders over sneakers is like blaming Dinah Shore, who endorsed Chevrolets, for the high rate of stolen Corvettes. But it would never occur to the Mushniks of the world to blame white celebrities for crimes they think nothing of laying at the feet of their black comparables. Were it so, Mushnik or some upscale colleague would perhaps at this hour be shoving the Donald McKinsey murder story under the nose of white celebrities who have endorsed the new target of a national rash of robberies and even murders: the Rolex watch.[72]

As the relationship between sneakers, urban fashion and commercialization became increasingly problematic for the industry, another sneaker-wearing model of masculine success emerged. Along with the black athlete and rap star, the Silicon Valley wonder boy showed up as a new model of male success. Simultaneously admired, derided and feared, millionaire tech moguls wore playground attire and

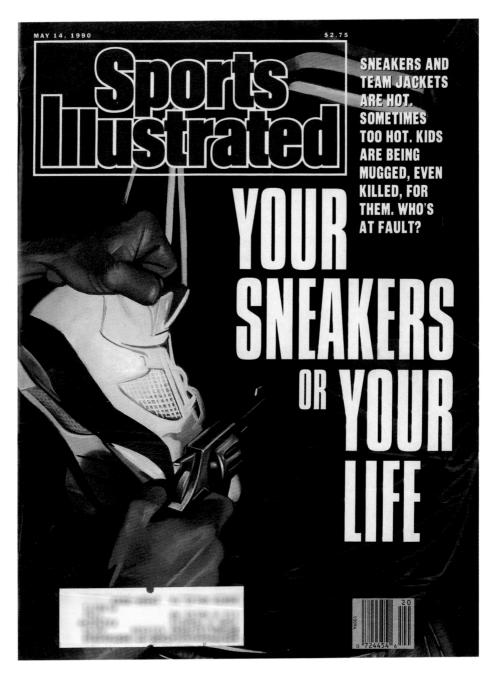

This controversial *Sports Illustrated* cover from 14 May 1990 featured a sneaker suggestive of the Air Jordan V.

sneakers into board meetings and suggested that the business brogue and the three-piece suit did not reflect the new world order. As one reporter remembered, 'In the era of 22-year-old dot-com millionaires who never had to go on an interview, let alone buy a suit for one, companies found the idea of dressing up to be somewhat dated.'[73]

As these shifts were being felt, the importance of the sneaker in the typical male wardrobe began to increase. The evolution of Casual Fridays in the late 1980s and into the 1990s was meant to relax workplace hierarchies and increase conviviality among employees, but it actually meant that men had to think more about their attire. For over a century, men in the white-collar workplace had been expected to don the uniform of the business suit. Status was expressed through expensive garments that conformed in general to a sameness of men's dress. Casual Friday, however, forced men to dip a toe into a fashion dictate traditionally directed at women: that fashion be used to express individuality. Indeed, they were being asked to reveal a little bit of their private selves, their true selves. Sneakers, which came in a variety of styles and colours reflecting a range of sports and subcultures, proved to be the perfect accessory with which to project individual identity. Even more importantly, the use of sneakers countered the potentially feminizing associations of fashion consumption by reaffirming rather than threatening masculinity through sneakers' long-standing associations with hypermasculine models of success, be it athlete, gangster or geek.

In contrast, for women, sneakers in relation to white-collar work attire drew derision. The pairing of women's business suits and sneakers was not greeted with enthusiasm. Throughout the 1980s, women in sneakers and suits were ridiculed in media from newspaper articles to *The Yuppie Handbook* (1984), which mocked nouveau riche privilege and featured a suited woman in Nike running shoes on the cover. In the effort to negotiate the predominately male white-collar workplace, women in the 1980s were encouraged to reference traditional men's business attire in their dress but with a feminine twist, such as by pairing broad-shouldered blazers with skirts and low-heeled pumps. Obviously, pumps were not as practical as business brogues, and women frequently carried their heels and wore running shoes or aerobic sneakers to and from the office. This use of sneakers underlined the fact that the women held positions for which they had to leave home and commute, an activity laden with socioeconomic implications. Many agreed with the author of the article 'Dress for Success in Sneakers? Not Her':

> The latest item to hit the streets leaves me cringing in disbelief ... No, I'm not referring to shoes appropriately 'teamed' with sweat socks and jogging shorts for a swift run around the track. These are the ones paired with stockings, business suits and tailored shirts for a brisk trot to the office.[74]

Whatever appeal sneakers may have held in the gym – and it should be acknowledged that the most fashionable gym activity, aerobics, was often done barefoot or in legwarmers pushed down over sneakers – was apparently not transferable into women's workaday world.

Although sneakers were gaining traction in women's fashion, for men the importance of sneakers continued to grow. With the popularization of sneaker culture, sneaker connoisseurs began to search for rare and forgotten models, setting the stage for the eager consumption of dead stock via online vendors such as eBay at the end of the century. The increasing appetite for sneakers also encouraged couture fashion houses to begin to offer them. Gucci was the first, in the 1980s, followed by Prada in the 1990s. Then Adidas set the trend for designer collaborations by working with two of the industry's most avant-garde designers, Yohji Yamamoto and Jeremy Scott, in 2002. That same year, Nike collaborated with Supreme, the famous skateboard fashion brand, and in 2005 Nike turned to Jeff Ng of Staple Design in New York to create the Staples × Nike Dunk Low Pro SB 'Pigeon', the limited release of which prompted a 'sneaker riot' in 2005 and revived mainstream concerns about violence, sneaker culture and racial issues. Despite this controversy, limited-edition collaborations and the creation of high-end sneakers continued unabated as men's interest in using sneakers to diversify their vocabulary of style grew stronger. The meanings associated with sneakers and those interested in wearing them were becoming increasingly varied and participation in sneaker culture grew exponentially. In 2005, the same year that just 150 pairs of Pigeons were released worldwide, vintagekicks.com opened Flight Club, a bricks-and-mortar shop in New York, where vintage sneakers could be consigned and purchased. Interest in acquiring deadstock (sneakers forgotten in store warehouses and still in their original boxes) OG (original issue) sneakers soared. The term sneakerhead came into common parlance and by the middle of the 'noughties', sneaker magazines, books and websites attracted thousands of readers. Sneaker release parties were thronged with attendees and sneaker conventions were attracting thousands of participants worldwide. Even sneaker designers such as Nike's Tinker Hatfield were becoming household names and were part of the larger cultural trend that celebrated footwear designers such as Christian Louboutin and Manolo Blahnik.

Seizing on the public's hunger for the collectible, the scarce and the nostalgic, companies began to release retro models. The Air Jordan III, the first AJ to be designed by Tinker Hatfield, was rereleased in 1994. This was followed by many other 'retros', and soon other companies were reissuing their signature models to eager consumers who would line up or even camp overnight outside sneaker stores to ensure that they could acquire the release, often for the purpose of tapping into the lucrative resale market rather than simply to wear. Sneaker brands sought to offer consumers a 'retail experience' and sneaker stores such as London's Niketown became destinations in and of themselves. More intimate boutiques like Kith in New York and Colette in Paris also became premium footwear destinations disseminating limited editions of exclusive sneakers at exorbitant prices. Those who wanted unique footwear also sought out customization. Nike had debuted NIKEiD in 1999, which allows purchasers to individualize their sneakers, but for those seeking the truly exclusive, such globally admired artists

American designer Jeremy Scott is known for pushing boundaries. His highly controversial Adidas collaboration, the 2013 Totem collection, was criticized for cultural misappropriation. Totem, American, 2013.

as Methamphibian, Eric Haze, Sekure D and Mache transformed sneakers into wearable art.

In 2009 the rapper Kanye West worked with luxury couture house Louis Vuitton to create a number of sneakers that quickly sold out, but it was the massive hype over his work with Mark Smith at Nike to create the Nike Air Yeezy 1 in 2009 and the Yeezy 2 in 2012 that secured his own designer cred. When it was rumoured that a pair of Yeezy 2s with the suggested retail price of $250 had sold on eBay for $90,300, international prominence of both Nike and Kanye West only increased. True or not, like Michael Jordan's fines for wearing the Air Jordan 1 in 1984, better publicity could not have been purchased. As highly successful rappers morphed into businessmen in their haute couture suits and high-end sneakers, the links between traditional and new sartorial signifiers and masculine success were validated.

Since 2004, thousands of people have come to Houston for the annual H-town Sneaker Summit, the largest sneaker convention in the United States, to buy, trade and admire rare sneakers. *Crowd at the Toyota Center*, American, 23 January 2011.

Not all exclusives are put out by major brands: some of the rarest sneakers are the ones customized by artists such as Mache, whose work has garnered him an international reputation and a celebrity client list. Air Force XXV Mache Customs, American, 2012.

The connection between fashion and sneakers continued to be linked to basketball, especially after Nike brokered deals with Kobe Bryant and LeBron James. Both players were recognized for their fashion sense, but James in particular was already a style icon in his own right. He was the first African American man to feature on the cover of American *Vogue* and his sartorial choices, which frequently saw him not wearing sneakers, were often the focus of media attention. James's ease with shifting between brogues and sneakers was illustrative of the larger social trend focusing on interest in men's attire, as evidenced by this snippet from the men's fashion and lifestyle magazine *GQ*:

> The two-time NBA MVP and Olympic gold medal holder is in London to promote his new Nike range, including the Lebron 9 he's currently wearing. However in addition to his show-stopping performances on the court for Miami Heat, James is increasingly known for his off court style, from wearing custom tailoring to games to front row appearances at New York Fashion Week.[75]

Just as with rap celebrities Jay Z and Kanye West, LeBron James was central to changing the image of masculine success and its expression through the wearing and consuming of desirable sneakers.

Fabled fashion houses began to offer men's sneakers, including Lanvin, the oldest haute couture house in Paris, in 2005 and Yves Saint Laurent in 2008, the year of its retired founder's death. By the 2010s, high-fashion designer collaborations with sneaker manufacturers were becoming increasingly common. Hussein Chalayan, Alexander McQueen and Mihara Yasuhiro created designs for Puma. Raf Simons's interest in creating a 'radically different image of masculinity'[76] was tapped by Adidas, while Riccardo Tisci designed for Nike, Marc Jacobs for Vans, and Missoni collaborated with Converse.

One of the most interesting developments in sneaker culture has been the entrance of high-end designers of women's shoes into the men's sneaker market. In 2011 Christian Louboutin opened his

NBA superstar LeBron James is a style icon on and off the court, linking fashion and sneakers to the changing image of masculine success. The bold graphics and cartoon-like quality of this pair of exceptionally rare sneakers were inspired by LeBron's favourite character, Stewie, from the animated television show *Family Guy*. The shoe was never put into production and just 24 pairs were made, available only through a 'Friends and Family' promotion. Stewie Griffin LeBron VI, American, 2009.

first men's boutique and offered sneakers. In an interview with *Women's Wear Daily* Louboutin stated, 'There is a group of men that is thinking a little bit more like women . . . They treat shoes very much as objects, as collectors' items.'[77] Indeed, sneakers are inducting men into a system in which expression of individuality through fashion demands constant consumption, hypervigilance to trends and a willingness to stand out by sporting footwear not worn by others. The abandonment of the pose of indifference to fashion and dress, while possibly liberating men in terms of choice and expression of personality, brings with it obligations that can in many ways be taxing.

This use of sneakers in fashion has been predominantly for and by males. In part, women's participation has been limited by the fact that the majority of the most coveted sneakers were not made in women's sizes. This was especially ironic when the Alien Stomper, worn by Sigourney Weaver in the sci-fi film *Aliens* (1986), was re-issued by Reebok in men's sizes only. Frustrated sneakerheads such as London ad executives Emilie Riis and Emily Hodgson, who started the Purple Unicorn Planet website in 2013 to petition Nike to make some sneakers in smaller sizes, have seen some changes. Air Jordan is one of the few brands available in a range of sizes. Many classics, such as the Adidas Stan Smith and Superstar, are available in men's and women's sizes. Often, however, sneakers for women are offered in styles and colours that do not attract sneaker aficionados, as Riis and Hodgson have noted. There are women 'from all across the globe who were in search for the perfect pair that weren't pink, purple or banana yellow',[78] and female interest in sneaker culture has often been redirected to shoes that reference sneakers and yet are not sneakers. The high-heeled sneakers offered by Norma Kamali in the 1980s and Donna Karan in the 1990s, as well as the wedged sneakers designed by Isabel Marant in 2013, are part of a larger continuum dating back to the nineteenth century that has allowed women to flirt with the

This pair of gold pony-skin uppers embellished with aggressive studs was designed by Christian Louboutin. As with his women's shoes, the footwear he makes for men features a red sole. Roller-Boats, French, 2012.

sneaker game but ultimately denying their admittance in to it. Karl Lagerfeld's Chanel Spring/Summer 2015 show, which featured flat-soled sneakers of his own design, perhaps signalled a challenge to the prominence of one of the most ubiquitous symbols of femininity, the high heel, and may suggest that sneakers are becoming a staple of women's fashion.

An interesting recent twist has been men's newfound desire for sneakers created specifically for women. Céline offered a sneaker for its 2014 collection that many men wanted to wear, despite it only being available in women's sizes. And Rihanna's collection for Puma included her Puma Creeper, and although it was originally released only for women it received so much interest from men that it was rereleased in men's sizes. Men's interest in women's footwear also occurred when the phenomenal basketball player Sheryl Swoopes became the first female athlete to get her own signature shoe, in 1996. A more indicative sign that sneakers are finally integrating themselves into the female wardrobe is the increasing presence of women wearing sneakers in men's erotica. Fashions that appear in men's pornography tend to have longer staying power.

The glamorization of sneakers within both men's and women's fashion has not been without its detractors. The pejorative term 'hypebeast', used to belittle someone extremely label-conscious, also carries with it racial overtones, as many people identified as hype-beasts are Asian. Hong Kong resident Kevin Ma embraced the term in 2005 when he started his blog Hypebeast, today one of the most authoritative voices in relation to 'hyped' sneakers and brands. The short-lived 'normcore' trend, which emerged in 2014 as an antidote to brand obsession, was a move towards 'anonymous', anti-fashion fashion that took inspiration from the banal and understated. It was as part of this low-key trend that luxury brands such as Visvim and Common Projects rose to fame by crafting understated sneakers, achieving cult status. Many of the anti-hype classic sneakers, such as the Converse Jack Purcell and the Adidas Stan Smith, were revived as part of normcore. The Stan Smith had been a popular tennis shoe in the late 1970s and 1980s. Its first iteration was created for

Until recently, the most desirable sneakers have been designed by men specifically for men. The Puma Creeper designed by superstar musician Rihanna suggests that the male-centric landscape of sneaker culture may be changing. It was first offered as a woman's shoe, but was so desirable that it was later made in men's sizes. The design features the thick platform sole of a traditional 'brothel creeper' and a classic Puma upper. Germany, 2015.

the great French tennis player Robert Haillet in 1964. In keeping with the all-white rule for tennis clothes, embellishment on these sneakers was limited to Haillet's signature and a small green felt tab at the heel. Adidas's classic three stripes were rendered in perforated holes to increase air circulation. In 1971 Adidas asked tennis legend Stan Smith to endorse one of its Haillet tennis shoes, and for a brief moment in the model's evolution the sneaker featured two endorsements: Haillet's signature on the upper and Smith's portrait and signature on the tongue. By 1978, when Haillet had retired from tennis, his name was dropped from the shoe. By the 1980s the sneaker featured only Smith's image and signature, and the shoe became a classic. A few years before it was relaunched in 2014 it was withdrawn by Adidas to create desire for the shoe, and indeed it came back with a bang. *Footwear News* declared the Stan Smith the 'Shoe of the Year' in 2014 and *The Guardian* wrote that the 'Stan Smith could well be to the teenies (we still don't have an official name for 2010 onwards, do we?) what skinny jeans were to the noughties.'[79] *Business*

This pair of Visvim sneakers was designed by Hiroki Nakamura, who combines his interest in traditional footwear from around the world with the Japanese aesthetic of *wabi-sabi*, which privileges authenticity and embraces imperfection. FBT Elston, Japanese, 2010.

*Insider* even noted that the Stan Smith had been hailed the most important sneaker in the world in 2015.[80] Indeed, the sneaker was worn globally.

The global importance of sneakers, and with them hip hop-inspired fashion, brought questions of exploitation and exclusion into the discussion once more. Some saw the potential for unity across ethic divisions. Early hip hop promoter and chairman and CEO of Rush Communications, Russell Simmons, said in 1998 in an interview for *Jet* magazine that 'Hip hop has transcended beyond just music. It has become a lifestyle and/or a culture for people worldwide. Hip hop is an attitude and hip hop is a language in which a kid from Detroit can relate to a kid from Hong Kong.'[81] The global embrace of hip hop fashion, including sneakers, is also seen by some as cultural appropriation. Indeed, although African American consumers remain a principal means by which many companies establish brand authenticity, there is little diversity within the design and innovation arm of the industry.

Concerns about industry wages and labour conditions, especially in Indonesia, Vietnam and China, have also dogged sneaker companies. The gap between offshore workers' inadequate pay and the remuneration of endorsers, corporate executives and even returns to stockholders is incomprehensible to many. The working conditions of these offshore employees also shocked many consumers, representing a continuity of concerns around production extending back to the brutal conditions of rubber cultivation at the turn of the twentieth century.[82] In 2000 the National Labor Committee accused a number of sneaker producers as well as other manufacturers of engaging in 'indentured servitude and abhorrent working conditions' in China. They reported that 'Women working at a Nike contracted factory were earning roughly 25 cents an hour and being made to sleep in a small room. When they went on strike complaining of the overtime and low pay, they were all fired.'[83] In the 2000s websites and articles on where to buy 'sweatshop-free sneakers' were available online, giving consumers information about brands and their labour practices and encouraging more thoughtful consumption.

In addition to raising awareness of sneaker manufacturing processes and labour issues in Asia, many in the U.S. bemoaned the loss of manufacturing jobs in America due to sneaker production being moved to foreign countries by the end of the twentieth century (with the exception only of New Balance, which has for the most part maintained sneaker production in Massachusetts). The steady increase in the use of robots in the manufacturing of sneakers worldwide suggests that we are heading into a post-labour economy. The humorist Art Buchwald wrote a prescient article in 1983 about a sneaker manufacturer who, sick of dealing with the complications of working with humans, gleefully fires all his workers and turns to robots: 'I don't even have to worry about the robots taking coffee breaks. No Social Security, no health care payments, no pensions.' The manufacturer notes that he is making so many sneakers that he has a surplus but is unsure why he is flooded with sneakers. Buchwald suggests that 'Maybe the reason is that robots don't wear sneakers . . . This country's success was based on the fact that the people who made our products could afford to buy them. You've replaced your workers with robots and you're saving a fortune in salaries, but you're now up to your ears in sneakers.'[84] Thirty-three years after Buchwald wrote his article, Adidas announced in 2016 that it was returning to making sneakers in Germany, but this time using robots rather than human workers. Concern was immediately expressed about the million or so workers in China who would be displaced.[85] The company cited increased labour costs in China for the change, and it was noted that Nike was also moving towards a robot manufacturing model.

Environmental concerns have also plagued contemporary sneaker production. One clothing recycling company reports that an estimated twenty billion pairs of running shoes are produced annually, and that three hundred million pairs are thrown away each year.[86] Researchers at MIT in 2013 reported that the life cycle of one shoe in their study generated 30 pounds (13.5 kg) of carbon emissions. It was 'made from 26 different materials, and required 360 different steps to manufacture and assemble. Many of those units, where the shoes were produced on small machines, were powered by coal. "It's

the many small parts – the making it, the manufacturing – cutting
out the pieces, injection-molding the rubber, sewing it together"' that
create the problem, said Elsa Olivetti, one co-author of the study.[87]

Environmentalists are also concerned about toxic materials use
and manufacturing wastage related to sneaker production and consumption. The craze for light-up sneakers that swept the children's
market in the mid-1990s resulted in mercury leaking into the environment after the sneakers were discarded. LA Gear agreed to pay the
state of Minnesota $70,000 to help recycle the shoes, which were said
to have the equivalent amount of mercury in one pair as in 2,200

Sneakers and sustainability began to become a concern for environmentalists,
consumers and sneaker companies in the 1990s. Nike's Reuse-a-Shoe
programme sought to turn recycled sneakers into flooring and mats.
American, 1996.

significantly contaminated northern pike.[88] Many sneaker companies have sought to address these issues. Nike's Flyknit construction was created in part to reduce material wastage, as 'the one-piece upper does not use the multiple materials and material cuts used in traditional sports footwear manufacture.'[89] Adidas partnered with the organization Parley for the Oceans to create prototype running shoes using fibres made from recycled ocean-polluting plastics, including illegal gill nets.

Where sneakers may be leading the way is through their increasing ability to be customized. It is a trend that suggests a post-industrial future in which the bespoke aspects of pre-industrial footwear production are revived and footwear is once again made at the request of the customer to his or her specifications. 3D printing, flyknit technology, and colour customizations stand at the brink of providing customers with the most exclusive form of footwear, made-to-order and made-to-measure.

The desire for the new and novel has inspired sneaker innovation since the moment rubber first became of serious interest in the West, and remains a driving force in sneaker consumption. Interest in proclaiming one's privilege likewise continues to inform sneaker culture, as it did in the nineteenth century. The sneaker's intimate connection to athleticism also remains important, although its ever-increasing consumption as an item of fashion, especially in men's dress, reflects profound social shifts. This interest in sneaker-driven sartorial expression has encouraged men to participate in the fashion system in new ways. The widespread interest in urban men's fashion allows for greater expressions of individualism and challenges or reinterprets traditional notions of masculinity – in particular of what masculine success now looks like. The increasingly complex nexus between individuals and sneaker brands is expanding the vocabulary of style and making sneakers one of the most culturally important forms of footwear at the moment.

In 2015, Adidas collaborated with Parley for the Oceans, an organization dedicated to raising awareness about the state of the world's oceans, to work with designer Alexander Taylor on creating sneakers that made use of plastic ocean waste. The resulting prototype was made using filaments from illegal deep-sea gill nets collected off the coast of West Africa. German, 2015.

# Conclusion

# GRANDS MAGASINS DU LOUVRE

PARIS — Les plus vastes du Monde — PARIS

## COMPTOIR SPÉCIAL DE CHAUSSURES POUR DAMES ET ENFANTS

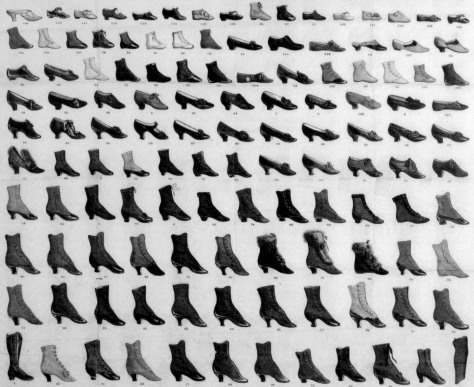

The family of mankind, ever growing and increasing, with its varied wants, its constant changes of fortune and alterations in its tastes, its coquetry, and its caprice, will find for the industry of the world quite enough to keep it employed.

'Vulcanization of India Rubber', *Mechanics Magazine*, 1856

Let's face it, no matter how much heat we have in our closets, we can only stunt one sneaker at a time. But now there's a solution to this 'problem.' . . . tiny rubberized sneaker keychains perfect for everyday flexing . . . Granted, they aren't as good as the real thing. But still, it's a fun, affordable way to show you're a diehard sneakerhead.

Rajah Allery, 'These Keychains are the Closest You'll Get to Owning Some of Your Grails', 29 June 2015

In the late twentieth century, interest in shoes had come to be seen by many as an expression of femininity verging on a biological need. As one reporter among many put it, 'women need no explanations. They simply accept the shoe thing as a force of female nature, a strappy leather siren's song, an attraction as irresistible and intoxicating as sea air to a sailor.'[1] Yet the phenomenon was not limited to women; many men too became increasingly obsessed with footwear, especially sneakers. Indeed, by the turn of the twenty-first century, footwear had become a cultural focus with the power to convey significant social meanings. The flip-flop sandal signalled summer holidays and leisure; the boot suggested hardworking a thenticity or ominous domination. The high heel was a metonym for femininity, its image clearly demarcating a public toilet door as the 'women's room' or linking readers to the 'women's section' of online newspapers, and the sneaker represented sports and urban culture. Moreover, specific brands from Blahnik to Birkenstock were used to create highly legible punctuations to sartorial statements and in turn became part of consumers' constructions of their own 'personal brands'. In this way,

Industrialization brought myriad styles of footwear into the reach of many by the end of the 19th century, as can be seen in this selection of women's and children's footwear. *Grands Magasins du Louvre*, 1875–90.

a necklace featuring a charm in the shape of a high heel might be worn to proclaim sexualized femininity, while the brand of high heels donned might be used to convey socioeconomic standing. These layered meanings embodied in the immense variety of footwear and shoe-related commodities was only made possible because of industrialization.

Although there had long been shoemakers who made shoes on spec for the general public without a guarantee of sales – the sale of ready-made footwear had dramatically increased over the course of the eighteenth century – the majority of shoes in the early years of the nineteenth century were still made to the specifications of the individual consumer.[2] Bespoke footwear involved input from the customer, including a discussion of which style of footwear was to be made as well as the material to be used, which was often supplied by the client directly. This relationship between maker and consumer was in effect collaborative and the final product was a unique reflection of both producer and consumer.

This pair of 18th-century shoes was preserved with a large piece of silk brocade, indicating that they were probably made from dressmaking remnants. The shoemaker who crafted this pair carefully positioned the brocaded motifs to produce a design of engaging asymmetric balance. English, 1730–50.

In many ways, the traditional shoemaker's shop was a micro-manufacturing enterprise. The tasks required to make a pair of shoes were apportioned among the people in the shop: the sewing of the uppers of textile might be done by the shoemaker's wife, the lasting might be given to a journeyman, the sewing of the sole to the insole the responsibility of the master. In Europe, shoemakers were tradition-ally part of the guild system and thus had laboured for centuries under a kind of protectionism and oversight that sought the best interests of the industry, offering both assistance and discipline to individual shoemakers. Production levels were modest compared to current concepts of fast fashion; experienced shoemakers could produce approximately two pairs of shoes or one pair of boots a day. In general, the constant need for footwear kept shoemakers employed and while it was not a profession that led to riches it allowed for a steady income and a respectable social standing. It was not until the middle of the eighteenth century that some shoemakers began to institute a nas-cent assembly line process in which each individual in a workshop

This print depicts a busy shoemaker's establishment; completed shoes and boots have been placed in the window as an enticement to customers. German, 1845.

specialized in only one aspect of shoemaking. As production capabilities increased, larger quantities of shoes were no longer custom-made for specific clients, yet the majority were also not being made on spec for the local market. Instead, many shoemakers began making footwear specifically for middlemen, called jobbers, who provided the materials to make the shoes that would then be sold to retailers, often in urban centres. Concern for quality control and efforts to limit wastage paved the way for some of these middlemen to seek greater control over the means of production, with many becoming shoe manufacturers in the next century. Wars in both Europe and the colonies, that were soon to become the United States, drove cost-cutting and time-saving innovations, including the further division of labour.

(*above*) In the 19th century, as some shoemakers expanded their production, the sewing and embellishment of uppers was sent out to independent seamstresses who did piecework at home. Charles Philippon, *La Laboreuse cordonnière*, c. 1830s.

(*right*) Just as shoemaking was being transformed by industrialization, genteel women began to make elaborate needlework uppers that were made into slippers for their husbands. This pair of Berlin work slippers features extremely fine pegging on the sole that would have been done by a professional shoemaker. English, c. 1860s.

At the dawn of the nineteenth century, hide cutting, or clicking, was carefully overseen to ensure minimal loss, while binding, or the sewing together of the component parts of an upper, was farmed out as piecework to be completed by women working at home. Completed uppers were then sent to shoemakers along with rough-cut soles to be lasted and bottomed, meaning the adding of the soles. Innovations in manufacturing technology sped up the process further. The pegging machine was designed to 'peg' soles to shoes using wooden pegs, thereby relieving the shoemaker from sewing the sole to the shoe. The sole cutter, invented in 1844, standardized the sizes and shapes of soles, and the rolling machine invented the following year compressed the fibres of sole leather with powerful rollers, thus relieving shoemakers of the task of pounding leather. 'But the crowning invention which has supplemented and given practical value to all other kinds of machinery in the manufacture of boots and shoes is the Sewing Machine,'[3] declared James Madison Edmunds, writing on manufacturing in the United States for the government in 1865. He continued,

> Its use has introduced a new era in the trade. Without it the partial use of machinery upon the bottoms of boots and shoes was attended with little economy, because the cost of stitching and binding the uppers, which was the larger item of expense, was not reduced in the corresponding degree. Although of quite recent introduction in this branch of industry, its employment, along with the sole-cutting machine, and other appliances, is gradually bringing about a silent revolution in the boot and shoe manufacture, this is daily assuming the characteristics of a factory system, being conducted in large establishments of several stories, each floor devoted to a separate part of the work, the aid of steam-power, and all the labor-saving contrivances known to the trade. It is safe to predict that this change will go on until the little 'workshop' of the shoemaker, with its 'bench' and 'kit,' shall become a thing of the past, as the 'handcard' and the great and little 'spinning wheel' have disappeared from the other branches of the clothing manufacture.[4]

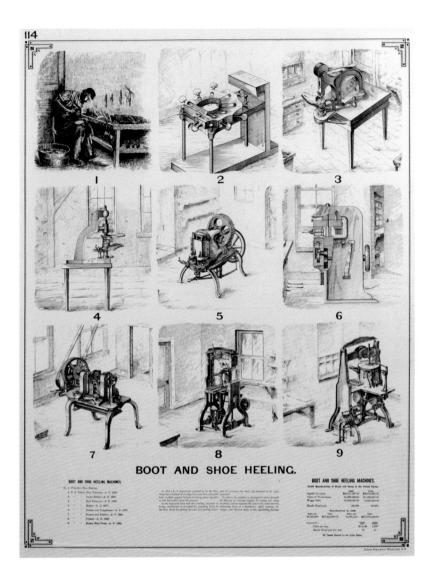

**BOOT AND SHOE HEELING.**

The industrialization that Edmunds championed had created frustration among shoe industry workers, who feared mechanization and its concomitant wage losses. This distress, combined with a depressed economy, reached a boiling point in the U.S. in 1860 among 3,000 shoemaker members of the Mechanics Association in Lynn,

Industrialization transformed shoe production as machine after machine was invented to replace skilled labour. *Boot and Shoe Heeling*, 1885.

Massachusetts, who called the largest strike in the United States before the Civil War. Howard Zinn, reporting, wrote:

> The economic crisis of 1857 brought the shoe business to a halt, and the workers of Lynn lost their jobs . . . When the manufacturers refused to meet with their committees, the workers called a strike for Washington's Birthday. That morning 3,000 shoemakers met in the Lyceum Hall in Lynn . . . In a week, strikes had begun in all the shoe towns of New England, with Mechanics Associations in twenty-five towns and twenty thousand shoe workers on strike.[5]

Despite these labour disruptions, the industrialization of footwear production continued unabated. The American Civil War, which broke out in 1861, pushed mechanization and step by step all aspects of shoemaking were mechanized. The invention in 1869 of the Goodyear welting machine made one of the most complicated construction techniques used in the making of high-quality shoes – welted construction – mass-producible.[6] The one aspect

As the industrialization of footwear increased production, some foresaw an almost unimaginably widespread availability of footwear, as illustrated in this trade card. American, c. 1870s.

of shoemaking thought to be safe from mechanization was lasting, which is when the upper is stretched over a shoe last and the sole is attached. Yet this too became mechanized when Jan Ernst Matzeliger, an immigrant to the U.S. from Dutch Guiana, received a patent in 1883 for a machine that allowed operators to last between three hundred and seven hundred pairs of shoes a day, compared to the fifty pairs hand-lasters could make. Matzeliger's invention, complained the hand-lasters, sounded as if it was taunting them, singing 'I've got your job, I've got your job' as it worked.[7] By the end of the nineteenth century, Edmunds's prediction had come true. The bespoke shoemaker had all but disappeared throughout North America; the wage-earning shoe-factory worker had replaced him in both the United States and in many parts of Europe, and production soared.

Concomitant with industrialization came mass-media advertising and branding. As customers lost personal contact with the makers of their footwear and as competition for consumers' attention grew stronger, advertisements and brand identity became increasingly important. Shoemakers had put labels in their shoes since the

This label from a late 18th-century shoe identifies its maker as Jonas S. Bass. The pair may have been bespoke but more likely was sold on spec. American, 1790s.

eighteenth century as a means of identifying who had made them, but it was shoe manufacturers who would now attempt to promote themselves through widespread marketing. Fairs or exhibitions of industry became one means of being seen and standing out. The Great Exhibition held in London in 1851, by far the largest and the most international industrial fair to that date, spoke to the global potential for industry. 'It is impossible to doubt that this great Exhibition gave a most powerful impulse to commerce and the industrial arts all the world over,' waxed T. S. Taylor as he recounted its impact.[8]

The awards won at industrial fairs had lasting effects on producers. François Pinet's hand-sewn footwear, for example, included the stamp of the Exposition Universelle in Paris from 1867, identifying the firm as an award-winner, and the stamp was used well into the early twentieth century to help customers differentiate between the company's finer offerings and their more affordable machine-sewn shoes. The fairs also highlighted to manufacturers the potential to reach global markets as industrialization dramatically increased and production began outstripping the capacities of domestic markets. With no awareness that globalization would eventually lead to their own demise, shoe manufactures in Europe and America only saw opportunity in foreign markets. Reporting in 1893, the *Shoe and Leather Reporter* commented that:

> if all the people in the world wore shoes to half the extent we do . . . the consumption would be immeasurably larger than it is now. It is a natural bent of exporters to throw all the temptations in the way of consumers abroad, that their ingenuity can conceive of and in that way augment the sales of their products . . . It is the way in which markets for all commodities are widened and shoes are articles with which persons who have once worn them will never do without afterword.[9]

While dreams of foreign markets gave producers hope, competition for customers domestically became increasingly competitive as production levels reached new highs. The ever-increasing availability

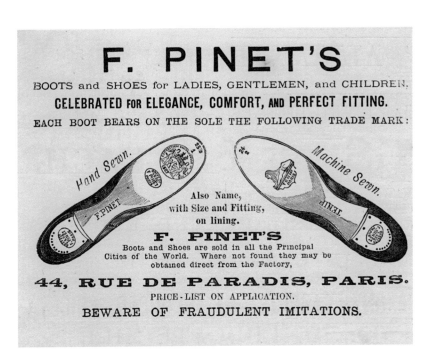

of shoes in domestic markets encouraged, or, more accurately, demanded, that manufacturers differentiate their products from their competitors'. As a result, branding became a necessity and selling became an art. Wholesalers, like earlier jobbers, were essential to getting shoes to retailers, but salesmen within retail establish-ments were becoming of particular importance. These workers, especially those in the newly developed department stores, where myriad goods from multiple makers were sold under one roof, were central to making a sale. They were responsible for assisting customers by providing advice concerning fit as well as guidance regarding the multiple brands and styles on offer, while simultaneously promoting the overarching brand of the establishment for which they worked. Many consumers needed assistance. Mass production meant fit was less individualized and salesmen were expected to provide advice that verged on the medical, taking into account all their customers' chiropodial complaints. Mass production had also confused the formerly clear demarcations between rich and poor in relation to footwear fashions.

Advert for Pinet shoes touting the differences between their two lines of shoes. French, late 19th century.

Consistency of product and the use of machine embroidery as well as embellishments such as tassels, bows and shiny buttons added just the right amount of glamour to even lower-priced footwear. As more and more people sought to consume ready-made fashionable footwear, socioeconomic difference became expressed through brand choice, and brand awareness was increased through a range of initiatives. Illustrated advertisements began to be placed in newspapers and periodicals, while trade cards featuring pictures of shoes were popular giveaways, as were small functional items such as button hooks and shoe horns.

Shoe-themed gifts, however, were not limited to shoe manufacturers. Footwear-inspired collectibles also became increasingly common as the nineteenth century progressed, reflecting the growing importance of footwear culturally. Greeting cards featuring illustrations of women's footwear were popular. Women's boot-shaped 'whimsies' made by Haudenosaunee (Six Nations Iroquois) seamstresses for sale at tourist destinations such as Niagara Falls did a brisk business, as did small ceramic or glass sculptures of women's high-heeled shoes which the invention of pressed glass in the mid-nineteenth century made particularly inexpensive. High-heel shaped pin cushions in silver or pewter were also common gifts.

(*above*) Stylish footwear became objects of desire at the new temples of consumption – the department stores – that sprang up in the second half of the 19th century. Mass production made a wide variety of fashionable footwear, such as these L. P. Perchellet boots, available to women at many different price points. French, 1875.

(*opposite left*) The sentiment conveyed by the forget-me-not flowers on this late 19th-century Christmas card is clear but the use of the single woman's shoe is more perplexing. American, 1895–1905.

(*opposite right*) 'Whimsies' were made by Six Nations Iroquois women and sold at tourist sites such as Niagara Falls. One of the most popular types were shaped like fashionable women's boots. Haudenosaunee, late 19th century.

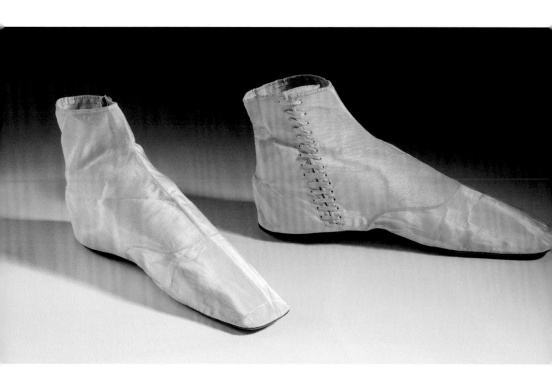

Actual footwear was also increasingly collected. The poet Johann Wolfgang von Goethe famously asked his mistress to send him a pair of her slippers to hold close. Likewise, a pair of boots worn by Empress Elisabeth of Austria was given to Colonel Louis de Schweiger, one of the countless men who had fallen under her spell, as a 'tendre souvenir' in the 1850s.[10] The footwear of famous people was also preserved, for less intimate reasons. In 1904 an article on various collections discussed one that included shoes worn by notables such as Queen Victoria and a pair of slippers said to have belonged to Madame de Pompadour.[11] Footwear was also collected when people travelled the world. Shoes had long been used as evidence of cultural difference. The frontispiece of the publication *Museum Wormianum* (1654), about Ole Worm's cabinet of curiosities, depicts a pair of heeled Central Asian boots hanging on the wall, and Sir Hans Sloane collected footwear from around the world in the middle of the

This pair of narrow boots belonged to Empress Elisabeth of Austria and was gifted to Colonel Louis de Schweiger. Austrian, 1850s.

eighteenth century, which is today housed in the British Museum. The collection and study of footwear would continue in the twentieth century with the establishment of the Northampton Shoe Museum at the Northampton Museum and Art Gallery, followed by the Musée International de la Chaussure in France, the Nederlands Leder en Schoenenmuseum in the Netherlands, the Deutsches Ledermuseum in Germany, the Museo Salvatore Ferragamo in Italy and the Bata Shoe Museum in Canada. As travel opened up in the nineteenth century, increasing numbers of people returned from exotic locations with examples of local shoes, among the most evocative mementos of the exotic being the tiny Han Chinese shoes for bound feet, many of which were made specially to meet the tourists' desires.

By the turn of the twentieth century, shoes and shoe-like ephemera were clearly capable of conveying a wide range of social information about individuals, as well as cultures and societies in general. This increased interest in footwear, combined with the death of

This pair of *gin lian* for bound feet measures only 11.5 cm (4.5 in.) in length. Probably made by a young bride, the symbolism on the shoes speaks to dreams of love and happiness. Han Chinese, 1875–95.

hand-shoemaking as a craft, made exquisite footwear collectible and gave birth to the shoemaker as artist. As *Vogue* wrote in 1920,

> It is when the soul-less machine takes the place of the craftsman, and the manufactured product begins to be advertised as any other unromantic commodity, that shoemaking becomes only a business proposition and the shoemaker degenerates from a philosophising master-workman to the puncher of the time clock.[12]

High-priced footwear by manufacturers such as François Pinet and Hellstern & Sons met the needs of many elite customers at the end of the nineteenth century, but the dream of owning luxury footwear made by a shoemaker deemed both a genius and an artist was embodied in the work of the Italian shoemaker Pietro Yantorny. In 1908 he set up shop in Paris's Place Vendôme and famously hung a sign reading, 'Most Expensive Shoemaker in the World' in his window. Like being dressed by the couturier Charles Frederick Worth, those who wished to be shod by Yantorny had to submit to his wishes. He was temperamental, eccentric and a strict vegetarian. The daughter of a client remembered years later that while visiting the shoemaker with her mother she had to eat gritty health bread that he had made himself from seeds he had sown by moonlight.[13] He was also demanding, requiring a significant downpayment of $1,000 for a client's first order, but later charging up to $5,000.[14] Yantorny took years to finish his orders and clients were allowed no input – only the wealthiest and most patient of women could own his shoes. As *Vogue* noted in 1915, 'Yantorny, in his "sky parlor" overlooking the place Vendôme, is intent on fashioning footwear which, from the price, might be studded with pearls and diamonds. His footgear is so highly specialized that one cannot say that he favors this or that particular shape or heel.'[15] Those who owned his shoes prized them. The famous American socialite Rita de Acosta Lydig kept the numerous pairs that she commissioned in shoe trunks specially made by Yantorny 'to the exact measure of the shoes which are to be encased in them'.[16] Her Yantorny trunks

This Yantorny shoe was made bespoke for a wealthy French customer in the late 1910s or early '20s. As with all Yantorny shoes, this pair came with beautifully crafted shoe-trees. French, late 1910s.

and shoes are now in the Metropolitan Museum of Art. Lucy, Lady Duff-Gordon, the famous fashion designer who designed under the name Lucile, wrote to her sister of being happy that although she had lost a treasured fur coat when the *Titanic* sank, she had been able to wear a pair of Yantorny mules into the lifeboat.[17] *Vogue* included a similar story in an article on Yantorny in 1920, claiming that in 1918 the glamorous Elsie de Wolfe, fleeing the approaching German Army, chose her Yantornys as her most valuable treasure as she escaped from Compiègne.[18] The magazine also reported on a visit to a 'most artistic élégante', who allowed a look into her shoe closet. 'A very spacious closet it was this, all shelves and with walls entirely covered in white satin. On the shelves, hundreds of the most beautiful Yantorny shoes

This advertisement is from the early years of the Keds brand which was established in 1916. American, 1919.

were aligned, tier above tier . . . all were beautiful, all works of art.'[19] Indeed, one of Yantorny's wishes was that his shoes, such as the pair made using the throat feathers of a hummingbird, currently held in the Musée International de la Chaussure, would someday be kept in a museum collection.

Although few could afford such exclusive shoes, many people sought out known footwear brands that aligned with either their class or their social aspirations. Some of these brands wove themselves into the fabric of popular culture. The famous comic strip characters Buster Brown, his dog Tige and his little sister Mary Jane were purchased from the cartoonist Richard F. Outcault in 1904 to promote Brown's children's shoes. This marketing was extremely successful; the characters became American icons and instep-strap shoes began to be known as Mary Janes, a term still in use today. Other companies, such as Keds and Converse, which debuted during the First World War, in 1916 and 1917 respectively, went on to become enduring American brands.

The post-war period also saw an increase in footwear production, particularly in the United States, and manufacturers pushed the idea of multiple types of shoes being required in the female wardrobe: 'Manufacturers again recommend that dealers promote the idea of shoes for the occasion. They are now making the style so distinctly and the walking shoe is so decidedly a walking shoe that it is out of place when worn on any other occasions.'[20] With shoes no longer hidden beneath voluminous skirts, they promised to become significant fashion accessories and manufacturers and shoe retailers promoted the importance of appropriate footwear through events such as 'pretty foot contests', in which the most beautifully shod were awarded with fleeting fame and new shoes. As if in collusion with the industry, newspaper articles warned women of the potential missteps of being seen wearing the wrong shoes at the wrong time. One fashion writer cautioned,

> If a patent leather shoe is worn in the morning, it should be of the tailored variety and the heel a low Louis or military.

Well known merchants, fashion writers and clever salesmen have stressed the poor taste of the satin pumps until, say, after 4 o'clock in the afternoon; but for some unexplainable reason women continue to wear satin pump slippers in the morning, and sad to relate often with strictly tailored suits.[21]

By the 1920s, a well-dressed woman was expected to have a wide variety of footwear to meet the needs represented by the range of activities that comprised her day. Boudoir slippers, dancing shoes, tennis shoes, evening shoes and walking shoes – all would now be deemed appropriate for the well-appointed closet, and with this increased consumption came the flaunting of such excess. Louis Vuitton shoe trunks were designed to hold thirty pairs of shoes and declared the extensive shoe wardrobe of the traveller, while increasingly starlets were photographed surrounded by the dozens of pairs that comprised their shoe wardrobes.

Following the war, shoe designers as opposed to shoemakers emerged and came to be revered as creative geniuses. Shoes by these exalted creators were sold in sumptuous shoe salons. In 1926 New York purveyor Israel Miller had one of the most luxurious of these, on the corner of 46th and Broadway, in which he sold shoes designed by fêted makers such as André Perugia, whose artistry was promoted in *Vogue* and other high-fashion publications. In the 1920s, Perugia, who first collaborated with Paul Poiret, a couturier who thought of himself as an artist, engaged with footwear design as if he were a sculptor. Unsurprisingly, Perugia later collaborated with Elsa Schiaparelli, the fashion designer who in the following decade became closely aligned with the art world through Surrealist creations that blurred the lines between fashion and art. One of the most famous was her shoe hat with its red sole, a prescient affair that presaged the work of Christian Louboutin.

A 'well-heeled' woman in the 1920s required myriad types of footwear, from athletic shoes to evening high heels. For women who could afford the luxury of leisure travel, a well-appointed Louis Vuitton shoe trunk with discreet compartments for thirty pairs of shoes was the means of travelling in style. French, 1920s.

Despite the increasing numbers of shoes in many women's wardrobes in the 1920s, shoe manufactures were dissatisfied with the volume of their sales and sought also to stimulate men's interest. To this end the National Shoe Retailers Association voted in 1927 to dedicate $4 million 'to induce men to buy shoes', but the efforts failed.[22]

During the Great Depression the footwear industry fared better than many others. Increased financial woes actually amplified the importance of footwear in women's fashion, as donning a pair of visually striking shoes did more to transform an outfit than any other accessory of the day. Clinton W. Bennett, in an article on the shoe industry for the National Association of Cost Accountants in 1934, wrote that, 'During the current, well-advertised depression, the shoe industry has been, in at least one respect, singularly fortunate in that it has enjoyed a splendid volume of business.'[23] Despite the high turnover in women's footwear, men's shoe sales continued to lag even after women's platforms had begun to exert some influence on men's footwear design. 'The interest in women's platform shoes has developed a corresponding interest in heavy soled shoes for men in leather, crêpe rubber and sport type uppers,' the *New York Times* reported at the end of the 1930s.[24] Indeed, men's footwear was offered in greater diversity than in the previous decade, with spectator shoes complementing the traditional business brogue and casual sneaker, but efforts to encourage consumption did little to spur sales. Perhaps the greatest boon to the price-conscious consumer was the ever-increasing importation of footwear from abroad. As American shoe manufactures noted with distress, American machines and production methods were being exported to other countries whose labour costs were negligible, giving the shoes they exported to the U.S. a price tag that no American manufacturer could meet. These inexpensive imported shoes, particularly sneakers, were extremely attractive to the financially strapped buyer and flooded in from Japan and Czechoslovakia. The threat to the health of the U.S. shoe-making industry was real and would result in the domestic industry's collapse by the end of the century.

This pair of shoes dates to the early 1920s and shows the influence of Paul Poiret's aesthetic on André Perugia. The gilt kid roses appliquéd on the uppers and the small rose-shaped gold buttons used to secure the T-straps are clear quotes from Poiret's designs. French, 1923–6.

During the Second World War, women's footwear consumption was central to keeping the domestic shoe industry alive. Although shoe rationing and consumer restraint made durable and practical shoes the most commonly purchased types, retailers advocated the continued promotion of multiple styles of shoes to the female customer. The *Boot and Shoe Recorder* of 17 January 1942 reported:

> For off-duty hours there are plenty of colourful, exotic styles... Some are on very high heels with thick clog soles and are exotic and extravagant looking. We advise you not to miss including at least a few pairs of these shoes. They may look like a lot of foolishness to you, but you'd be surprised how many, even so-called very sensible women, like a thoroughly frivolous shoe now and then.[25]

Having adequate footwear became an increasing issue as the war raged on, but it was the piles of shoes left behind by the victims of the unimaginable horrors unfolding in Europe that helped bring the scale of the atrocities being committed into perspective. Bill Lawrence, writing for the *New York Times* in 1944, described the shoes left in just one German concentration camp:

> But I have been in a wooden warehouse at the camp, approximately 150 feet long, in which I walked across literally tens of thousands of shoes spread across the floor like grain in a half-filled elevator. There I saw shoes of children as young as 1 year old. There were shoes of young and old men or women. Those I saw were all in bad shape – since the Germans used this camp not only to exterminate their victims, but also as means of obtaining clothing for the German people – but some obviously had been quite expensive. At least one pair had come from America, for it bore a stamp, 'Goodyear welt.'[26]

Despite the long tradition of using empty shoes to convey a sense of loss, from caparisoned horses carrying the deceased's boots backwards in the stirrups to sentiments such as someone's shoes being hard to fill, the shock conveyed by the seemingly endless multitudes of shoes once worn by the victims of the Holocaust went on to inspire memorials after the war. These included the bronze sculpture of empty shoes along the banks of the Danube honouring the 3,500 people murdered in Budapest and the shoe room at the United States Holocaust Museum. Empty shoes are also used to commemorate other deaths including recent temporary installations of shoes set up to encourage people to remember the lives lost to gun violence in the twenty-first century. As Jonathan Frater wrote in 2011:

> Shoes are intensely personal items that we use to define ourselves as people ... is there any item of human manufacture that speaks to civilization and our place in it more than footwear? We discard shoes only when we've destroyed them. Or, in this case, destroyed the people in them.[27]

The post-war era saw increased shoe consumption. Owning multiple pairs of shoes was slowly becoming standard regardless of gender and even across socioeconomic ranges. Hush Puppies, desert boots, motorcycle boots and sneakers formed part of the male wardrobe while stilettos, sandals and ballet flats were central to women's fashion. The way shoes were acquired was also rapidly changing. The opening of Pay-Less National in Topeka, Kansas, in 1956 signalled the new direction. Louis and Shaol Pozez, two enterprising cousins, opened Pay-Less stores in converted super-markets. They offered a no-frills, self-service shopping experience and ultra-low-priced footwear. Their success signalled the death of the salesman. No longer would the shoe salesman mediate between the customer and the product. Instead, branding and advertising would have to bear the weight of convincing potential buyers. In light of this, national brands and 'genius' shoe designers became increasingly popular.

In the 1960s, growth in the domestic shoemaking industries in the U.S. and UK decreased even further, despite an increase in footwear consumption. Many international trade negotiations sought to reduce imports but the tide could not be stemmed. The one bright spot seemed to be the booming and consuming youth demographic, but these young customers did not show a preference for domestically made shoes – style made the sale. The popularity of the German brands Adidas and Puma, which were first introduced into the American market in the late 1960s, was evidence of this and highlighted the increasing importance of branding. The Japanese sneaker manufacturer Onitsuka Tiger also began to make inroads into the American market through the efforts of Phil Knight, but by 1972 he and his partner Bill Bowerman had created Nike, a sneaker company that would set the example of having their footwear produced overseas, mainly in Asia, while maintaining company headquarters in the U.S., where design development and branding would be carried out. Nike as well as other sneaker manufacturers declined to highlight the skills of their individual footwear designers as was becoming increasingly important in the sale of women's high-end footwear, but rather turned to celebrity athletes for endorsements. This linking of brand identity to male athletic prowess served, in part, to make male interest in and consumption of footwear seem expressly masculine, in spite of the fact that in reality it mirrored women's.

By the mid-1980s, as the importance of sneakers increased in men's fashion, rare deadstock and hard-to-find sneakers became collectors' items and more and more companies began to vie for market share. The most successful was the Nike Air Jordan brand, which numbered each season's sneakers – Air Jordan II, Air Jordan III, Air Jordan VI – in a move that created anticipation but also fed into the collecting mindset. As sneaker collecting, particularly as an urban male activity, began to be noticed, it was often assessed with racist undertones that suggested these collectors were a bit irrational. The article 'For Joggers and Muggers, the Trendy Sneaker' written by Greg Donaldson for the *New York Times* in 1979 included an interview with an eighteen-year-old high school student from Brooklyn whose six pairs of sneakers are remarked upon with some amazement: 'I asked Rickey if it wasn't a little strange to have so many pairs of sneakers and he laughed, "Hell,

no." . . . He thought for a moment and added, "Besides, my brother Ray's got five pair of Pumas – five pair, just Pumas. Now that's crazy.'"[28]

Women's collecting likewise garnered attention. In 1986, Imelda Marcos's abandoned shoe collection numbering in the thousands of pairs captured the world's attention at the end of her husband's dictatorial reign. Michele Ingrassia, reporting for *Newsday*, wrote, 'nothing . . . better captured the world's sense of outrage over the excesses of the Marcos' regime than Imelda's 3,000 pairs of size 8½ shoes.'[29] The article goes on to puzzle about why any woman would own so many shoes. The people interviewed gave responses ranging from suggesting that Marcos must have a physiological disorder to dreaming of having such a generous collection themselves, albeit without the political baggage. The general tone, however, was that a shoe collection of such size was an indicator that the owner was a bit off-kilter. Yet the fact that some shoes had value was made clear by the auction price of $150,000 attained in 1988 for one of the

This pair of Beltrami slingbacks was owned by Imelda Marcos and probably acquired by her while she was in exile. Italian, 1980s.

Miniature sculptures of shoes were desirable collectables in the 1900s and early 2000s. Assortment of Just the Right Shoes, American, 2000s.

pairs of ruby slippers worn by Judy Garland in the film *The Wizard of Oz* (1939) – a figure topped in 2000 when the pair was sold again for $666,000.

In the late 1990s, the television show *Sex and the City* reflected the growing idea that women harboured insatiable desires for footwear. Indeed, for many women, the buying and amassing of collections of shoes had shifted from being an aberration to becoming a mainstream, even aspirational, activity. Many women proclaimed themselves shoeaholics and saw their desire as akin to an addiction. It was not just shoes that women were buying, however; sales of shoe-related items also soared. In 1997 the Metropolitan Museum of Art started to offer Christmas tree ornaments inspired by shoes in its collection. Sensing that a 'shoe thing was definitely happening,'[30] Richard Stevens, the museum's manager of three-dimensional reproductions, ordered a few ornaments and within three years the museum had sold almost 300,000, to the tune of $4.3 million, becoming the best-selling objects in the history of the museum's store.[31] In 1999, Just the Right Shoe capitalized on the trend and started offering small collectible sculptures of women's shoes. Greeting cards, napkins, necklaces and tote bags featuring illustrations of shoes became increasingly popular, and so did books that offered shoe-based eye candy.

The majority of these goods reflected the growing importance of the high heel not only as an icon of femininity, but more importantly as *the* icon of hypersexualized femininity. Even the rejection of the high heel in various countries served to reinforce ideas of its power to eroticize and its importance in the construction of Western ideals of femininity. In 1999, Sheikh Abd al-Aziz ibn Baz banned high heels in Saudi Arabia, in part on the grounds that they made women more alluring by increasing their height.[32]

Just as women's shoe collecting increased, so did men's. By the early 2000s, sneaker collecting had grown exponentially. The media also wavered between discussing such collecting as either foolish or cutting-edge, but more often than not it was contrasted with women's footwear acquisition by insinuating that men's collecting was not simply driven by desire but was often calculated to

produce a profit. Sean Conway, a sneaker collector in Annapolis, Maryland, was described as having

> devoted his life to footwear. In fact, his main source of income is buying shoes and reselling them once they have appreciated in value. Conway has so many shoes that he converted his second bedroom into a storage room. 'I love the shoes – the material, colorways and collaborations,' he said. 'Some people think I'm crazy until I show them that there are shoes that sell online for $4,000. I think of it as a collection and an investment. The shoes are always going to be collectibles.'[33]

In the same article, Vasilios Christofilakos, chairman of the Accessories Design department at the Fashion Institute of Technology in New York City, also promoted the idea that the ways men and women

An image of a jumble of fashionable shoes decorates this shirt designed for a young girl. American, 2016.

collect shoes is different: 'While women tend to go for variety in their shoe collections (picture the heels, boots, sandals, flats and more filling the closets of the notorious Imelda Marcos and the fictitious Carrie Bradshaw from *Sex and the City*), men tend to collect a certain type.'[34] This is a point affirmed by another collector:

> Those shoes those women buy have no story behind them . . . Women buying shoes and shoe collectors are much different. If I was buying Prada, Gucci and Louboutins, that would be one thing, but I'm buying Nikes and Jordans. I don't think those other shoes have a retail value.[35]

Indeed, retail value has become central to how footwear is valued. At a time of unprecedented production capacity, the rare and exclusive have come to drive fever-pitched desire. Scarcity has

Sneaker collector Rick Kosow is shown standing in his storage room surrounded by his impressive collection, which forms the core of his Sneaker Museum. American, 2015.

become a defining feature of the post-scarcity market. The most exclusive women's designer shoes have price tags in the multiple thousands, with men's high-end footwear not far behind, especially sneakers. Rare sneakers in particular have reached resale prices in the tens of thousands of dollars, reflecting their value as investment-level collectibles. Major sneaker brands have created scarcity through exclusive collaborations made available in very small quantities, first with high-end fashion designers and then with other designers, celebrities, sports figures and famous musicians. Even blue-chip artists such as Tom Sachs and Damien Hirst have done highly limited-edition sneakers with major brands, blurring the line between fashion and art. This was followed by luxury women's shoe brands getting into the sneaker market and collaborating with celebrity designers. Niche or specialist producers of hand-crafted sneakers emerged that manufactured only in small batches, in a way similar to traditional high-end women's footwear. Other brands also began to seek out trendsetters with whom to work: both Birkenstock and Dr Martens have done collaborations with other fashion houses, and even Manolo Blahnik collaborated in 2016 with the singer Rihanna – the year after she debuted a collaboration with Puma.

As brands and collaborations blossomed, the rhetoric of shoes as individualized expressions of self also pushed the customization market. It seems ironic that it would be the most industrialized of all footwear types, the sneaker, that would be the first to offer mass customization, paving the way for a reinterpretation of pre-industrialized bespoke footwear production. Many aspects of these sneakers are customizable, but model shape and branded logo remain immutable, allowing for both individualization and a retention of brand identity. Yet while the consumption of footwear may become more of a bespoke experience, the making of shoes may be transformed into a fully automated enterprise. The announcement in 2016 of Adidas's new robot-run 'Speedfactory' in Germany seemed to make Art Buchwald's 1983 vision of a robot-based production model a reality. *The Guardian*, in a report on 'sewbots' being primed to replace 90 per cent of all garment- and footwear-producing workers, noted

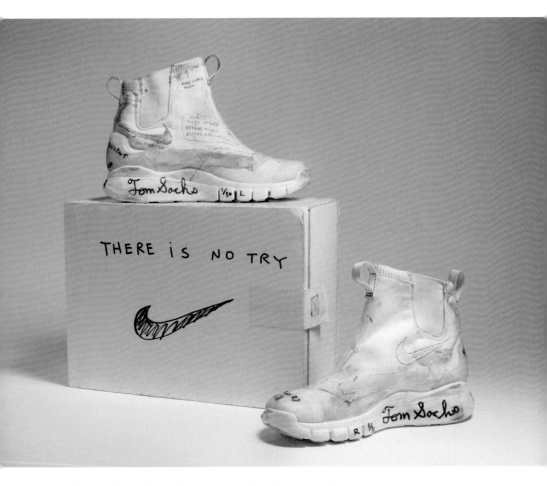

Responding to the perfected anonymity of mass-produced consumer goods, American artist Tom Sachs strives to retain the mark of the maker in his work. With these principles at the forefront of his practice, his collaboration with Nike, called NikeCraft, offered unique challenges. The moon boot was a prototype for the collection. Tom Sachs, *NikeCraft Lunar Underboot Aeroply Experimentation Research Boot Prototype*, 2008–12.

that the Speedfactory would 'employ just 160 people: one robotic production line will make soles, the other production line the upper part of shoes . . . Currently an Adidas shoe takes 18 months to produce from idea to shelf. The aim is to reduce this to five hours, with consumers able to customize their orders in stores.'[36] The most efficient production method may be 3D printing – a technology that could also allow footwear to take on new, yet to be imagined forms, leading to perhaps new social meanings.

This decentralization of labour may be one way of dealing with the long-standing abuses and abhorrent working conditions endured by many offshore workers, who have produced Western footwear for decades. Yet despite the profound need for improvements to their working conditions, the ultimate result of automation threatens unemployment on a massive scale. The increasing move towards individualization in both production and consumption reflects fundamental changes in the societies and economies in which they are embedded, and perhaps also signals changes to the meaning and function of fashion. But despite the yet unimagined technological possibilities, the paradox of personal expression being achieved through brand identification will most likely continue. The future may see us putting even greater importance on footwear, in its multiple forms, as very few elements of dress can be so easily adapted to new production methods, and are invested with so much meaning.

The Adidas Futurecraft sneaker features a 3D printed sole. The goal is to eventually offer customizable printed footwear. Futurecraft prototype, German, 2015.

# References

## I Sandals: Eccentricity

1 Fort Rock sandals are the oldest known footwear in the world, carbon dated to more than 9,000 years ago. Thomas J. Connolly, 'Fort Rock Sandals', www.oregonencyclopedia.org, accessed 23 May 2016.

2 André J. Veldmeijer and Alan J. Clapham, *Tutankhamun's Footwear: Studies of Ancient Egyptian Footwear* (Leiden, 2010). See also other research by Veldmeijer.

3 Carol van Driel-Murray, 'Vindolanda and the Dating of Roman Footwear', *Britannia*, XXXII (2001), p. 185.

4 Charles Brockden Brown, ed., 'French Private Ball', *The Literary Magazine and American Register*, II/15 (1804), p. 708.

5 Thomas Thornton, *A Sporting Tour through Various Parts of France, in the Year 1802* (London, 1804).

6 'Domestic Occurrences, Fashions for January 1810', *The Hibernia Magazine*, January 1810, p. 62.

7 This anecdote would be repeated later in the twentieth century regarding Roger Vivier. 'The London Shoemaker', *The Lady's Miscellany, or, Weekly Visitor, for the Use and Amusement of Both Sexes*, V/29 (1807), p. 227. See also J. Bell, ed., *La Belle Assemblée, or, Bell's Court and Fashionable Magazine*, II (1807), p. 56.

8 'Little Punch: Street Thoughts by a Surgeon', *Littell's Living Age*, IV/35 (1845), p. 76.

9 E. Littell, 'Minor Matters in Dress', *Littell's Living Age*, VI/60 (1845), p. 142.

10 By the end of the eighteenth century, ballet had transformed from an elegant court art to a discipline that required greater athleticism. Included among the new feats of *ballet d'action* was the ability to rise *en pointe*. The earliest reference to going up *en pointe* dates to the 1721–2 ballet season at Lincoln's Inn Fields when a Mr Sandham thrilled audiences by going up on his toes. Later in the century, another male dancer, named Antoine Pitrot, also stunned audiences with his athletic prowess and ability to rise *en pointe*. Both these dancers, however, performed their feats without the aid of specialized footwear.

11 'Fashions for the Seaside', *Warehousemen and Drapers' Trade Journal*, V (1876), p. 347.

12 Joseph F. Edwards, ed., 'Notes and Comments: Torture for Fashion', *Annals of Hygiene*, II/3 (1887), p. 108.

13 Jeffery S. Cramer, *I to Myself: An Annotated Selection from the Journal of Henry D. Thoreau* (New Haven, CT, 2007), p. 48.

14 Vi-An Nguyen, '10 Things You Didn't Know About the Statue of Liberty (She Was Almost Gold!)', www.parade.com, 2 July 2014.

15 Garance Franke-Ruta, 'When America Was Female', *The Atlantic*, 5 March 2013.

16 George Orwell, *The Road to Wigan Pier* (London, 1937), p. 121, n. 13.

17 'The Dress and Undress of the Kibbo Kift Kindred', *Costume Society News*, www.costumesociety.org.uk, 30 November 2015.

18 Edward Carpenter, 'Simplification of Life', in *England's Ideal, and Other Papers on Social Subjects* (London, 1887), p. 94.

19 Tony Brown and Thomas N. Corns, *Edward Carpenter and Late Victorian Radicalism* (Abingdon-on-Thames, Oxon, 2013), p. 157.

20 'Garden City – Within the Gates of the City of the Simple Life', *New York Times*, 6 October 1907, p. 85.

21 'Bare Legged Boy Shocks a Policeman', *New York Times*, 9 January 1910, p. 3.

22 'The Sandal Craze: A Medical Opinion on the Latest Fad', *Daily Telegraph*, 5 August 1901, p. 2.

23 'The Parisian Idea of Fashionable Footwear: Well Shod Is Well Dressed', *Saint Paul Globe*, 1 June 1902, p. 12.

24 'Sandals for Children: Present Fad in England – Americas: Children Go Barefooted', *Indianapolis Journal*, 21 July 1901, p. 20.

25 'Women Discard Stockings: Seaside Sojourners Take to Sandals or Low-cut Shoes', *New York Times*, 11 August 1912, p. C2.

26 'Sandals New Paris Fad: They Display Wearer's Bare Feet and Toe Rings Go with Them', *New York Times*, 7 April 1914, p. 1.

27 Ibid.

28 'Let's Wear Sandals', *San Jose Evening News*, 4 October 1917.

29 'Trouserless Home Greets Menalkas . . . Police Restore Isadora Duncan's Nephew to His Ancient Greek Milieu. Boy Sighs for Modernity . . . Wanted to Enjoy His New Clothes and Know at Least One Non-vegetarian Christmas', *New York Times*, 26 December 1920, p. 7.

30 His attire emulated the dress of the poorest in India and his willingness to work with leather challenged the traditional caste system, which relegated leatherwork to the lowest castes.

31 In the 1930s, lido came to be the name used for public swimming pools in the uk.

32 This preference for sandals with a soupçon of folkloric costume was matched by the interest in blouses that featured traditional Eastern European embroidery, as the traditional dress of other nations inspired fashion.

33 'Fashion: Shoes for Resorts', *Vogue*, 15 November 1926, pp. 56, 57, 174.

34 'Fashion: Pen and Snapshots from the Lido, Venice', *Vogue*, 1 October 1926, p. 74.

35 Ibid.

36 'Mere Male Kicks at Homely Dress: London Reformers Seek to Make Garb Healthy and Picturesque', *The Globe*, 13 January 1929.

37 Frank Hillary, 'Hot Weather Togas for Men Suggested by Californian: The Matter of Pockets Again Bobs Up Along with Ties and Suspenders and Somebody Pokes Fun at Mr Warner', *New York Times*, 29 July 1928.

38 'Current History in Gloves and Shoes', *Vogue*, 15 August 1931, p. 52.

39 'Shirt to Slip on for Beach Wear', *Indianapolis Star*, 8 June 1930, p. 46.

40 *Boot and Shoe Recorder*, 2 May 1931.

41 'Cool Sandals to Wear in Summer . . .', *Rochester Evening Journal and the Post Express*, 6 June 1931.

42 Carl Carmer, 'Features: American Holiday', *Vogue*, 1 July 1936, p. 48.

43 'Fashion: Autumn Shoes – A More Complicated Matter', *Vogue*, 15 September 1931, pp. 94, 95.

44 'Fashion Forecast (from Our London Correspondent)', *Sydney Morning Herald*, 18 January 1933.

45 Elsie Pierce, 'Pedicure Fad Will Reduce Foot Ills, Elsie Pierce Says', *Milwaukee Sentinel*, 18 May 1932, p. 8.

46 'Close-up of the Paris Collections', *Vogue*, 15 March 1935, p. 51.

47 'Schiaparelli among the Berber', *Vogue*, 15 August 1936, p. 44.

48 Salvatore Ferragamo, *Shoemaker of Dreams* (London, 1957), pp. 56–7.

49 Ibid.

50 For detailed information on the history of both the Spanish and Venetian chopine, see Elizabeth Semmelhack, *On a Pedestal: From Renaissance Chopines to Baroque Heels* (Toronto, 2009).

51 Ruth Matilda Anderson, 'El chapin y otros zapatos afines', *Cuadernos de la Alhambra*, 5 (1969), p. 38.

52 Elizabeth R. Duval, 'New Things in City Shops: Shoes as a Storm Center', *New York Times*, 31 March 1940, p. 53.

53 Cosmo Agnelli, *Amorevole aviso circa gli abusi delle donne vane* (Bologna, 1592).

54 'We Fear the Worst', *Pittsburgh Press*, 25 September 1948, p. 4.

55 'Spring Styles Ready for Action', *Shoe and Boot Recorder*, 17 January 1942.

56 'Popularity of "Slack Suit" Brings Mr American Around, Finally, to Becoming Stylish', *Palm Beach Post*, 14 July 1939, pp. 1, 5.

57 Orwell, *The Road to Wigan Pier*, p. 121, n. 13.

58 Ibid.

59 'Barefoot Sandals', *Vogue*, 1 December 1944, pp. 86, 87.

60 'Fashion: Looking Back at Paris Fashions, 1940–1944', *Vogue*, 1 January 1945, p. 70.

61 For more information see Elizabeth Semmelhack, *Roger Vivier: Process to Perfection* (Toronto, 2012).

62 'Fashion: Thong Sandals', *Vogue*, 15 March 1945, pp. 114, 115.

63 'Roman Sandals', *Vogue*, 1 June 1952, p. 114.

64 Rand Richards, 'North Beach: 225 Columbus Avenue – Vesuvio Café (since 1949)', *Historic Walks in San Francisco* (San Francisco, CA, 2008), p. 299.

65 'We Fear the Worst', *Pittsburgh Press*, 25 September 1948, p. 4.

66 John Cameron Swazye, 'The Historian of the Streets of Manhattan', *Toledo Blade*, 13 July 1951.

67 In Australia the rubber sandal was simply called a thong, but in New Zealand it was called a jandal, a conflation of the words Japanese and sandal, and its origins are the subject of great controversy. Morris Yock trademarked the name 'Jandal' in 1957 and was given credit for the term, but the family of John Cowie, a friend of Yock, hotly contests this, arguing that Cowie was the one to coin the term in the 1940s. Regardless of the origin of their names, rubber sandals were gaining widespread popularity at the exact moment that sandals were becoming increasingly politicized.

68 'The Jelly Shoe by Jean Dauphant AKA La Méduse', www.thehistorialist.com, 30 October 1955.

69 Marc Lacey, 'For Eritrean Guerrillas, War Was Hell (and Calluses)', *New York Times*, 2 May 2002.

70 Hunter S. Thompson, 'The "Hashbury" Is the Capital of the Hippies', *New York Times Magazine*, 14 May 1967, pp. 14ff.

71 Rebecca Mead, 'On and Off the Avenue: Sole Cycle – The Homely Birkenstock Gets a Fashion Makeover', www.newyorker.com, 23 March 2015.

72 'Exercise Sandal at Work While You Play', *Quebec Chronicle-Telegraph*, 11 May 1970, p. 4.

73 Judith Siess, 'The Sock-O Look', *Time*, CV/5 (1975), p. 72.

74 Ted Morgan, 'Little Ladies of the Night: Today's Runaway Is No Norman Rockwell Tyke. Instead, She May Well Be a 14-year-old in Hot Pants on New York's Minnesota Strip', *New York Times*, 16 November 1975, p. 273.

75 'Goodbye Boots . . . Hello Sandals', *Vogue*, 1 March 1977, p. 190.

76 John Traynor, 'Open Toes for the Open Road', *Geographical*, LXVII/2 (1995), p. 47.

77 'Take a Journey through the History of Havaianas!', www.us.havaianas.com, 29 May 2015.

78 Frankie Cadwell, 'Opinion: Don't Thank the Boss for "Casual Friday"; Men's Wear Angst', *New York Times*, 26 July 1994.

79 Ginia Bellafante, 'The Nation: Footwear Politics; Just Who, Really, Is a Birkenstock Voter?', *New York Times*, 5 October 2003.

80 Rosie Swash, '"Ugly", 50 Years Old and Stepping Right Back into Fashion: Birkenstock Orthopaedic Footwear Is Flying out of the Stores after Being a New Hit on the Catwalks', *The Observer*, 15 June 2014, p. 12.

81 Mead, 'On and Off the Avenue'.

82 Jennifer Fermino, 'That's Quite a Feet! Bam First Flip-flop President', www.nypost.com, 5 January 2011.

83 Ibid.

84 'Petty Controversy: Presidential Flip-flops!', www.nypost.com, 6 January 2011.

85 Russell Smith, 'How to Solve the Gnarly Issue of Men's Feet? Wear Shoes', *Globe and Mail*, 19 July 2008, p. L4.

86 'Minor Matters in Dress', *Littell's Living Age*, VI/62 (1845), p. 139.

87 Alana Hope Levinson, 'Why Does Society Hate Men in Flip-flops? It's Not Because Men Have Disgusting Feet', www.melmagazine.com, 6 July 2016.

88 Ian Lang, 'Pedicures for Guys: Why You Should Get a Pedicure', www.askmen.com, accessed 31 October 2016.

89 David Hayes, 'Socks and the City: The Rise of the Man-sandal', *Financial Times*, 17 August 2013, p. 4.

90 D. E. Lieberman, M. Venkadesan, W. A. Werbel et al., 'Foot Strike Patterns and Collision Forces in Habitually Barefoot versus Shod Runners', *Nature*, CDLXIII/7280 (2010), pp. 531–5.

91 Dennis Yang, 'GQ Fitness: Five-toed Shoes Are Ugly and Bad for Your Feet', www.gq.com, 14 May 2014.

92 Sean Sweeney, '5 Ways to Look Fly in Your New Slide', www.blog.champssports.com, 16 April 2015.

93 Stu Woo and Ray A. Smith, 'I'll Be Darned, Wearing Socks with Sandals Is Fashionable', www.wsj.com, 15 September 2015.

**II Boots: Inclusivity**

1 Thomas Dekker, 'Apishnesse: Or The Fift Dayes Triumph', in *The Seven Deadly Sins of London, Drawn in Seven Several Coaches, Through the Seven Several Gates of the City; Bringing the Plague with Them* (London, 1606/1879), p. 37.

2 Thomas Middleton, 'Father Hubburd's Tales 1604', quoted in John Dover Wilson, 'Dress and Fashion: The Portrait of a Dandy', in *Life in Shakespeare's England* (Cambridge, 1920), p. 127.

3 Christopher Breward, 'Men in Heels: From Power to Perversity', in *Shoes: Pleasure and Pain*, ed. Helen Persson, exh. cat., Victoria and Albert Museum, London (2015), p. 132.

4 Margarette Lincoln, *British Pirates and Society, 1680–1730* (London and New York, 2014), p. 12.

5 The boots worn by postilion riders, who rode the forwardmost horse in a team of four or more horses harnessed in tandem, had to withstand the weight of the forwardmost horses' bodies which, when colliding against each other, could crush the postilion rider's leg.

6 Georgiana Hill, *A History of English Dress from the Saxon Period to the Present Day* (New York, 1893), vol. II, p. 29.

7 Charles Dickens, ed., *Household Words: A Weekly Journal*, XI/254 (1855), p. 348.

8 Edward Dubois (pseud.), *Fashionable Biography; or, Specimens of Public Characters by a Connoisseur* (London, 1808), p. 86.

9 George Cruikshank, 'My Last Pair of Hessian Boots', in *George Cruikshank's Omnibus, Parts 1–9*, ed. Samuel Laman Blanchard (London, 1842), p. 8.

10 Robert Forby, *The Vocabulary of East Anglia*, quoted in June Swann, *Shoes* (London, 1983), p. 35.

11 See Nancy E. Rexford, *Women's Shoes in America, 1795–1930* (Kent, OH, 2000). See also Blanche E. Hazard, *The Organization of the Boot and Shoe Industry in Massachusetts Before 1875* [1921] (New York, 1969).

12 Wilma A. Dunaway, *The African-American Family in Slavery and Emancipation* (Cambridge, 2003), p. 87.

13 W. Chambers and R. Chambers, 'Things as They Are in America: Boston – Lowell', *Chamber's Journal of Popular Literature, Science and Arts*, 25 (Edinburgh, 1854), p. 394.

14 Helen Bradley Griebel, 'New Raiments of Self: African American Clothing in the Antebellum South', dissertation, University of Pennsylvania (1994), p. 239.

15 A Sufferer, 'Boot-blackmail', *Life*, VII/165 (1886), p. 117.

16 John MacGregor, Esq., 'Ragamuffins', *Ragged School Union Magazine* (London, 1866), p. 182.

17 Ibid., p. 189.

18 'Tilting Hoops', *Circular*, 2 July 1866.

19 Lola Montez, *The Arts of Beauty; or, Secrets of a Lady's Toilet* (New York, 1858), p. 70.

20 'The Footprints on the Sands', *Every Week: A Journal of Entertaining Literature*, 24 October 1888.

21 Anna Cora Mowatt Ritchie, 'Ladies' Legs', *Evening Telegraph*, 14 April 1870, p. 2.

22 Richard Krafft-Ebing, *Psychopathia Sexualis*, trans. Charles Gilbert Chaddock (Philadelphia, PA, and London, 1894), p. 126.

23 Ibid., p. 130.

24 'The Cult of the Bloomer: Demonstration at Reading', *Times of India*, 19 October 1899, p. 6.

25 Annie de Montaigu, 'The *Tête à Tête* Wheel: Fashion, Fact, and Fancy: Conducted by the Countess Annie de Montaigu', *Godey's Magazine*, CXXXII/70 (New York, 1896), p. 444.

26 James Naismith and Luther Halsey Gulick, eds, 'Cross-saddle Riding for Women', in *Physical Education* (Springfield, MA, 1892), p. 34.

27 Barbara Brackman, 'Legend Posing as History: Hyer, Justin, and the Origin of the Cowboy Boot', *Kansas History: A Journal of the Central Plains*, XVIII/1 (1995), p. 35.

28 Ibid., p. 34.

29 Winthrop, 'With the "Cowboys" in Wyoming', *Puck*, XVI/404 (New York, 1884), p. 219.

30 'William F. Cody "Buffalo Bill" (1846–1917)', www.pbs.org, accessed 28 October 2016.

31 Richard Harding Davis, 'The Germans Enter Brussels', www.gwpda.org, accessed 28 October 2016.

32 For more information see Alison Matthews David, 'War and Wellingtons: Military Footwear in the Age of Empire', in *Shoes: A History from Sandals to Sneakers*, ed. Giorgio Riello and Peter McNeil (London and New York, 2006), pp. 116–36.

33 The importance of boots is evinced in Erich Maria Remarque's novel *All Quiet on the Western Front* (1929).

34 'Saw War in the Trenches: Dutchman Horrified When Belgians Took the Boots of Dead Germans', *New York Times*, 14 November 1914, p. 2.

35 '8 Precautions against Trench Feet and Frost Bite', *Orders Sent Out to Troops of the Warwickshire Regiment, September–November 1916*, www.nationalarchives. gov.uk, accessed 28 October 2016.

36 See www.hunter-boot.com, accessed 21 June 2016.

37 'Flappers Flaunt Fads in Footwear/Unbuckled Galoshes Flop Around their Legs and Winter Sport Shoes Emphasize their Feet. Stockings Scare Dogs. Arctic Leg and Foot Equipment Has Been Adopted for Street Wear', *New York Times*, 29 January 1922.

38 'Concerning the Flapper-galosh Situation', *Life*, 16 March 1922.

39 'Go West, Young Dude, Go West: Where Ranch Life Provides New Delights in the Lines of Riding, Roping and Round-ups', *Vogue*, 15 June 1928, p. 45.

40 Ibid., p. 47.

41 Peter Stanfield, *Horse Opera: The Strange History of the 1930s Singing Cowboy* (Urbana and Chicago, IL, 2002).

42 '15,000 Nazis Defy Ban in Graz March for Seyss-Inquart', *New York Times*, 2 March 1938, p. 1.

43 'Dore Schary Finds Films Dominated by Men', *New York Times*, 31 December 1959, p. 11.

44 Chukka is a polo term for a period of play.

45 Bill Hayes, *Hell on Wheels: An Illustrated History of Outlaw Motorcycle Clubs* (Minneapolis, MN, 2014).

46 See www.chippewaboots.com, accessed June 2016.

47 While the two factions had had numerous scuffles, in 1964 over the long weekend of 18–19 May, in the seaside towns of Margate, Broadstairs and

Brighton, large numbers of mods and rockers clashed. As in Hollister, the media sensationalized the fighting, shining a spotlight on the two groups.

48 'What Are They Wearing on the West Coast in '66?', *Madera Tribune*, 15 March 1966, p. 11.

49 'Fashion in the 1960s – Decade of the Peacock Revolution', *Eugene Register-Guard*, 25 December 1969, p. D1.

50 Doug Marshall, *Ottawa Citizen*, 19 February 1964, p. 25.

51 Ibid.

52 'Fashion: Paris 1964: Vogue's First Report on the Spring Collections', *Vogue*, 1 March 1964, p. 131.

53 'Vogue's Eye View: Boots for a Heroine', *Vogue*, 1 October 1966.

54 'Dr Martens at 50: These Boots Were Made for . . . Everyone', www.theguardian.com, 31 October 2010.

55 Gloria Emerson, 'British Youth's Latest Turn: The Skinhead', *New York Times*, 16 December 1969, p. 12.

56 'Dr Martens at 50'.

57 Ibid.

58 Marian Christy, 'Leg-hugging Boots "In" for Fall', *Beaver County Times*, 17 June 1970, p. a23.

59 Ibid.

60 'Saint Laurent "Russian" Styles Have Rolled on to Victory', *Sarasota Herald-Tribune*, 6 February 1977, p. 4G.

61 William K. Stevens, 'Urban Cowboy, 1978 Style', *New York Times*, 20 June 1978, p. 1.

62 'Tailored for President?', *Washington Post and Times Herald*, 24 September 1967.

63 'Vogue's View: Well-bred Style: Designers Go Equestrian', *Vogue*, 1 November 1988.

64 'Fashion: On the Street; In Jodhpurs, Standing Out from the Herd', *New York Times*, 17 September 1989.

65 Jane L. Thompson, 'Getting the Boot and Loving It', *National Post*, 25 September 1999, p. 9.

66 Leslie Rabine, 'Fashion and the Racial Construction of Gender', in *'Culture' and the Problem of the Disciplines*, ed. John Carlos Rowe (New York, 1998), pp. 121–40.

67 George Hosker, 'Hiking Boots as High Fashion? These Days Yes', *The Telegraph*, 2 November 1993, p. 26.

68 See www.ugg.com, accessed 28 October 2016.

69 Stephanie Kang, 'Style and Substance; Uggs Again: What Last Year's "It" Gift Does for an Encore', *Wall Street Journal*, 9 December 2005.

70 Me: What's with all these scarves and yoga pants? I just don't get it. Friend: Ahhh, white girls.

Friend: They be like: 'What color uggs should I wear? Tan? Or slightly darker tan?'
71 'Dressed in Sexy Fashions, Bratz Dolls Popular with Young Girls', *Pittsburgh Post-Gazette*, 23 November 2003.

## III High Heels: Instability

1 Jeffrey A. Trachtenberg, 'Take My Advice: Book by Comic Steve Harvey Gets Boost from Radio Show', www.wsj.com, 7 February 2009.
2 For more information see Elizabeth Semmelhack, *Standing Tall: The Curious History of Men in Heels* (Toronto, 2016).
3 Florin Curta, *The Earliest Avar-age Stirrups, Or the 'Stirrup Controversy' Revisited* (Leiden, Boston, MA, and Tokyo, 2007).
4 The fact that today's cowboy boot retains the high heel is evidence of its usefulness in keeping the foot in the stirrup.
5 Semmelhack, *Standing Tall*, pp. 14–25.
6 The household accounts of Queen Elizabeth I in 1595 record the request for 'one payre of spanyshe lether shoes with highe heels and arches'. Janet Arnold, *Queen Elizabeth's Wardrobe Unlock'd* (Leeds, 1988).
7 June Swann, *Shoes* (London, 1983), p. 12. Although Swann suggests that this means that footwear was unisex, if such were the case the remark would not have called them men's shoes.
8 *Hic Mulier; or, The Man-woman: Being a Medicine to Cure the Coltish Disease of the Staggers in the Masculine-feminines of Our Times. Exprest in a briefe Declamation* (1620), www.books.google.ca, accessed 28 October 2016.
9 As items of fashion, stacked leather heels begin to show up in men's footwear by the 1620s. In contrast to self-covered heels – that is, heels of wood covered in leather – the structure of stacked leather heels remained fully visible. Stacked leather heels could be found in some Persian examples but the inspiration for this type of heel probably lay beyond Persia, reaching into places such as those areas that are now Afghanistan and Uzbekistan. In England, this type of heel seems to have been called polony, but the reasons for this have not yet been fully established; polony boot was a term used to describe knee-high boots in the mid-sixteenth century, before the introduction of the heel. Polish attire, including heels, was inspired by Persian models and featured self-covered heels, so the use of the term to describe this newer heel is of interest. Certainly, the mounted Polish hussar, like the Persian mounted warrior, garnered great respect at this time. Whatever the origin, as the century wore on, the two types of heels available to men came to express two distinct forms of masculinity, one of refined elegance and the other of action. The argument that patches added to the heel area of shoes led to the development of the heel remains unsatisfactory.

10 How red came to be favoured for heels and the origin of this fashion require more research. There was a long history of Byzantine rulers wearing red shoes and it was a fashion assumed by the papacy after the Schism of 1054 divided Christianity into Eastern Orthodox and Roman Catholic sects. The association of red footwear and the right to rule may have informed the politicization of red heels in the court of Louis XIV, but this is simply conjecture. What is known, however, is that red heels were already in fashion prior to their use by Louis XIV and that during the time of his rule, red heels became important signifiers of court privilege.

11 Sir John Suckling, 'A Ballad Upon a Wedding', www.bartleby.com, accessed 28 October 2016.

12 Charles Perrault's story 'Cinderella', which debuted in the French court in the late seventeenth century as part of his collection of moral tales, clearly articulated this new ideal. Cinderella's extraordinarily tiny feet are the physical embodiment of her natural nobility and her unyielding glass slippers transparently confirm this inborn grace and lead to her social elevation. In sharp contrast to Cinderella are her stepsisters, whose large feet signify their intrinsic lack of beauty. Perhaps the more important role they played, however, was to illustrate how fashion can be used to deceive. For the eighteenth-century audience, as well as for subsequent generations, the tale suggested that a small foot was an indicator of the wearer's natural goodness and beauty. However, in reality a small foot might be fictive, an illusion created by fashionable high heels. The high heel, like other aspects of dressy attempts to deceive, had the potential to be used as a devious contrivance that could conceal the wearer's true nature and deceive the (male) admirer.

13 John Evelyn, *The Diary of John Evelyn, 1665–1706* (New York and London, 1901).

14 Judith Drake, *An Essay in Defence of the Female Sex: In Which Are Inserted the Characters of a Pedant, a Squire, a Beau, a Vertuoso, a Poetaster, a City-critick, &c.: In a Letter to a Lady* (London, 1696), p. 68.

15 'Obituary of Remarkable Persons; with Biographical Anecdotes [January 1797]', *The Gentleman's Magazine* (London, 1797), p. 85.

16 Sir Thomas Parkins, 'Treatise on Wrestling', commenting on men's dress in 1714. As quoted in Frederick William Fairholt, *Costume in England: A History of Dress from the Earliest Period until the Close of the Eighteenth Century* (London, 1860), p. 393.

17 Despite the fact that increasing numbers of women began to participate in intellectual life, and some, like Catherine the Great, were hailed as paragons of Enlightenment virtue, these women were noted exceptions that simply proved the rule.

18 Bernard Mandeville, *The Virgin Unmasked; or, Female Dialogues, betwixt an Elderly Maiden Lady and Her Niece on Several Diverting Discourses* (London, 1724), p. 10.

19 'The Delineator', *The Hibernian Magazine; or, Compendium of Entertaining Knowledge* (Dublin, 1781), p. 342.

20 Male height was closely linked to ideals of masculinity, a point made very clearly in a 1830s guide to men's fashion that devotes a whole section to the challenges faced by men of shorter stature and advocates discreet ways to wear heels:

> Now I compute – if a man 5 feet 4 inches thus dressed, wears heels an inch and a-half, at three or four yards distance he will appear 5 feet 8 inches; while at twenty yards he will seem a tall man. So much for what may be done by a little attention . . . Then the tight-looking legs of course elonge the figure; the reason why I strenuously recommend Hessians . . . [the dress boot] is particularly applicable to those who wish to heighten their stature, a thing this will enable them to do in any degree that an undress boot will admit of, by having high heels. These can be two or even three inches if required: only two things should be observed: when they are very high, the aforesaid heels should be tipped with cork at least half an inch in thickness, so that no more reverberation need be made than with a pump to screen them completely from 'human ken'; the trousers should be made very long, even to touching the ground, and strapped. Oh! What a transformation is here, my countrymen, in a diminutive man! . . . if followed in the manner my instructions have pointed out, cannot give the slightest cause to suspect you are actually walking upon *raisers*.

*The Whole Art of Dress! or, The Road to Elegance and Fashion at the Enormous Saving of Thirty Per Cent!!! Being a Treatise upon That Essential and Much-cultivated Requisite of the Present Day, Gentlemen's Costume; . . . by a Cavalry Officer* (London, 1830), p. 67.

21 James Dacres Devlin, *Critica Crispiana; or, the Boots and Shoes, British and Foreign, of the Great Exhibition* (London, 1852), p. 69.

22 Grace Greenwood, 'The Heroic in Common Life: A Lecture by Grace Greenwood', *Christian Inquirer*, XIV/11 (1859).

23 Bellamy Brownjohn, 'A Severe Family Affliction', in *The Grecian Bend* (New York, 1868), p. 3.

24 *New York Times*, 2 September 1871, p. 4.

25 This was famously observed and critiqued by Thorstein Veblen in his seminal text *The Theory of the Leisure Class* (1899).

26 M.E.W. Sherwood, 'How Shall Our Girls Behave?', *Ladies' Home Journal and Practical Housekeeper*, V/11 (1888), p. 2.

27 'The Social Problem: Young Men Responsible for the Fashions of Young Women', *Circular*, VI/35 (Oneida, NY, 1869), p. 279.

28 George Wood Wingate, *Through the Yellowstone Park on Horseback* (New York, 1886), p. 21.

29 Julian Ralph, *Our Great West: A Study of the Present Conditions and Future Possibilities of the New Commonwealths and Capitals of the United States* (Chicago, IL, 1893), p. 388.

30 An article in *Cosmopolitan* magazine from 1886 on the Montana cowboy included this explanation for the heels on cowboy boots: 'For foot gear they invariably wear high boots, with very high heels . . . [that] are for a special purpose: or, to put it in the current scientific jargon, this highly specialized form of the heel has been developed by the requirements of the animal for some mechanical means to prevent the slipping of the foot through the aperture of the stirrup.' William T. Hornaday, 'The Cowboys of the Northwest', *The Cosmopolitan Monthly Magazine*, II (1986), p. 222.

31 Dorothy Dunbar Bromley, 'Feminist – New Style', www.harpers.org, October 1927.

32 'Lay the High Heel Low', *Washington Post*, 6 May 1920, p. 6.

33 'Hooch and High Heels Are Driving Nation to Perdition Fast', *Lebanon Daily News* (Lebanon, PA, 1929), p. 16.

34 'Writes a Bill Limiting Heels to Mere Inch: Texas Solon Would Protect Public Health, Starting at Shoe Bottoms', *The Detroit Free Press*, 3 February 1929, p.28.

35 'Stand By High Heels: Massachusetts Shoe Men Oppose Law Banning Them', *New York Times*, 15 February 1921, p. 6. 'Shoe manufacturers and dealers who appeared before a Legislative committee at the State House today in opposition to the bill designed to prevent the wearing of high heels by women . . . characterized it as "a freak and foolish measure." One dealer asserted that 60 per cent of women now wear shoes that come within the proposed law which would prevent the manufacture and sale of shoes the heels of which are more than an inch and a half in height.'

36 'Use of Footgear in Costumes: Part Played by Shoes and Hosiery Takes on Importance in Ensemble Effects', *New York Times*, 18 April 1926.

37 Ibid.

38 'What Women Will Wear When Another Hundred Years Becomes Fashion History', *Spokane Daily Chronicle*, 18 April 1936, p. 5.

39 Paul Popenoe, *Applied Eugenics* (New York, 1920), p. 301.

40 Knight Dunlap, *Personal Beauty and Racial Betterment* (St Louis, MO, 1920), p. 22.

41 C. J. Gerling, *Short Stature and Height Increase* (New York, 1939), p. 148. The book advises just such devices, explaining that while high heels are helpful to women, 'high heels look effeminate and grotesque on a man and men are more in need of stature aid than are women.' The author continues: 'Naturally, the ideal shoe of this sort must effect a considerable elevation of the feet from the ground while presenting an external appearance no different from that of an ordinary shoe.'

42 Elizabeth R. Duval, 'Fashion's Fantasies for Feet', *New York Times,* 14 April 1940.

43 'Pinups Ruin Perspective, Veteran Says', *Washington Post*, 12 March 1945.

44 '2,000 mph Flying Stiletto Readied for Advanced Tests', *United Press International*, 17 November 1953.

45 Frances Walker, 'Steel Heel Holds Up New Shoe', *Pittsburgh Post-Gazette,* 8 November 1951.

46 See Elizabeth Semmelhack, *Roger Vivier: Process to Perfection* (Toronto, 2012).

47 Thomas Meehan, 'Where Did All the Women Go?', *Saturday Evening Post*, 11 September 1965, pp. 26–30.

48 'As Hemlines Go Up, Up, Up, Heels Go Down, Down, Down', *New York Times*, 27 January 1966.

49 *Women's Wear Daily*, 22 March 1968, p. 8.

50 'The Shape of Shoes', *Time*, LXXXV/15 (9 April 1965).

51 Ann Hencken, 'Men's Fashions Become Elegant During 1972', *Daily Republic*, 9 March 1972, p. 15.

52 Ibid.

53 Hollie I. West, 'A Tinseled Pimp-hero', *Washington Post*, 21 April 1973.

54 De Fen, 'Fee Waybill of The Tubes Discusses Music, Theater and the Merger of the Two', www.punkglobe.com, accessed 28 October 2016.

55 Some artists, such as David Bowie, did attempt to subvert traditional gender roles.

56 'The Monsters', *Time*, XCVI/4 (27 July 1970), p. 46.

57 Bernadine Morris, 'On Heels, There's No Firm Stand: "More Functional-minded" Stiletto Heels', *New York Times*, 8 August 1978, p. C2.

58 Gloria Emerson, 'Women Now: Your Clothes: What They Tell about Your Politics', *Vogue*, 1 September 1979, p. 300.

59 'Reagan White House Gift: "Ronald Reagan" Cowboy Boot with Presidential Seal', www.maxrambod.com, accessed 25 August 2016.

60 E. Salholz, R. Michael, M. Starr et al., 'Too Late for Prince Charming?', *Newsweek*, CVII/22 (1986), pp. 54–7, 61.

61 'Sex and the City: Carrie Bradshaw Quotes', www.tvfanatic.com, 17 August 2010.

62 Leora Tanenbaum, 'Our Stripper Shoes, Ourselves', www.huffingtonpost.com, 25 May 2016.

63 Jennifer Finn, 'Survivor's Shoes Symbolize Distress, Despair', www.911memorial.org, 10 July 2014.

64 'The Armadillo Shoes by Alexander McQueen: History of an Icon', www.icon-icon.com, 18 May 2016.

65 Rachael Allen, 'Alexander McQueen Armadillo Shoes Bring In $295,000 at Christie's', www.footwearnews.com, 24 July 2015.

66 The economists Nicola Persico and Andrew Postlewaite of the University of Pennsylvania, along with Dan Silverman of the University of Michigan,

published a paper in 2004 suggesting that as early as one's teenage years, height directly influences later earnings. Later, Dr Anne Case and Dr Christina Paxson, economists at Princeton University, released their paper 'Stature and Status: Height, Ability and Labor Market Outcomes', which likewise discussed advantages related to height. Both papers asked nuanced questions related to social status, shame, the impact of nutrition and other factors. Nicola Persico, Andrew Postlewaite and Dan Silverman, 'The Effect of Adolescent Experience on Labor Market Outcomes: The Case of Height', *Journal of Political Economy*, cxii/5 (2004), pp. 1019–53; Anne Case and Christina Paxson, 'Stature and Status: Height, Ability, and Labor Market Outcomes', *Journal of Political Economy*, cxvi/3 (2008), pp. 499–532.

67 Joel Waldfogel, 'Tall on Intelligence', *National Post*, 14 September 2006.
68 'Uplifting Speech, Mr Sarkozy', *Daily Mail*, 10 June 2009, p. 26.
69 Katya Foreman, 'Prince, He's Got the Look', www.bbc.com, 29 September 2014. As Questlove of the band The Roots wrote in a *Rolling Stone* tribute to Prince, 'I wonder what his mind state was in 1981, standing onstage in kiddie briefs, leg warmers and high heels without a number one hit.'
70 Georgina Littlejohn, 'Lenny Kravitz Dresses Like an American Woman as He Strolls around New York', www.dailymail.co.uk, 24 September 2010.
71 Stacy Lambe, 'The Five Fiercest Men Dancing in Heels', www.queerty.com, 24 July 2013.
72 Alyssa Norwin, 'Bruce Jenner: His "Girl Parties" at Home and New Love of Heels', www.hollywoodlife.com, 29 April 2015.
73 'Cannes Film Festival "Turns Away Women in Flat Shoes"', www.bbc.com, 19 May 2015. Richter was eventually admitted.
74 Rachael Revesz, 'Waitress Forced to Wear High Heels at Work Shares Photo of Her Bleeding Feet', www.independent.co.uk, 12 May 2016.

**IV Sneakers: Exclusivity**

1 This chapter builds upon the work done for the Toronto Bata Shoe Museum exhibition 'Out of the Box: The Rise of Sneaker Culture' and subsequent travelling exhibition, under the auspices of the American Federation of Arts, and the book by Elizabeth Semmelhack, *Out of the Box: The Rise of Sneaker Culture* (New York, 2015).
2 Charles Macintosh in England found a way to rubberize fabric, giving birth to the iconic rubberized raincoat that still bears the name Mackintosh.
3 Salo Vinocur Coslovsky, 'The Rise and Decline of the Amazonian Rubber Shoe Industry: A Tale of Technology, International Trade, and Industrialization in the Early 19th Century', unpublished working paper (Cambridge, 2006), pp. 11–12.

4 L. Johnson, *The Journal of Health*, 1/6 (Philadelphia, PA, 1829), p. 81.

5 'Without stopping to test the nature of the gum . . . the anxious speculator, and the enthusiastic manufacturer plunged boldly into the sea of trade . . . but the "bubble" soon burst, goods manufactured . . . in April became a sticky mass of useless rubbish in July. The warm weather literally melted the hopes and expectations of the incautious adventurer. A panic was the consequence . . . an enterprise so promising but a few months before, was swept as by a hurricane.' William H. Richardson, ed., Book III, chap. 1: 'Discovery of the Sulphurization and Vulcanization of India-rubber in America', in *The Boot and Shoe Manufacturers' Assistant and Guide: Containing a Brief History of the Trade. History of India-rubber and Gutta-percha . . . With an Elaborate Treatise on Tanning* (Boston, MA, 1858), p. 113.

6 'History: The Charles Goodyear Story', http://corporate.goodyear.com, accessed 2 November 2016.

7 Thomas Hancock, *Personal Narrative of the Origin and Progress of the Caoutchouc or India-rubber Manufacture in England* (Cambridge, 2014), p. 107.

8 *Manufactures of the United States in 1860: Compiled from the Original Returns of the Eighth Census, under the Direction of the Secretary of the Interior* (Washington, DC, 1865), p. lxxviii.

9 *Public Documents of Massachusetts*, vol. IV (1835).

10 R. Newton, ed., 'The Science of Croquet', *The Gentleman's Magazine*, V/1 (London, 1868), p. 235. Confusingly, later in the century many ladies' shoes of varying descriptions were called croquet shoes.

11 Nancy Rexford, *Women's Shoes in America, 1795–1930* (Kent, OH, and London, 2000), also says that rubber overshoes were called croquet sandals, p. 157.

12 'Lawn Tennis – Costumes for, and Customs of, the Game', *Harper's Bazaar Toronto Mail*, 28 July 1881, p. 3.

13 Ibid.

14 R. K. Munkittrick, 'My Shoes – A Cursory Glance through the Closet', *Puck*, 26 August 1885.

15 Mary Anne Everett Green, ed., 'Petitions 17. May 1, 1660', in *Calendar of State Papers, Domestic Series, of the Reign of Charles II. 1660–1661*, vol. II (London, 1860), p. 18.

16 'Tennis Courts in Brooklyn Parks', *New York Times*, 20 April 1884, p. 3.

17 Dr Tahir P. Hussain, 'Concept of Physical Education: Physical Culture: Origins', in *History, Foundation of Physical Education and Educational Psychology* (New Delhi, 2012).

18 Archibald Maclaren, 'Rules and Regulations for the Gymnasium', in *A System of Physical Education: Theoretical and Practical* (London, 1869), p. 1.

19 Moses Coit Tyler, 'Fragmentary Manhood', *The Independent . . . Devoted to the*

*Consideration of Politics, Social and Economic Tendencies, History, Literature, and the Arts*, 18 November 1869.

20 Josiah Flynt, 'Club Life among Outcasts', *Harper's New Monthly Magazine*, XC/539 (1894), p. 716.

21 'Sporting Shoes: Tennis Shoes', in *Shoe and Leather Reporter*, XLIII (New York, Boston, Philadelphia and Chicago, 1887), p. 683.

22 Frederick William Robinson, *Female Life in Prison*, vol. I (London, 1862), p. 209.

23 James Greenwood, 'Christmas in Limbo', in *In Strange Company: Being the Experiences of a Roving Correspondent* (London, 1863), p. 321.

24 '"Sandbagging" in Chicago', *Barnstable Patriot*, 8 February 1887.

25 'Guyer's Shoe Store', *Sacred Heart Review*, 5 August 1895.

26 James Naismith, 'The Need of a New Game', in *Basketball: Its Origin and Development* (Lincoln, NB, and London, 1941), p. 29.

27 'Active Woman's Game: Basket-ball the Rage for Society's Buds and Matrons. Line-up of Opposing Teams at the Berkeley Ladies Athletic Club. Young Matrons Play Against Unmarried Girls, who Wear White Blouses – Keeping the Ball in Motion – Mrs. Astor One of the Captains – Hard Work for the Forwards – Play that Reduces Flesh. Qualities of the Game. Women Who Throw Straight. The Underhand Toss', *Washington Post*, 12 January 1896, p. 22. The all-female Smith College student body embraced the game. The *Washington Post* even claimed basketball was invented by college girls.

28 'Girls Play Basket Ball: How the Game Looks to One Seeing It for the First Time', *New York Times*, 14 May 1896, p. 27.

29 C. Gilbert Percival, 'Basket Ball for Women', *Health*, LVII/5 (1907), p. 294.

30 James Naismith, 'The Uniforms', in *Basketball: Its Origins and Development* (Lincoln, NB, and London, 1941), p. 90.

31 'A Plea for Sports', *Telegraph Herald*, 24 June 1917.

32 'National Disgrace, Says Senator Wadsworth', *Physical Culture Magazine*, XXVIII/4 (1917).

33 'Find No Sure Guide to Women's Weight: Reduction Methods Discussed by Physicians in Seeking Proper Health Scale', *New York Times*, 23 February 1926.

34 'Sure-footed We Stand', *Vogue*, 15 July 1927, p. 69.

35 'Barefoot Bathers Warned of Flat Feet: Girls in High Heeled Pumps Have the Right Idea, Say Doctors – Advise Standing Pigeon-toed', *New York Times*, 16 July 1922, p. E6.

36 'The Business World: Good Sales in Rubber Footwear', *New York Times*, 10 August 1923.

37 'Rubber-soled Footgear: All Classes of French Take More to Shoes of This Type', *New York Times*, 11 November 1923.

38 *Shoe and Boot Recorder*, 14 April 1934, p. 24.

39 Adidas archive, conversations with the author, 2014.

40 Adolf Hitler, *Mein Kampf*, trans. James Murphy (London, 1939), p. 418.

41 DeWitt MacKenzie, 'Fitness Becomes State Objective: Interesting Conditions Grow Out of Upheaval in Europe and Orient', *Kentucky New Era*, 20 July 1939.

42 'Women and Sport: Physical Culture in Europe. News from Many Centres', *The Age*, 27 December 1935.

43 'Heritage: Episode 02, Bata's Golden Age', www.bata.com, accessed 1 November 2016. See also 'Bata World News: Bata Tennis: An Old Favorite from Bata India is Launched Worldwide' [2014], www.bata.com, accessed 1 November 2016: 'Bata began making sneakers in India in 1933. Bata opened its Batanagar factory near Kolkata in 1934 to fulfill Tomas Bata's vision to shoe mankind. The Bata Tennis was first manufactured there two years later for Indian schoolchildren to wear to physical education classes.'

44 'Rubber in the Military', *Milwaukee Journal*, 1 February 1942.

45 Stephen L. Harp, *A World History of Rubber: Empire, Industry, and the Everyday* (Chichester, 2016), p. 103.

46 *The Billboard*, LVI/9 (1944), p. 10.

47 Harp, *A World History of Rubber*, p. 103 (Buna); D. C. Blackley, *Synthetic Rubbers: Their Chemistry and Technology* (London and New York, 2012), p. 20 (Neoprene).

48 Harp, *A World History of Rubber*, p. 105. See also 'Here Are Chief Facts and Figures About Rubber', *Milwaukee Journal*, 1 February 1942.

49 'Something Afoot', *Globe and Mail*, 13 May 1978.

50 Melvyn P. Cheskin, Kel J. Sherkin and Barry T. Bates, *The Complete Handbook of Athletic Footwear* (New York, 1987), p. 16.

51 Jack Anderson, 'Some Insight on the Flabby American', *Nevada Daily Mail*, 12 April 1973, p. 4.

52 Lara O'Reilly, '11 Things Hardly Anyone Knows About Nike', www.businessinsider.com, 4 November 2014.

53 It should be noted that Davidson was given an undisclosed amount of Nike stock by Phil Knight as a thank you in 1983. See 'Origin of the Swoosh' at https://web.archive.org/web/20071023034940/http://www.nike.com/nikebiz/nikebiz.jhtml?page=5&item=origin.

54 'Something Afoot'.

55 'Everything You've Ever Wanted To Know about Running, Tennis Gadgetry and Sneakers', *Battle Creek Enquirer*, 14 May 1978, p. 35.

56 Dave Barry, 'Sneaker Plague Threatens to Sap the Strength of This Great Nation', *Bangor Daily News*, 25 January 1991, p. 155.

57 Christopher B. Doob, *The Anatomy of Competition in Sports: The Struggle for Success in Major U.S. Professional Leagues* (Lanham, MD, 2015), p. 99.

58 Chuck Taylor was an American basketball coach. Robert Haillet was a French tennis player. Jack Purcell played badminton for Canada.

59 Bobbito Garcia, *Where'd You Get Those? New York City's Sneaker Culture, 1960–1987* (New York, 2003), p. 12.

60 Andrew Pollack, 'Case Study: A Onetime Highflier; Nike Struggles to Hit Its Stride Again', *New York Times*, 19 May 1985.

61 Ibid.

62 Ibid.

63 Some have argued that Jordan was banned for wearing the Nike Air Ship High, but although he did wear that model briefly, the NBA specifically banned the Air Jordan, as stated in the letter they sent to Nike, which is held in the Nike archives. Nike Archives, correspondence with the author, 2015.

64 The term had earlier been used for all-white Pro-Keds.

65 It has been suggested that the song was written in part to counter the rap created by the social activist Dr Gerald Deas called 'Felon Shoes', in which the doctor links lace-less sneakers with degeneracy and advises young black men to tighten up their laces and 'put a goal in your mind, put your nose to that grindstone and success in life, you will find.'

66 *International Directory of Company Histories*, V/18 (Farmington Hills, MI, 1997), p. 266.

67 Nathan Cobb, 'Hey, Check It Out – Soles with Soul', www.highbeam.com, 18 December 1988.

68 Semmelhack, *Out of the Box*, p. 162.

69 Bill Brubaker, 'Had to Be the Shoe: An Explosion of Sole', *Washington Post*, 15 August 1991.

70 Rick Telander, 'Your Sneakers or Your Life', *Sports Illustrated*, 14 May 1990, pp. 36–8, 43–9.

71 Ira Berkow, 'Sports of the Times; The Murders Over the Sneakers', *New York Times*, 14 May 1990.

72 Les Payne, 'Black Superstars Get Dunked for Nothing', *Newsday*, 2 September 1990, p. 11.

73 Jane Rinzler Buckingham, 'Trend Watch: Skip Casual: Dress Up to Stand Out', *Ocala Star-Banner*, 11 July 2001.

74 'Dress for Success with Sneakers? Not Her', *Pittsburgh Post-Gazette*, 27 August 1983, p. 17.

75 Oliver Franklin-Wallis, 'Personal Style: LeBron James', *Gentleman's Quarterly*, 14 November 2012.

76 'Raf Simons: About', www.rafsimons.com, accessed 1 November 2016.

77 Katie Abel, 'FN Home: Influencers: Power Players: Red State: Q&A With Christian Louboutin', *Footwear News*, 19 November 2012.

78 'Hey Nike, Women Like Trainers Too', www.wonderlandmagazine.com, 5 August 2013.

79 Imogen Fox, 'How 2015 Was the Year the Stan Smith Went Mass',
   *The Guardian*, 22 December 2015.

80 Dennis Green, 'A Tennis Shoe from 1963 Has Suddenly Taken the Fashion
   World by Surprise', *Business Insider*, 26 July 2015.

81 'Is Rap Music Here to Stay?', *Jet*, 17 August 1998, p. 59.

82 For more information, see 'The Rubber Terror', www.takingthelane.com,
   25 October 2011, and Andre C. James, 'The Butcher of Congo: King Leopold
   II of Belgium', www.digitaljournal.com, 4 April 2011. See also Juan Velez-
   Ocampo, Carolina Herrera-Cano and Maria Alejandra Gonzalez-Perez, 'The
   Peruvian Amazon Company's Death: The Jungle Devoured Them', in *Dead
   Firms: Causes and Effects of Cross-border Corporate Insolvency*, ed. Miguel M.
   Torres, Virginia Cathro and Maria Alejandra Gonzalez-Perez (Bingley, West
   Yorkshire, 2016), pp. 35–46.

83 'Labor Slams Nike for Unfair Labor Practices', *Philippine Daily Inquirer*,
   12 May 2000, p. B10.

84 Art Buchwald, 'Mister Robots', *Ellensburg Daily Record*, 25 April 1983, p. 4.

85 'Reboot: Adidas to Make Shoes in Germany Again – But Using Robots',
   *The Guardian*, 25 May 2016.

86 'The Shoe Waste Epidemic', www.usagainblog.com, 17 May 2013.

87 Suzanne Goldenberg, 'Running Shoes Leave Large Carbon Footprint, Study
   Shows', *The Guardian*, 23 May 2013.

88 'Shoemaker Settles Mercury Suit', *Eugene Register-Guard*, 14 July 1994.

89 'Nike Engineers Knit for Performance', http://news.nike.com, 21 February
   2012.

**Conclusion**

1 Barbara Brotman, 'Sole Sisters Possessed, Obsessed and Completely
   Infatuated with Footwear', *Chicago Tribune*, 19 May 1999.

2 See Giorgio Riello, *A Foot in the Past: Consumers, Producers and Footwear in
   the Long Eighteenth Century* (Oxford, 2006).

3 James Madison Edmunds, 'Introduction', in Edmunds, *Manufactures of
   the United States in 1860; Compiled from the Original Returns of the Eighth
   Census, under the Direction of the Secretary of the Interior* (Washington, DC,
   1865), p. lxxi.

4 Ibid.

5 Howard Zinn, 'The Lynn Shoe Strike, 1860', in *A People's History of the United
   States*, www.libcom.org, 9 September 2006.

6 Welt construction is done when a lasted shoe upper – that is an upper that has
   been stretched over a foot-shaped last and tacked in place – has a welt, which
   is a narrow strip of leather, sewn along both the lasting margin of the upper
   and the insole. The sole is then stitched to the welt.

7 Fred A. Gannon, *Shoe Making, Old and New* (Salem, MA, 1911), p. 36.

8 T. S. Taylor, 'Thirteen Remarkable Events: 7. First Great Exhibition', in *First Principles of English History: 1850–1879* (London, 1880), p. 117.

9 'Searching Out for Trade', *Shoe and Leather Reporter*, 2 March 1893, p. 541.

10 Note that accompanied the boots and gloves; all held in the collection of the Bata Shoe Museum, Toronto.

11 'Old Clothes Fad', *Lewiston Evening Journal*, 4 January 1904, p. 8.

12 'Fashion: A Modern Compatriot of Trilby', *Vogue*, 15 September 1920, p. 70.

13 Private donor of multiple Yantorny shoes to the Bata Shoe Museum, conversation with the author. His bread and diet were also discussed in his *New York Times* obituary: 'Pierre Yantorny, Bootmaker, Dead', *New York Times*, 15 December 1936, p. 25.

14 Baron de Meyer, 'The Pursuit of Elegance', *Vogue*, 15 November 1915, p. 51.

15 'Fashion Adds Half a Cubit to Our Stature', *Vogue*, 1 October 1915, p. 44.

16 'The Fine Art of Cobbling', *Vogue*, 1 January 1914, p. 70.

17 Hugh Brewster, 'To the Lifeboats', in Brewster, *Gilded Lives, Fatal Voyage: The Titanic's First-class Passengers and Their World* (New York, 2012), chap. 13, n. 17.

18 'Fashion: A Modern Compatriot of Trilby', *Vogue*, 15 September 1920, p. 70.

19 De Meyer, 'The Pursuit of Elegance', *Vogue*, 15 November 1915, p. 51.

20 'Fancier Footwear to Rule This Year: Manufacturers Include Lizard and Alligator Effects in Their Style Program', *New York Times*, 16 January 1924, p. 24.

21 Unnamed fashion writer, 'Whole Wardrobe Scheme Is Dependent on Shoe', source and date unknown.

22 'Men's Shoes', *Washington Post*, 9 October 1927, p. 51.

23 Clinton W. Bennett, 'A Cost Plan for the Women's Shoe Industry', *National Association of Cost Accountants Bulletin*, XVI/12 (1935), p. 677.

24 'Shoes Are Bought in "Fast Fashions": Volume Buyers Book Orders for August Deliveries at Boston Fair', *New York Times*, 8 June 1939, p. 34.

25 'Spring Styles Ready for Action', *Shoe and Boot Recorder*, 17 January 1942, p. 17.

26 W. H. Lawrence, 'Nazi Mass Killing Laid Bare in Camp: Victims Put at 1,500,000 in Huge Death Factory of Gas Chambers and Crematories', *New York Times*, 30 August 1944, p. 1.

27 Jonathan Frater, 'The Shoe Room, and What I Learned There: A Visit to the U.S. Holocaust Museum', www.roguescholar.blogs.com, 9 August 2011.

28 Greg Donaldson, 'For Joggers and Muggers, the Trendy Sneaker', *New York Times*, 7 July 1979.

29 Michele Ingrassia, 'Fashion Shoes for Imelda Laid Heel to Heel, the 3,000 Pairs of Shoes She Left Behind Would Stretch for More Than a Mile', *Newsday*, 1 April 1986, p. 3.

30 Rita Reif, 'They Won't Fit Your Foot, They Wear Well', *New York Times*, 10 December 2000, p. 40.

31 Ibid.

32 'High-heel Shoes Banned in Saudi', *Irish Times*, 18 March 1996.

33 John-John Williams, 'If the Shoe Fits: Avid Sneaker Fans Prove Collecting Shoes Is No Longer a Woman's Game', *Baltimore Sun*, 31 March 2011, p. C1.

34 Ibid.

35 Ibid.

36 Tansy Hoskins, 'Robot Factories Could Threaten Jobs of Millions of Garment Workers', www.theguardian.com, 16 July 2016.

# Bibliography

Agnelli, Cosmo, *Amorevole aviso circa gli abusi delle donne vane* (Bologna, 1592)

Anderson, Ruth Matilda, 'El chapin y otros zapatos afines', *Cuadernos de la Alhambra*, 5 (1969), pp. 17–41

—, *Hispanic Costume, 1480–1530* (New York, 1979)

Arnold, Janet, *Queen Elizabeth's Wardrobe Unlock'd* (Leeds, 1988)

Blackley, D. C., *Synthetic Rubbers: Their Chemistry and Technology* (London and New York, 2012)

Brackman, Barbara, *Hyer, Justin, and the Origin of the Cowboy Boot* (Topeka, KS, 1995)

Breward, Christopher, 'Men in Heels: From Power to Perversity', in *Shoes: Pleasure and Pain*, ed. Helen Persson (London, 2015)

Brewster, Hugh, 'To the Lifeboats', in *Gilded Lives, Fatal Voyage: The Titanic's First-class Passengers and Their World* (New York, 2012)

Brown, Tony, and Thomas N. Corns, *Edward Carpenter and Late Victorian Radicalism* (Abingdon-on-Thames, Oxon, 2013)

Canby, Sheila R., *Shah 'Abbas: The Remaking of Iran* (London, 2009)

Carpenter, Edward, 'Simplification of Life', in *England's Ideal, and Other Papers on Social Subjects* (London, 1887)

Case, Anne, and Christina Paxson, 'Stature and Status: Height, Ability, and Labor Market Outcomes', *Journal of Political Economy*, CXVI/3 (2008), pp. 499–532

Cheskin, Melvyn P., Kel J. Sherkin and Barry T. Bates, *The Complete Handbook of Athletic Footwear* (New York, 1987)

Coslovsky, Salo Vinocur, 'The Rise and Decline of the Amazonian Rubber Shoe Industry: A Tale of Technology, International Trade, and Industrialization in the Early 19th Century', unpublished working paper (Cambridge, 2006)

Cramer, Jeffery S., *I to Myself: An Annotated Selection from the Journal of Henry D. Thoreau* (New Haven, CT, 2007)

'Cross-saddle Riding for Women', *Physical Education*, III/2, ed. James Naismith and Luther Halsey Gulick (Springfield, MA, 1894)

Curta, Florin, *The Earliest Avar-age Stirrups, Or the 'Stirrup Controversy' Revisited* (Leiden, Boston, MA, and Tokyo, 2007)

David, Alison Matthews, 'War and Wellingtons: Military Footwear in the Age of Empire', in *Shoes: A History from Sandals to Sneakers*, ed. Giorgio Riello and Peter McNeil (London and New York, 2006)

Dekker, Thomas, 'Apishnesse: Or the Fift Dayes Triumph', in *The Seven Deadly Sins of London, Drawn in Seven Several Coaches, Through the Seven Several Gates of the City; Bringing the Plague with Them*, ed. Edward Arber (London, 1606/1879)

Devlin, James Dacres, *Critica Crispiana; or, The Boots and Shoes, British and Foreign, of the Great Exhibition* (London, 1852)

Doob, Christopher B., *The Anatomy of Competition in Sports: The Struggle for Success in Major U.S. Professional Leagues* (Lanham, MD, 2015)

Drake, Judith, and Mary Astell, *An Essay in Defence of the Female Sex: In Which are Inserted the Characters of a Pedant, a Squire, a Beau, a Vertuoso, a Poetaster, a City-critick, &c.: In a Letter to a Lady* (London, 1696)

Dubois, Edward (pseud.), *Fashionable Biography; or, Specimens of Public Characters by a Connoisseur* (London, 1808)

Dunaway, Wilma A., *The African-American Family in Slavery and Emancipation* (Cambridge, 2003)

Dunlap, Knight, *Personal Beauty and Racial Betterment* (St Louis, MO, 1920)

Edmunds, James Madison, 'Introduction', in *Manufactures of the United States in 1860; Compiled from the Original Returns of the Eighth Census, under the Direction of the Secretary of the Interior* (Washington, DC, 1865)

Evelyn, John, *The Diary of John Evelyn* (Woodbridge, Suffolk, 2004)

Fairholt, Frederick William, *Costume in England: A History of Dress from the Earliest Period until the Close of the Eighteenth Century* (London, 1860)

Faotto, Gabriella Giuriato, *L'arte dei calegheri e dei zavateri di Venezia dal Medioevo ad oggi: due importanti epigrafi in piazza San Marco* (Venice, 1999)

Ferragamo, Savaltore, *Shoemaker of Dreams: The Autobiography of Salvatore Ferragamo* (Florence, 1985)

Ferrier, R. W., 'The European Diplomacy of Shāh Abbās I and the First Persian Embassy to England', *Iran*, XI (1973), pp. 75–92

—, 'The First English Guide Book to Persia: A Discription of the Persian Monarchy', *Iran*, XV (1977), pp. 75–88

—, 'The Terms and Conditions Under Which English Trade Was Transacted with Safavid Persia', *Bulletin of the School of Oriental and African Studies, University of London*, XLIX/1 (1986), pp. 48–66

Garcia, Bobbito, *Where'd You Get Those? New York City's Sneaker Culture, 1960–1987* (New York, 2003)

Gerling, C. J., *Short Stature and Height Increase* (New York, 1939)

Green, Mary Anne Everett, ed., 'Petitions 17. May 1, 1660', in *Calendar of State Papers, Domestic Series, of the Reign of Charles II, 1660–1661*, vol. II (London, 1860)

Griebel, Helen Bradley, 'New Raiments of Self: African American Clothing in the Antebellum South', dissertation, University of Pennsylvania (1994)

Hancock, Thomas, *Personal Narrative of the Origin and Progress of the Caoutchouc, or India-rubber Manufacture in England* (Cambridge, 2014)

Harp, Stephen L., *A World History of Rubber: Empire, Industry, and the Everyday* (Chichester, 2016)

Hayes, Bill, *Hell on Wheels: An Illustrated History of Outlaw Motorcycle Clubs* (Minneapolis, MN, 2014)

Hazard, Blanche E., *The Organization of the Boot and Shoe Industry in Massachusetts before 1875* [1921] (reprint, New York, 1969)

*Hic Mulier; or, The Man-woman: Being a Medicine to Cure the Coltish Disease of the Staggers in the Masculine-feminines of Our Times. Exprest in a Briefe Declamation* (London, 1620)

Hill, Georgiana, *A History of English Dress from the Saxon Period to the Present Day* (New York, 1893)

Hussain, Dr Tahir P., 'Concept of Physical Education: Physical Culture: Origins', in *History, Foundation of Physical Education and Educational Psychology* (New Delhi, 2012)

*International Directory of Company Histories*, vol. XVIII (Farmington Hills, MI, 1997)

Jacoby, David, 'Silk Economics and Cross-cultural Artistic Interaction: Byzantium, the Muslim World, and the Christian West', *Dumbarton Oaks Papers*, LVIII (2004), pp. 197–240

Jirousek, Charlotte, 'Ottoman Influences in Western Dress', in *Ottoman Costumes: From Textile to Identity*, ed. Suraiya Faroqhi and Christoph K. Neumann (Istanbul, 2004)

Jones, Ann Rosalind, and Peter Stallybrass, *Renaissance Clothing and the Materials of Memory* (Cambridge, 2000)

Knolles, Richard., *The Generall Historie of the Turkes, from the First Beginning of That Nation to the Rising of the Othoman Familie: With All the Notable Expeditions of the Christian Princes against Them: Together with the Lives and Conquests of the Othoman Kings and Emperours unto the Yeare 1610* (London, 1610)

Krafft-Ebing, Richard, *Psychopathia Sexualis* (Philadelphia, PA, and London, 1894)

Kuchta, David, *The Three-piece Suit and Modern Masculinity: England, 1550–1850* (Berkeley and Los Angeles, CA, 2002)

Lincoln, Margarette, *British Pirates and Society, 1680–1730* (London and New York, 2014)

Mandeville, Bernard, *The Virgin Unmasked; or, Female Dialogues, betwixt an Elderly Maiden Lady and Her Niece on Several Diverting Discourses* (London, 1724)

*Manufactures of the United States in 1860: Compiled from the Original Returns of the Eighth Census, under the Direction of the Secretary of the Interior* (Washington, DC, 1865)

Matthee, Rudolph P., 'Between Venice and Surat: The Trade in Gold in Late Safavid Iran', *Modern Asian Studies*, XXXIV/1 (February 2000), pp. 223–55

—, *The Politics of Trade in Safavid Iran: Silk for Silver, 1600–1730* (Cambridge, 1999)

Middleton, Thomas, 'Father Hubburd's Tales 1604', in *Life in Shakespeare's England*, ed. John Dover Wilson (Cambridge, 1920)

Montez, Lola, *The Arts of Beauty; or, Secrets of a Lady's Toilet* (New York, 1858)

Morrow, Katherine Dohan, *Greek Footwear and the Dating of Sculpture* (Madison, WI, 1985)

Naismith, James, *Basketball: Its Origin and Development* (Lincoln, NE, and London, 1941)

Orwell, George, *The Road to Wigan Pier* (London, 1937)

Perrault, Charles, *Cinderella, and Other Tales from Perrault* (New York, 1989)

Persico, Nicola, Andrew Postlewaite and Dan Silverman, 'The Effect of Adolescent Experience on Labor Market Outcomes: The Case of Height', *Journal of Political Economy*, CXII/5 (2004), pp. 1019–53

Popenoe, Paul, *Applied Eugenics* (New York, 1920)

Ralph, Julian, *Our Great West: A Study of the Present Conditions and Future Possibilities of the New Commonwealths and Capitals of the United States* (Chicago, IL, 1893)

Remarque, Erich Maria, *All Quiet on the Western Front* (New York, 1930)

Rexford, Nancy E., *Women's Shoes in America, 1795–1930* (Kent, OH, and London, 2000)

Ribeiro, Aileen, *Dress in 18th-century Europe, 1715–1789* (New Haven, CT, and London, 2002)

—, *Fashion and Fiction: Dress in Art and Literature in Stuart England* (New Haven, CT, 2006)

Richardson, William H., ed., 'Discovery of the Sulphurization and Vulcanization of India-rubber in America', in *The Boot and Shoe Manufacturers' Assistant and Guide: Containing a Brief History of the Trade. History of India-rubber and Gutta-percha . . . With an Elaborate Treatise on Tanning* (Boston, MA, 1858)

Richter, Gisela M. A., 'Greeks in Persia', *American Journal of Archaeology*, L/1 (1946), pp. 15–30

Riefstahl, R. M., 'A Persian Figural Velvet of the Shah Abbas Period', *Bulletin of the Art Institute of Chicago*, XIX/1 (January 1925), pp. 1–5

Riello, Giorgio, *A Foot in the Past: Consumers, Producers and Footwear in the Long Eighteenth Century* (Oxford, 2006)

—, and Peter McNeil, eds, *Shoes: A History from Sandals to Sneakers* (London and New York, 2006)

Robinson, Frederick William, *Female Life in Prison*, vol. I (London, 1862)

Semmelhack, Elizabeth, 'A Delicate Balance: Women, Power and High Heels', in *Shoes: A History from Sandals to Sneakers*, ed. Giorgio Riello and Peter McNeil (Oxford and New York, 2006)

—, *Icons of Elegance: The Most Influential Shoe Designers of the 20th Century* (Toronto, 2005)

—, *On a Pedestal: Renaissance Chopines to Baroque Heels* (Toronto, 2005)

—, *Out of the Box: The Rise of Sneaker Culture* (New York, 2015)

—, *Roger Vivier: Process to Perfection* (Toronto, 2012)

—, *Standing Tall: The Curious History of Men in Heels* (Toronto, 2016)

Stanfield, Peter, *Horse Opera: The Strange History of the 1930s Singing Cowboy* (Urbana and Chicago, IL, 2002)

Swann, June, *History of Footwear: In Norway, Sweden and Finland Prehistory to 1950* (Stockholm, 2001)

—, *Shoes* (London, 1983)

Taylor, T. S., *First Principles of English History, 1850–1879* (London, 1880)

Tosh, John, 'Gentlemanly Politeness and Manly Simplicity in Victorian England', in *Transactions of the Royal Historical Society*, vol. XII (2002), pp. 455–72

Van Driel-Murray, Carol, 'Vindolanda and the Dating of Roman Footwear', *Britannia*, XXXII (2001), pp. 185–97

Veldmeijer, André J., and Alan J. Clapham, *Tutankhamun's Footwear: Studies of Ancient Egyptian Footwear* (Leiden, 2010)

Velez-Ocampo, Juan, Carolina Herrera-Cano and Maria Alejandra Gonzalez-Perez, 'The Peruvian Amazon Company's Death: The Jungle Devoured Them', in *Dead Firms: Causes and Effects of Cross-border Corporate Insolvency*, ed. Miguel M. Torres, Virginia Cathro and Maria Alejandra Gonzalez-Perez (Bingley, West Yorkshire, 2016)

*The Whole Art of Dress! or, The Road to Elegance and Fashion at the Enormous Saving of Thirty Per Cent!!! Being a Treatise upon That Essential and Much-cultivated Requisite of the Present Day, Gentlemen's Costume; . . . by a Cavalry Officer* (London, 1830)

Wingate, George Wood, *Through the Yellowstone Park on Horseback* (New York, 1886)

# Acknowledgements

First, I would like to thank Vivian Constantinopoulos, Editorial Director at Reaktion Books. Her patience, kindness, good council and commitment to this book have made working on it a true pleasure and are greatly appreciated. I also thank Jess Chandler, Editor at Reaktion, for her clear questions and excellent suggestions which made the final edits painless. I would like to thank Sophie Kullmann who did a beautiful job laying out the book and to Simon McFadden for the excellent cover design.

I am indebted to Mrs Sonja Bata, Founder and Chairman of the Board of the Bata Shoe Museum. I thank her for choosing me to be the Museum's Senior Curator and allowing me to wander down whatever path my research into footwear history has taken me. Her collection of over 13,000 footwear-related artefacts inspires me every day and many feature prominently in this book. I am very grateful to the museum for allowing me to use so many images from its incredible collection.

I am also thankful to my wonderful Bata Shoe Museum colleagues. Special thanks are given to: Dr Emanuele Lepri, Bata Shoe Museum Director, who has always supported my desire to write this book; Nishi Bassi, Assistant Curator, who patiently read through each chapter offering encouragement with her comments; Suzanne Peterson, Collections Manager, who manages the museum's image rights as well as taking quite a few wonderful photographs herself, many of which grace the pages of this book; and Ada Hopkins, the Conservator, whose diligence and care keeps the museum's objects in peak condition. Many thanks also to Ron Wood, our photographer of choice. His stunning images of shoes from the Bata Shoe Museum collection are highlights of this publication.

In addition, my thanks go to all of the other people and institutions who graciously and generously contributed images to this book. Rebecca Shawcross, the Senior Shoe Curator at the Northampton Museum and Art Gallery; Martin Herde, the Collection's Manager at adidas Archives; Sam Smallidge, the Archivist at Converse; Kristi Keifer, Records Manager at Nike Archive; Jennifer Schmidt at Puma; Nazim Mustafaev, collector at Shoe Icons; and Marc Ransdell at the Tom of Finland Foundation, are all warmly thanked for their collegiality and generosity. Likewise, I would also like to thank Dee Wells from Obsessive Sneaker Disorder for his wonderful photographs and Rick Kosow from the Sneaker Museum for agreeing to be in one of those shots. Mayan Rajendran and Ross McIntyre are thanked for their willingness to take some much needed shots on short notice. Tom Sachs and Darryl McDaniels are also greatly thanked for their generosity

Heartfelt thanks to Linda Bien, my long-suffering mother-in-law/editor, for all her thoughtful comments and corrections on the numerous versions of my text. Her ability and willingness to read my work over and over again is both remarkable and not taken for granted. I also want to thank my husband Daniel, likewise, for his ability to consider the same text repeatedly without complaint as well as his willingness to engage in endless conversations about history and the social implications of footwear, offering at each turn new insights and points to consider. My children Benjamin and Isabelle's keen yet distinctive intellects have likewise suggested many new perspectives for me to consider as I worked on the book. I also want to thank my dearest friends: Dr Jennifer Sage Holmes, whose lifelong friendship has been, and always will be, there to fill my life with laughter and comfort; Sonia Tanazefti-Dahmen, who appeared as if by magic and whose elegance and eloquence always provide encouragement; and Dr Alison Matthews David, with whom I have been known to spend many a pleasant hour researching and discussing fashion and footwear.

Lastly, I want to thank my parents. Recently we were going through old papers that my mother had saved and found a Christmas list of mine from when I was three. It simply said 'more'. Clearly, I was already enjoying my life but little did I know how much more my parents would give over the years. They have filled my life with love, encouragement and support. They have led by example. They have dreamed and dared for their whole lives and their belief in following one's path has led me to write this book.

## Photo Acknowledgements

The author and publishers offer great thanks to the Bata Shoe Museum for generously providing the majority of the images for this book: collection of the Bata Shoe Museum: pp. 194 (photo: © Bata Shoe Museum); 65, 70, 74, 139, 147 (photos: Tanya Higgins © Bata Shoe Museum); 20, 31, 112, 171, 173 (above and below), 184, 186, 298 (photos: Tanya Higgins and Fiona Rutka © Bata Shoe Museum); 22, 136 (photos: Brian Hillier © Bata Shoe Museum); 52, 98, 141, 153, 209, 255, 291, 323 (photos: Shannon Linde and Hayley Mills © Bata Shoe Museum); 263 (photo: Christine McLean); 85, 296, 303, 308 (left), 311 (photos: Christine McLean and Nicole Dawkins © Bata Shoe Museum); 113, 317 (photos: Faraz Olfat and Celina Hoang © Bata Shoe Museum); 68 (photo: Faraz Olfat and Thalia Stafford © Bata Shoe Museum); 8, 32, 39, 63, 66, 97, 115, 150, 199, 231, 257, 275, 299, 300, 319, 324 (photos: Suzanne Peterson © Bata Shoe Museum); 19, 25, 99, 127 (photos: Hal Roth © Bata Shoe Museum); 314 (photo: Alex Sandison © Bata Shoe Museum); 47, 53, 56, 58–9, 67, 72, 75, 100, 129, 189, 191, 207, 210, 247, 305, 308 (right), 313 (photos: David Stevenson and Eva Tkaczuk © Bata Shoe Museum); 16, 18, 21, 44, 88, 92, 93, 96, 104, 107, 109, 131, 132, 144, 155, 160, 163, 167, 168, 174, 177, 181, 200, 203, 204, 213, 215, 224, 227, 228, 234, 272, 279, 285, 301, 309, 310 (photos: Ron Wood © Bata Shoe Museum).

All other images were kindly provided courtesy of the following: collection of Adidas Archive: pp. 271 (photo: ©adidas Archive), 293 (photo: ©adidas AG), 258 (photo: ©adidas Archive/studio waldeck), 331 (photo: ©adidas AG); The British Library: p. 238 (HS85-10-18314); collection of Converse Archives (© Converse Archives): pp. 245, 249; published by Currier and Ives, American, c. 1868: p. 179; collection of the Tom of Finland Foundation (© Tom of Finland Foundation): p. 135; collection of Chad Jones: p. 283 (photo: Ron Wood © Bata Shoe Museum); Library of Congress Prints and Photographs Collection, Washington, DC: pp. 29, 30, 36 (photo: Bain News Service, NYC), 40, 94, 101, 103, 111, 117, 118, 121, 123 (photo: C. W. Turner), 125 (photo: Russell Lee), 188, 195, 196 (photo: Alfred T. Palmer), 233 (photo: Frances Benjamin Johnston), 241, 243, 251, 304; collection of Mache: p. 281 (photo: Ron Wood © Bata Shoe Museum); photo © Yanis Marshall: p. 221; collection of Ross McIntyre, Fleece 'n Stuff: pp. 69, 76 (photos: © Ross McIntyre, Fleece 'n Stuff); The Metropolitan Museum of Art, New York: pp. 91 (gift of George A. Hearn/ photo: © The Metropolitan Museum of Art), 162 (purchased with Joseph Pulitzer Bequest, 1952), 165 (Marquand Collection, Gift of Henry G. Marquand, 1889), 166 (The Elisha Whittelsey Collection, The Elisha Whittelsey Fund, 1953); collection of Muzeum jihovýchodní Moravy ve Zlíně, Czech Republic (© Muzeum jihovýchodní Moravy ve Zlíně): p. 253; © The National Portrait Gallery, London: p. 35; collection of Nike Archives: pp. 268, 269 (photo: Ron Wood © Bata Shoe Museum); collection of the Northampton Museums and Art Gallery: pp. 237 (photo: Greg Washington © Bata Shoe Museum), 261 (photo: Ron Wood © Bata Shoe Museum); Public.Resource.org (flickr): p. 43; collection of PUMA Archives: p. 264 (photo: Ron Wood © Bata Shoe Museum); photo © Puma: p. 287; photo © Mayan Rajendran: p. 83; collection of Mayan Rajendran: p. 288 (photo: Ron Wood © Bata Shoe Museum); REX Shutterstock: pp. 142 (Mark Henderson/PYMCA), 266 (Ted Polhemus/PYMCA); collection of Tom Sachs: p. 329 (photo: © Sperone Gallery); photo Elizabeth Semmelhack: p. 326; collection of Shoe Icons (© Shoe Icons Collection): pp. 183, 307; from Spalding's Athletic Library Official Collegiate Basket Ball Guide, American, 1907: p. 244; collection Museo Stibbert: p. 51 (photo: © Museo Stibbert); The Victoria and Albert Museum, London: p. 27; © Dee Wells: pp. 280, 327.

# Index